John
Banville

CONTEMPORARY IRISH WRITERS
a Bucknell series

Series Editor:
John Rickard

Irish studies is currently undergoing a renewal, not only in connection to major figures such as James Joyce and W. B. Yeats, but also within a larger framework, with particular attention to women's issues, nationalism, Northern Ireland and its writers, the Irish language, and the fiction, poetry, drama, and film of contemporary Ireland.

These short monographs bring newer, more theoretically informed perspectives to a consideration of the work and lives of single authors, and they provide a general discussion of interpretive issues and strategies for understanding this work. These books will appeal to a sophisticated but not solely professorial audience—that is, advanced undergraduates, graduate students, and independent readers and scholars as well as professors of Irish literature and culture.

Titles in Series

Richard R. Russell on Bernard MacLaverty

Jody Allen Randolph on Eavan Boland

Neil Murphy on John Banville

www.bucknell.edu/universitypress

CONTEMPORARY IRISH WRITERS

John Banville

Neil Murphy

BUCKNELL UNIVERSITY PRESS

Published by Bucknell University Press
Copublished by The Rowman & Littlefield Publishing Group, Inc.
4501 Forbes Boulevard, Suite 200, Lanham, Maryland 20706
www.rowman.com

Unit A, Whitacre Mews, 26-34 Stannary Street, London SE11 4AB, United Kingdom

Copyright © 2018 by Neil Murphy

Excerpts from *Birchwood*. (London: Panther Books, 1984); *Doctor Copernicus* (London: Panther Books, 1984); *Mefisto* (London: David R. Godine, 1989). Reprinted with Permission from the author ©John Banville.

Excerpts from *The Book of Evidence* (London: Secker & Warburg, 1989); *Ghosts* (London: Secker & Warburg, 1993); *Athena* (London: Secker & Warburg, 1995). Reprinted with Permission from the author ©John Banville.

Excerpts from *The Sea* (London: Picador, 2005). Reprinted with Permission from the author ©John Banville.

Excerpts from *Eclipse* (London: Picador, 2000); *Shroud* (London: Picador, 2002); *Ancient Light* (New York: Viking Penguin, 2012). Reprinted with Permission from the author ©John Banville.

Excerpts from *The Blue Guitar* (London: Viking Penguin, 2015). Reprinted with Permission from the author ©John Banville.

All rights reserved. No part of this book may be reproduced in any form or by any electronic or mechanical means, including information storage and retrieval systems, without written permission from the publisher, except by a reviewer who may quote passages in a review.

British Library Cataloguing in Publication Information Available

Library of Congress Cataloging-in-Publication Data available

ISBN: 978-1-61148-872-2 (cloth : alk. paper)
ISBN: 978-1-61148-873-9 (electronic)

∞™ The paper used in this publication meets the minimum requirements of American National Standard for Information Sciences—Permanence of Paper for Printed Library Materials, ANSI/NISO Z39.48-1992.

Printed in the United States of America

For Su

CONTENTS

	Acknowledgments	ix
	Abbreviations	xiii
	Introduction	1
1	The Early Evolution of an Aesthetic: From *Long Lankin* to *Mefisto*	27
2	The Frames Trilogy: *The Book of Evidence*, *Ghosts*, and *Athena*	63
3	Brushstrokes of Memory: *The Sea*	93
4	The Art of Self-Reflexivity: The Cleave Novels	119
5	John Banville and Heinrich von Kleist— The Art of Confusion: *The Broken Jug*, *God's Gift*, *Love in the Wars*, and *The Infinities*	139
6	Art and Crime: Benjamin Black's Quirke Novels	159
	Conclusion	187
	Bibliography	201
	Index	211
	About the Author	215

ACKNOWLEDGMENTS

This volume has been in process for several years, simmering away in the background while other projects elbowed themselves to the foreground. It thus contains the benefit of many voices over the years—of students, colleagues, and writers—all of whom have shaped my thinking.

Immense gratitude is initially offered to Declan Kiberd and Rüdiger Imhof both of whom were, in different ways, immensely helpful expert guides and always tolerant of the excesses of my early travels. Thanks too to John Moriarty and Pat Sheeran whose conversations on many subjects helped me to think about literature in ways that steadfastly remain with me. More recently, Gerald Dawe, Seán Golden, Dermot Healy, Aidan Higgins, Alannah Hopkin, and Annie Proulx have all continued the conversation in very special ways, always exemplifying extraordinary ways of thinking—there can be no greater gift. Thanks to you all for everything.

Many former and current students have contributed enormously to my thinking about Banville's work—this volume would have been very different without you: Hafizah Amid, Candice Balete, Zoea Chen, Adel Cheong, Joanne Chia, Kang Mengni, Patricia Karunungan, Li Lianghui, Keith Lim, Lim Yiru, Quyen Nguyen, and Yao Xiaoling. It's been my great privilege to work with you.

Similarly so with various colleagues and friends over the years whose imprint is felt on these pages: Boey Kim Cheng, Martin Constable, Jen Crawford, Terence Dawson, Jan Jedrewski, Peter van de Kamp, Geoffrey Keating, Bob Lumsden, Eugene O'Brien, May O Lwin, Niamh Moriarty, Donal McKay, Ondřej Pilný, Thierry Robin, Ron Schleifer, Seeto Wei Peng, John Tangney, and Wee Wan-ling. Deepest gratitude to you all.

Special thanks to Keith Hopper for both his friendship and rich insights, which are greatly cherished. Thanks too to Shirley Chew for her years of friendship and guidance. Huge thanks are also owed to Daniel Jernigan;

ACKNOWLEDGMENTS

friend, colleague, and fellow-schemer. And to Michelle Chiang, Jeremy Fernando, Cheryl Julia Lee, Lim Lee Ching, and Michelle Wang—former students who now teach me precious things every day; thank you all for your friendship and brilliance.

Special thanks are owed to several Banville scholars who have been welcoming and helpful. Derek Hand has been there since the beginning—and is owed particular, and warm, thanks. Thanks too to Hedwig Schwall, Hedda Friberg Harnesk, and Joe McMinn, fellow travelers all.

Several people helped with the text and research at various stages: thanks to Jeanette Pang for patiently and insightfully helping to bring everything to its final state. Thanks to Samuel Wee for his immense work on the earlier drafts, and to Pan Huiting for valuable early assistance with gathering everything in one place.

Particular thanks is offered to Dean Alan Chan for providing a nurturing academic context in the College of Humanities, Arts, and Social Sciences, Nanyang Technological University-Singapore, and for willingly providing the necessary time and space for this work to be completed.

Thanks to the endlessly resourceful staff at the School of Humanities and Social Sciences library, NTU, especially Vincent Wong, the English subject librarian.

Deep gratitude, as always, is offered to Rose, Ted, Con, and Tim. Special thanks to James and Mary, and their wonderful family for making our Summers, year after year, special oases of warmth.

My children, Maya, Nadia, Lia, and Dylan, deserve endless thanks for simply being there, and for always making the world brighter. And to Su I offer deepest thanks—for giving me the world—this book is yours as much as mine.

Over the years several grants and scholarships have enabled work on this book. I am grateful to Hermione Lee for supporting my Visiting Scholarship at Wolfson College, University of Oxford, in 2016, where several chapters of this book were written. In addition, this work was supported with the assistance of a Singapore, Ministry of Education ACRF Tier 1 research grant, for which thanks and appreciation are duly registered. Similarly, thanks are owed to the College of Humanities, Arts, and Social Sciences for funding several research and conferences trips which were immensely beneficial to the development of the work. Warm thanks too are due to Frank Finlay, John Whale, and Lance Pettitt, for hosting invited talks on Banville at the University of Leeds and St. Mary's University, respectively.

ACKNOWLEDGMENTS

It has been a pleasure to work with colleagues at Bucknell University Press, and Rowman & Littlefield, on the production of this book, in particular, Greg Clingham, Pam Dailey, John Rickard, and Zachary Nycum.

Thanks to John Banville for the words, and for permission to quote from his work.

Initial versions of some of the current work appeared previously in other publications and I thank the editors for their permission to reprint in modified form:

"John Banville and Heinrich von Kleist: The Art of Confusion." *The Review of Contemporary Fiction*, Volume XXXIV, No. 1, Spring 2014: 54–70.

"Crimes of Elegance: Benjamin Black's Impersonation of John Banville." *Moving Worlds*, Volume 13, No. 1, Spring, 2013: 19–32.

ILLUSTRATIONS/PERMISSIONS

Jean-Antoine Watteau, *Gilles* (1718–1719). Oil on canvas. 72.6 × 58.9 in. (184 x 149 cm). Musée du Louvre. ©RMN-Grand Palais/Art Resource, NY.

Jean-Antoine Watteau (1684-1721). *L'Embarquement pour Cythère* (Embarkation for Cythera), (1717). Oil on canvas. 50.8 × 76.4 in. (82 x 65 cm). Inv. No. INV8525. Photo Stéphane Maréchalle. Musée du Louvre. ©RMN-Grand Palais/Art Resource, NY.

Willem Drost, *Portrait of a Woman* (1653-5). Oil on canvas. 50.8 × 76.4 in. (129 x 195 cm). SzépművészetiMúzeum / Museum of Fine Arts, 2018.

Pierre Bonnard, *Nude in the Bath, and Small Dog* (1941-6). Oil on canvas. 48 1/4 x 59 1/4 in. (122.55 x 150.5 cm). Carnegie Museum of Art, Pittsburg. With thanks to the Artists Rights Society (ARS) and Carnegie Museum of Art. © Adagp, Paris [2018]

Pierre Bonnard, *Table in Front of the Window* (1934-5). Oil on canvas. 40 x 28.5 in. (101.5 x 72.5 cm). Private Collection. With thanks to the Artists Rights Society. © Adagp, Paris [2018]

Pablo Picasso (1881-1973), © ARS NY. *The Old Guitarist* (1903 - early 1904). Oil on Panel. 48 ⅜ x 32½ in. (122.9 x 82.6 cm). Helen Birch Bartlett Memorial Collection, 1926.253. The Art Institute of Chicago. Photo Credit: The Art Institute of Chicago/Art Resource, NY. ARS, NY. ©Succession Picasso 2018.

ACKNOWLEDGMENTS

Édouard Manet (1832-1883), *Déjeuner sur l'herbe* (Luncheon on the Grass), (1863). Oil on canvas. 48 ⅜ x 32½ in. (208 x 264.5 cm). Inv. RF1668. Photo: Benoît Touchard/Mathieu Rabeau. Musée d'Orsay. ©RMN-Grand Palais/Art Resource, NY.

ABBREVIATIONS

The Works of John Banville:

A	*Athena* (London: Secker & Warburg, 1995).
AL	*Ancient Light* (New York: Viking Penguin, 2012).
BG	*The Blue Guitar* (London: Viking Penguin, 2015).
BoE	*The Book of Evidence* (London: Secker & Warburg, 1989).
BW	*Birchwood* (London: Panther Books, 1984).
DC	*Doctor Copernicus* (London: Panther Books, 1984).
E	*Eclipse* (London: Picador, 2000).
G	*Ghosts* (London: Secker & Warburg, 1993).
K	*Kepler* (London: Panther Books, 1985).
LL	*Long Lankin* (London: Secker & Warburg, 1970).
M	*Mefisto* (New Hampshire: David R. Godine, 1989).
NL	*The Newton Letter: An Interlude* (London: Panther Books, 1984).
NS	*Nightspawn* (London: Secker & Warburg, 1971).
S	*Shroud* (London: Picador, 2002).
TI	*The Infinities* (London: Picador, 2009).
TS	*The Sea* (London: Picador, 2005).

The Works of Benjamin Black:

BEB	*The Black-Eyed Blonde* (New York: Henry Holt, 2014).
CF	*Christine Falls* (London: Picador, 2006).
DS	*A Death in Summer* (London: Mantle, 2011).
EA	*Elegy for April* (London: Picador, 2011).
ED	*Even the Dead* (London: Penguin, 2016).
HO	*Holy Orders* (New York: Henry Holt, 2013).

ABBREVIATIONS

L   *The Lemur* (London: Picador, 2008).
TSS   *The Silver Swan* (London: Picador, 2007).
V   *Vengeance* (London: Mantle, 2012).

Drama and Screenplays:

BJ   *The Broken Jug: After Heinrich von Kleist* (Oldcastle: Gallery Press, 1994. 1st prod, at the Peacock Theatre, Dublin, 1 June 1994. Dir. Ben Barnes).
GG   *God's Gift: A Version of Amphitryon by Heinrich von Kleist* (Oldcastle: Gallery, 2000. 1st prod, at the O'Reilly Theatre, Belvedere College, Dublin, 12 October 2000. Dir. Veronica Coburn).
LW   *Love in the Wars: After Kleist's Penthesilea* (Oldcastle: Gallery, 2005).

INTRODUCTION

"The autumn sun fell slantwise into the yard, making the cobbles bluely shine, and in the porch a pot of geraniums flourished aloft their last burning blossoms of the season. Honestly, this world."

(TS, 58)

In John Banville's novel, *The Blue Guitar* (2015), the painter-narrator, Oliver Orme, initiates a retrospective account of his ongoing artistic crisis in the following manner: "One day I saw the problem, just like that, and nothing was to be the same again. And what was the problem? It was this: that out there is the world and in here is the picture of it, and between the two yawns the man-killing crevasse."[1] What follows in the first section of the novel is the integration of a sequence of observations about his artistic crisis with the unfolding of his illicit love-affair with Polly. Oliver's description of Polly persistently resonates with his artistically motivated transformative eye; she seems to him "not newly beautiful, but to radiate something I hadn't noticed before, something that was hers, uniquely: the abundance of her, the very being of her" (*BG*, 6). But the elaborate observations about his painterly process offer an additional layer of significance: "Don't misunderstand me, my effort wasn't to reproduce the world, or even to represent it. The pictures I painted were intended as autonomous things, things to match the world's things, the unmanageable thereness of which had somehow to be managed" (*BG*, 58). In all of these aspects, Oliver could be referring to the pivotal sense of artistic process-crisis that defines all of Banville's work, reminding one of the extraordinary levels of cross-textual significance in his body of work. At one point, for instance, Oliver refers to himself as Gavrilo Princep, one of the

INTRODUCTION

Serbian assassins who murdered the Archduke Ferdinand, sparking World War 1, but Gavrilo is also the Serbian word for Gabriel, the narrator of Banville's second novel, *Birchwood* (1973), which arguably initiated the deeply integrated, self-conscious, artistic adventure that has recurred in modified forms for the past forty years.[2] Gabriel Godkin was consumed with artistic process in *Birchwood*—and all that that entailed—while Oliver Orme is a painter who seeks to articulate an artistic crisis that is both his and, simultaneously, that of all Banville's artist-creators in the intervening years.

The dominant significance of John Banville's fiction lies in its focused, cumulative development of an aesthetically self-conscious discourse that both defines the overt narrated concerns within each novel and also registers the status of the novels as works of art in their own right. This multitextured discourse extends far beyond the intricate network of allusions to the visual arts, literature and philosophy that characterizes his fictional storyworlds. Similarly, the overt self-conscious commentaries that emerge from his various characters' obsessions with paintings, forgeries, philosophy, and literature, as well as from the use of scientific and historical metaphoric frames, are all simply constituent components of richly textured fictive worlds that are themselves worthy of consideration as works of art of a specific kind. But Banville's body of fiction is far more sophisticated and ambitious than even such overt signals imply. His contention that a work of art "is not about something, it is something,"[3] offers a valuable indicator of aesthetic intent that alludes both to the diminished value of subject matter and representation in his work and to the principle that the work itself is not merely an attempt to replicate some potential world *out there* but to establish an artistic ontology with an inherent system of value. Banville's fictional storyworlds are intricate, multilayered, narrative structures that act as frames in which his medley of characters each extend what can be viewed as one long elaboration of the same impulse: to create art forms that self-consciously engage with, and are ultimately conditioned by, the meaning and presence of art. This is achieved by the construction of what is surely one of the most richly textured, imaginative universes in all of post-1950s fiction, and one which compares with the formal density and interconnectedness of writers like Joyce and Beckett.

Banville's insistence on the status of his own work as art, and on the pursuit of beauty as the proper aim of the artist, have long characterized his observations in interviews and commentaries.[4] Furthermore, his overall body of work is both representative of a very specific understanding of what art entails and is simultaneously exemplary of the process of its own evolution as art. As such, his work represents a particularly intricate form of contemporary self-reflexive fiction. Banville claims that he has "always been fascinated by the possibility of taking the form of the popular novel and turning it into an art form,"[5] although what he means by art is far more nuanced both in its conception and execution than such teasing statements suggest. Central to his understanding of art is a distinction between meaning—or what he names "translatable content"—and significance.[6] Echoing Nietzsche's rejection of "the identical" as a feasible artistic aim, Banville disputes the first principle of representative narrative fiction as a replica of life: "Nothing is translatable really. I don't think anything has meaning, in the sense that I define it."[7] In this context *meaning* suggests a mode of knowable signification or representation, or a sense of art as a vehicle of comment, opinion and rhetorical purpose. Art's *significance*, alternatively, lies in its capacity to "make vivid for the reader the mysterious predicament of being alive"[8] and aims to "go beyond mere human doing to the question of what it is to be, the question of being in the world. And that's what all artists do, however they work."[9]

At the heart of such observations lies the perennial aesthetic question of the significance of content, or subject-matter, in works of art and the tension between competing oppositions of utility and beauty, or logos and mythos. The aesthetic philosopher, Gordon Graham, for example, points to the obvious limitations of interpretive paraphrasing when compared with the actual works of literature from which the activity is derived.[10] He also argues that "a novel is not to be thought of as providing us with a faithful reflection of experience or a skilful summary of it, but as obliging us to view some aspect of experience through an image which allows us to attain an illuminating perspective on it."[11] The key point here relates to the capacity that art has to *illuminate* experience, rather than to reflect it, as with Banville's assertion that art may have significance rather than meaning. As Graham indicates, the confusion between meaning and significance is derived from the mistake of applying "aesthetic cognitivism to imaginative literature,"[12] resulting in a kind of educated summary of the work of art whose primary value lies precisely in that aspect which cannot be summarized:

> These difficulties arise chiefly because it is natural to think that any cognitive element in poetry or novels—what there is to be learned from them—is in *what* they say and not in the *form* in which they say it. Yet if the form of a poem or a novel is not central to its assessment as an artistic achievement, it would appear to follow that literary art cannot amount to more than "embroidery and embellishment"

INTRODUCTION

(to use John Locke's terms), and that paraphrase can replace poetry without significant loss of meaning.[13]

The complex form that is the literary work becomes reducible and is effectively erased as an art form in any full sense, when paraphrase occurs.

For Graham, the fraught relationship between the work of art and material reality is a key issue but this does not so much represent a refusal to acknowledge a significant connection between the work of art and the world as to assert a special nonrepresentational relationship: "the literary devices of poetry and the novel can be used to create images which oblige us to view our experience in certain ways and thus illuminate aspects of it."[14] The formative potential of the artistic on received experience is prioritized and ultimately Graham argues that works of art "actually create the world of that experience for us by fashioning master-images that become paradigms for thought and conduct."[15] Herein lies the true significance of the artistic impulse for Graham. His vision of the artwork as imaginative paradigm, as a form that reshapes experience, echoes Banville's explanation of his way of working: "I have no messages to deliver. I simply want to re-create the world as I see it and to provide delight to readers. No messages."[16] He has been remarkably consistent on this point and has repeatedly explained his work in terms of its distance from a literal relationship with representational or material reality: "I'm not interested in politics, I'm not interested in society, I'm not interested in Man. I seem to be just interested in this voice that goes on and on and on in my head."[17] In fact, he believes that any direct social engagement is problematic for the literary artist: "If you mix politics and art, you get bad politics and bad art.... For art, subject is always incidental, or at least secondary, to the work itself."[18]

While Banville has acknowledged that there is "something of me and my history" in all of the novels' characters,[19] the relationship between his work and life is muted, at best, with his basic biography offering little direct correlation with the subject matter of his novels. He was born in Wexford town, in S. E. Ireland, to a garage clerk father, and homemaker mother, and attended St. Peters College, Wexford. Instead of attending university he chose to work for the Irish airline *Aer Lingus* for several years after which he worked as a journalist for close to forty years, initially as a subeditor with the now defunct *Irish Press*, then as a subeditor and literary editor with the *Irish Times*. He remains a regular book reviewer. He has two children with the American artist Janet Durham, whom he married in 1969. While he admits that *The Sea*[20] is based in the fictionalized Rosslare, the seaside town where he spent every summer as a child,[21] and Cleave's house in *Eclipse*[22] is the Wexford house in which he was born,[23] he nevertheless insists that he has no interest in writing about himself at all, because he views true art to be impersonal.[24] In the recently published *Time Pieces: A Dublin Memoir* (2016), Banville comes as close as he ever has to writing about his own life and acknowledges, in particular, that certain places, locations, "imprint themselves on the memory with improbable vividness and clarity" (2), and indicates how a certain bend in the Avoca river found its way into *The Newton Letter* (3), and a flat in Mount Street in Dublin, where he once lived, was given to Quirke as his dwelling place (66). Similarly, the name of the Reck family, who lived in a flat above him in Dublin, appears in several Banville works (*The Broken Jug* [1994], *The Book of Evidence* [1989], for example).[25] Nevertheless, Banville's memoir of Dublin repeatedly acknowledges the essential elusiveness of the world about which he writes: "Let us say, the present is where we live, while the past is where we dream" (4). More emphatically, he insists in the memoir that he has never "paid much attention to my surroundings wherever it was I happened to find myself. . . . Art is a constant effort to strike past the daily doings of humankind in order to arrive at, or at least to approach as closely as possible to, the essence of what it is, simply, to be" (53).

Some peripheral fragments from his own life reappear in the later novels, particularly in the settings of *Eclipse*, *The Sea*, and *Ancient Light*,[26] but the subject matter of the novels has little connection with Banville's life. He does concede that the core subject of *The Book of Evidence*, Freddie's "failure of imagination" holds resonance for the Omagh bombing (1998) and the general failure of imagination that accompanied the violence in Ireland between the 1960s and 1990s.[27] Nonetheless, Banville doesn't regard himself as an Irish writer in the sense that he writes about explicitly Irish subject matter, even if he admits to sharing an oblique usage of language with an Irish tradition.[28] It's a key difference that is tied to his impersonal artistic perspective. Even if there is a linguistic grammar that he inevitably inherits, the role of the artist is not to represent reality in a discursive manner: "I think it's not that writers should be writing about Ireland and our crisis and so on. That's not what artists do. I don't think it is. I don't think it's even what novelists do."[29] Furthermore, he suggests that such essentially material matters cease to be of any significance during the act of writing:

> Away from his desk the novelist can care deeply about the social, political, moral aspects of what he is writing but when he sits down

> to write, all those concerns fall away and nothing matters except the putting down of one carefully chosen word after another carefully chosen word, until a sentence is finished, then a paragraph, then a page, then a chapter, then a book.[30]

Banville's repeated observation that subject matter, or content, is only of peripheral significance is, of course, closely related to his general refusal to write fiction that is explicitly derived from his life, or that of his general social milieu: "By what means, then, does fiction *get at* the world? Not by engagement, I am convinced, but precisely by disengagement, by adopting a posture of bland innocence, standing back with empty palms on show. . . . The subject matter hardly matters."[31]

Such views may appear anathema to socially inclined critics but Banville's observations reflect a relatively common position in aesthetic philosophy and among a certain tradition of writers. For example, Etienne Gilson argues that while "an element of signification necessarily enters into the composition of any poetry," because poetry is "fashioned" out of words, it "does not follow that poetry's object is to signify anything whatever: concepts, images or feelings. Poetry always does this, more or less, but this is not its proper end," and insists instead that the proper end of poetry is to "create beauty with words."[32] Similarly, using Stan Brakhage's cinema as an example, the philosopher Noël Carroll specifically points to the formal attributes of the filmmaker to illustrate his work's status as art, and highlights how Brakhage "searched for artistic strategies that would promote audience attention to the purely visual" and "excises narratorial and pictorial elements from his films so that they would not draw attention away from our concentration on the look of the film."[33] Again, the elevation of the form above content asserts itself as a measure of artistic activity that echoes Banville's insistence on the primacy of the formal and the incidental nature of subject-matter. In this, Banville's work echoes a distinct European novelistic tradition that includes authors as diverse as Nabokov, Calvino, and Kundera, and which the latter defines in terms of its distance from realism:

> Laurence Sterne's *Tristram Shandy* and Denis Diderot's *Jacques le Fataliste* are for me the two greatest novelistic works of the eighteenth century [. . .] They reached heights of playfulness, or lightness, never scaled before or since. Afterward the novel got itself tied to the imperative of verisimilitude, to realistic settings, to chronological order. It abandoned the possibilities opened up by these two masterpieces, which could have led to a different development of the novel.[34]

Realism, for Kundera, is fatally tied to the principle of the literary work as a storehouse of knowledge and suggests that those who "declare knowledge to be the novel's sole morality are betrayed by the metallic aura of 'knowledge,' a word too much compromised by its links with the sciences," and instead suggests, like Gilson, that "whatever aspects of existence the novel discovers, it discovers as the beautiful. The earliest novelists discovered adventure. Thanks to them we find adventure itself beautiful and wish to have it."[35] Banville too sees the pursuit of beauty as central to his artistic activity: "Beauty is a word that we haven't mentioned yet, but it's crucial to me. It's what I'm after constantly. Beauty is an almost nonhuman pursuit."[36] The "nonhuman" pursuit is directly linked to a particular kind of writing by those who have "abandoned the pretense of realism" and who have "ceased to speak about things in favor of speaking the things themselves, such as Beckett . . . or those who took old forms and worked a revolution from within, such as Henry James."[37]

The resonant influence of Henry James is crucial to Banville's aesthetic, particularly with respect to the manner in which his works openly announce the myriad ways that the imagining consciousness reshapes and illuminates the world of experience, or offers up self-evident artificial images to stand above or beyond "identical" worlds of referential reality. James, using the metaphor of the house of fiction, emphasizes the multiplicity of "apertures, of dissimilar shape and size," behind which is positioned "a figure with a pair of eyes, or at least with a field-glass, which forms again and again, for observation, a unique instrument, insuring to the person making use of it an impression distinct from every other."[38] It is this figure who then becomes an instrument of artistic creation:

> The spreading field, the human scene, is the "choice of subject"; the pierced aperture, either broad or balconied or slit-like and low-browed, is the "literary form"; but they are, singly or together, as nothing without the posted presence of the watcher—without, in other words, the consciousness of the artist. Tell me what the artist is, and I will tell you of what he has *been* conscious.[39]

In Banville's early novel *Birchwood*, alluding to James's "house of fiction," Gabriel Godkin promises to remain in his "house" alone and to "live a life different from any the house has ever known," a statement that Banville later claimed was the "only direct statement I've *ever* made in any book that I have written."[40] All of Banville's work occurs in one elaboration or another of this house of fiction of endlessly reimagined dimensions and features, replete with

INTRODUCTION

revisited obsessions, character types, and imagistic patterns, which ultimately map the topographical terrain of his aestheticized world. Inherent to these elaborations of the house is the perpetual presence of the artistic consciousness that informs everything either through direct first person narration, or via various interloper figures who frequently appear in the work. Irrespective of the apparent subject matter—morality, science, historical reconstruction, art forgeries, impersonation, acting, thieving, or painting—Banville's novels are always more concerned with art in a fundamental sense, with the positioning of the imagining consciousness, the watcher at the window, who seeks to prepare a glittering surface for the work of art.

The resistance to the referential impulse is also apparent in another of Banville's major influences, Nabokov,[41] who asserts a crucial distinction between what he calls "average reality" and a higher order of reality when he suggests that "[a]verage reality begins to rot and stink as soon as the act of individual creation ceases to animate a subjectively perceived texture."[42] Alternatively, the attainment of "true reality," as projected in literary fiction, involves a formal reconceiving of reality and allows one to reenvision the constituent parts of the reflected reality. Banville's works always project overtly artificial worlds, corresponding to Nabokov's "true reality," reflected in fiction only by the construction of "real, authentic worlds."[43] Realist fiction, for Nabokov, represents but a journalistic reality, or what he terms the reality of "general ideas, conventional forms of humdrummery, current editorials."[44] This contrast is again reflective of the critical gap between materialist expectations and artistic principles and is indicative of the fascination that one finds repeatedly in Banville's work, but it also underpins critical observations on the development of the novel in Europe. Milan Kundera, as indicated earlier, views Sterne's *Tristram Shandy* and Diderot's *Jacques le Fataliste* to be central antecedents to a nonrealist tradition, and pinpoints the qualities of playfulness and lightness that define their work.[45] Italo Calvino, similarly, writes of the "adventurous, picaresque inner rhythm" or the "quick light touch" that he aspired to as an antidote to the "weight, the inertia, the opacity of the world—qualities that stick to writing from the start, unless one finds some way of evading them."[46] Calvino's aesthetic desire to fashion images closely resonates with Banville's, or what he terms the "wrought and polished object itself," the "pictured world," in which the lovingly fashioned artificial is always vividly declared.[47] Within the novels, this accounts for the overt artificiality that is generated from the self-conscious mode, the rich allusory frame that defines the fictional universes, and from the comparative descriptions that frequently liken his worlds to artworks. For example, in *The Sea* Morden appears to admire the landscape—but only via his imaginative infusion of the fictional world with Tiepolo's frescoes: "It was a sumptuous, oh, truly a sumptuous day, all Byzantine coppers and golds under a Tiepolo sky of enameled blue, the countryside all fixed and glassy, seeming not so much itself as its own reflection in the still surface of a lake" (45). The world is both itself, on the primary level of plot and, simultaneously, resonant of other worlds derived from elegant composites of the visual arts, literature, mythology, and literature.

Banville's persistent identification of his fictions as works of art may seem faintly odd, or anachronistic, in contemporary literary circles, as is evident from the fact that reviewers and commentators persist in returning to his suggestion that it was "nice to see a work of art win the Booker prize," after *The Sea* was announced as the winner in 2005, as though it were somehow a controversial statement.[48] The designation of literature as a form of art has, after all, a very long tradition in Philosophical history, as eloquently summarized by Peter Lamarque in his *The Philosophy of Literature*, in which he claims, citing Aristotle, Horace, Abbé Charles Batteux, Hegel, among others, that literature, "primarily in the modes of poetry and drama," has been considered "an art form for over two millennia."[49] Similarly, Etienne Gilson argues that literature is one of the primary art forms, suggesting that there is "an art of the beautiful in literature each time that the end of a word is its own beauty, independently of its truth" and while he claims that poetry "finally, is the supreme form of the arts of language,"[50] he concedes that many novels are "works of art."[51] Frank Kermode assumes an even more assertive position with respect to prose fiction when he claims that "in our phase of civility, the novel is the central form of literary art,"[52] offering an indication not only of the primacy of the form in contemporary writing but also asserting its status as art whose "relation of fiction and reality is uniquely reimagined."[53] A renegotiation of the relation between reality and fiction, or between material reality and constructed images, has clear resonance for the world-making tendencies of the novel form which has had a consciousness of its own image-making tendencies throughout one part of its tradition—since novels like *Tristram Shandy*. Such tendencies are never empty formal gestures but instead acknowledge the complexity of the relationship between phenomenological reality and art, by developing the sophisticated form that the novel became, what Gordon Graham refers to as the "device of multilayered representation" that one finds in novels.[54] The aesthetic form into which the novel evolved declares its artistry in many ways, as Peter Lamarque suggests:

INTRODUCTION

> As the genre developed, now-familiar criteria emerged for judging better or worse novels: to do with plot, character, structure, good writing, thematic interest, verisimilitude, originality. Such criteria, which are not too distant from those proposed by Aristotle for tragedy, are artistic criteria in the sense that they concern the artifice of the whole and the pleasure to be derived from it.[55]

The artistry of all complex literary forms seeks to generate master images, paradigms that might speak of human experience in an imaginative fashion in order to "illuminate" aspects of that experience, to return to Graham's distinction between works of art and other narrative forms, and the implicit relationship between Banville's declaration that his works have significance but not meaning.

The tension between "meaning" and the aspirations of art generates a fundamental question in philosophical aesthetics. Gilson, for example, repeatedly draws our attention to the difference between knowledge and making, and argues that readers frequently err in confusing meaning with the true aspiration of the work of art: "What we look for in a beautiful work is often not its beauty, but the meaning, the moral or speculative information it contains. Nothing could be more legitimate, provided meaning is not mistaken for beauty."[56] Banville too tells us that it is precisely "beauty" to which he aspires.[57] Gilson's logic is derived from what he views to be the essential difference between the real, or knowledge, and art, or the beautiful. In other words, the images upon which the literary arts are based are "less imitations of ready-made things than models of things to be made. They are directly conceived and formed as prototypes of so many possible works, waiting for the artist to give them the actual existences they lack."[58] Echoing Graham's "master images,"[59] or Banville's insistence on "artifice,"[60] or perhaps even Kundera's "suddenly kindled light of the never-before-said,"[61] Gilson's focus on the artistic image, primarily as a unique nonrealist mode of expression, is central to the artistic ethos of nonrepresentational art, or art that seeks to alert the reader to the primacy of its artifice rather than to the content, the world, which it echoes across the artistic gulf. Banville's work needs to be considered in such an aesthetic context rather than excavated as a vehicle of meaning.

The production of illuminating images, or paradigms, as Graham has it, nevertheless holds implications for the manner in which aspects of the real world are embodied. For example, the manner in which Banville has depicted women, frequently at the very center of his narrators' philosophical and aesthetic focus, raises some crucial questions. Throughout the work there is a clear interconnection between the aesthetically driven transformative zeal of Banville's narrators and the way that female figures embody and focalize this zeal. As early as *Birchwood* the female characters are largely aspects of both Gabriel's artistic journey and his sexual development, a combination that offers a telling signal of Banville's persistent blending of a particular form of eroticism and aesthetic intent in future novels. For example, approximately four decades later, in *Ancient Light*, a youthful Alex Cleave recounts his affair with his friend's mother, Mrs. Celia Gray, and largely repeats the same pattern. While Alex depicts, in detail, his "plunging and gouging" of Mrs. Gray's insides (43), he simultaneously, and repeatedly, emphasizes an aestheticized attentiveness to his subject, in much the same manner that Banville has always done. He assures the reader that he has "never been so sharply conscious of the presence of another human being, this separate entity, this incommensurable not-I" (35), in terms that are strongly reminiscent of Freddie Montgomery's insistence, immediately before he murders Josie in *The Book of Evidence*, that he had "never felt another's presence so immediately and with such raw force" (113). While many critics of Banville have not closely analyzed the significance of his representation of female figures beyond a few cursory remarks, several have sought to address what is a clearly discernible pattern of representation.

Joseph McMinn was the first critic to observe a distinct pattern of gender representation when he suggested that Banville's main characters are men "who are almost invariably fascinated by images of women" and thus the work is "an anatomy, and a pathology, of a distinctively male psyche,"[62] although he largely views this tendency as a matter of representation, or content, and does not explore the role of women within Banville's larger aesthetic enterprise. In response to McMinn's comments, Derek Hand acknowledges that Banville "can be taken to task for his representation of women" but sees a correspondence between his narrator's general difficulty with the "unknowable" and the manner in which he describes women.[63] While it is not difficult to demonstrate that Banville's narrators are frequently puzzled by the strangeness of existence and that their representation of males is every bit as likely to be self-consciously subverted, it is the specific nature of the positioning and representation of women that invites closer consideration.

There are some very particular patterns of female representation evident throughout most of Banville. Ruth Frehner, for example, has argued that "complementary women figures," "the dark one and the fair, haunt most if not all of Banville's protagonists"[64] and that they are all "mediated through the mind of a male protagonist, a narrator, and more than anything else, they reflect his desires and fears."⁶⁵ Similarly, Elke D'Hoker, in her ethical reading of *The Book of Evidence* distinguishes between the "malleable" female figures in paintings and flesh-and-blood women. She suggests that art is more responsive to Freddie's subjective "imaginative interpretations" than is the resistant figure of the actual Josie Bell. Freddie thus feels "threatened both by Josie Bell's sudden difference from what he had assumed her to be and by her sudden similarity and proximity to him as a physical and entirely unartistic human being." He erases her alterity by killing her. While the primary function of such a reading is to argue for an ethical reading on *The Book of Evidence*, D'Hoker also argues that there is a gendered pattern to Freddie's actions, suggesting that he shares a "fear of physicality and of certain types of women with other Banville protagonists."⁶⁶

Patricia Coughlan also discerns a specific pattern of female representation and claims that there is an eroticized "insistent recurrence of threesomes" prevalent in Banville's work, in which a male and two females are featured, whose "typical dispositions are of a man watching and women watched."⁶⁷ Thus, the male voyeur watches the exhibitionist female(s) in classic gestures of supplication. Coughlan views this model as part of a Pygmalion-style aesthetic mode in which the male (Pygmalion) figures "visualize the sexually attractive female characters of their milieu as objects of aesthetic representation, entire works of art or figures from such works, who are brought to life by the galvanizing imaginative energies of these self-deluding heroes."⁶⁸ Coughlan's question, ultimately, is whether Banville in fact retains a conservative aesthetic model when it comes to the representation of women, despite his apparent progressive and deconstructive aesthetic model. Is Banville's "posthumanism," she asks, "despite itself a ruse of containment" that leaves "some foundations undisturbed?" Finally, she interprets the closing sequence of *Eclipse*, in which the dead Cass appears, as raising the possibility that perhaps at last "she is an other truly recognized as herself," although it is clear that certain reservations remain.⁶⁹ Anja Müller's exploration of the function of ekphrasis in the Frames Trilogy, with respect to the representation of women, also brings together several keys strands in Banville's aestheticization of women:

> In *The Book of Evidence*, the narrator tries to materialize a woman (i.e., to render her most vividly) through ekphrasis, while objectifying her as if she were a picture. In *Ghosts*, the woman gradually takes shape within the frame of a narrative, but this narrative is eventually revealed as nothing but an ekphrasis in disguise. In *Athena* the represented woman appears to assume enough agency to step out

of the frame of ekphrasis into the narrative, and, ultimately, out of that, as well; her body nevertheless remains strangely elusive and immaterial.[70]

For Müller the issue is whether Banville's female figures ever acquire agency beyond the subjective imaginings of their male Pygmalion narrators. While Flora in *Ghosts* appears on the threshold of attaining such a status, she is thereafter silenced by virtue of her depiction via numerous allusions to paintings—she is thus offered no genuine voice of her own and fails to genuinely materialize.[71] Alternatively, Müller sees A. in *Athena* as having come close to finally having achieved the "transformation of a female character from a statuesque or painterly representation into a full-fledged, material, live body because she is so mobile, evasive and fluctuating."[72] As such, A. represents a progressive development in female representation for Müller rather than merely another negative representation in the Banville pantheon of women characters.[73]

More recently, Carol Dell'Amico has characterized the critical response to Banville's depiction of women in general as being suggestive that "his writing is coincident with the masculinism of the histories summoned into the novels by problematic citations." This, she asserts, is because in novels like *Athena*, Banville offers uncritical commentary on the sequence of paintings that deal with "classical rape and seduction" resulting in "a distressed sexual atmosphere," although she also suggests that "uncritical citations of this sort outside of *Athena* are few."[74] Her rationale stems from the logic that while critics like Hand, Frehner, and Coughlan have assembled a "selection of gendered elements as reflections of Banville's corresponding gender and sexual imaginary," they continue to pass over contradictory elements and argue that "a masculinist aesthetic shapes the writing." In particular, she claims that despite Coughlan's identification of Banville's masculinist "visuality" there is no further development of this as an aesthetic process.[75] Dell'Amico identifies Müller's work on Banville as being the only attempt to specifically interrogate what a masculinist aesthetic means with respect to his work, via a detailed consideration of the novels' feminine ekphrasis which embodies "a masculinist way of knowing, as a reflection of Banville's core aesthetic." Ultimately, Dell'Amico's point is that Banville's work sometimes lacks an overt feminist sensibility. Nonetheless, she argues that his masculinist aesthetic is not a static condition and that there is a progressive movement in the more recent novels towards an integration of a self-conscious awareness of the very masculinist limits that seemed apparent in the earlier work. To support her argument she cites the examples of *Shroud*[76] and *The Infinities*,[77] both of which deploy

INTRODUCTION

a secondary omniscient narrator that "conspicuously illustrates the limits of his male protagonists' knowledge," as well a distinct pattern in the Benjamin Black novels that circles around "the social histories of feminist women with an emphasis on institutionalized masculinism—the species of gender crime to which the uncritical citations of Banville's other writings point."[78] Ultimately she sees Banville's more recent work as offering an "oblique" form of gendered corrective to the mundo constructed in the earlier work.

Whether this is a conscious corrective or not, it certainly seems apparent that there is progression in the post-2000's work. The manner in which Cass's point of view is rendered via free indirect discourse in several sections of *Shroud* contributes to a sense at least of an emergent agency, as well as a shift away from the primary male aesthetic consciousness. She is also intertextually connected to the figure of Phoebe in the Benjamin Black novels who frequently offers a corrective to Quirke's dominant point of view.[79] Banville has claimed that he intended Phoebe "to portray that rarest of things, an independent-minded young woman in 1950s Ireland" and she is certainly important as a central defining point of view in the later Black novels.[80] Even in recent Banville novels like *Ancient Light* and *The Blue Guitar*, in which the primary female characters are still *initially* positioned at the center of their narrators' aesthetic aspirations, they each conclude with the female figures having asserted their individual agency and moved beyond the imagining claims of the males who initially held them in thrall. Although Dell'Amico's suggestion that Banville's later work offers an intentional corrective remains a little speculative, there appears to be ample evidence of at least some progressive development both in his representation of women and in their direct significance for the development of a less masculinist aesthetic than had been evident, particularly in the Frames Trilogy.

In some respects the gender question in Banville exemplifies the familiar conflict between content, or representation, and aesthetic form even if in Banville it is exceedingly difficult to separate content from aesthetic intent, given the high degree of art-related content in his plots. Susan Sontag's compelling argument that modern interpretative strategies prioritize "content" above the work of art itself echoes Gilson's distinction between image and knowledge in that "the perennial never consummated project of *interpretation*," effectively becomes an act of translation of the work of art into a mere "set of elements (the X, the Y, the Z, and so forth) from the whole work."[81] Citing Freud, Sontag suggests that the search for "manifest content" then defines the interpretive act and represents a kind of "revenge of the intellect" on the impermeability of works of art.[82] Banville's own association of "translatable content" with meaning further stresses the fundamental distinction between these apparent oppositions and also firmly positions his work in a very recognizable aesthetic mode that asserts both the complex relationship between art and life and, simultaneously, the essential distinction between the two. The absence of "real life" is replaced by the aestheticized artificial, a model that both resembles that which it echoes—life—and yet attains its own essential attributes of strangeness and self-contained otherness.

By generating a persistent sense of otherness Banville's fictional worlds also register the essential remoteness and indifference of material reality. As Max (or Morden), in *The Sea*, informs us, "I marveled, not for the first time, at the cruel complacency of ordinary things. But no, not cruel, not complacent, only indifferent, as how could they be otherwise?" (20). This indifference is frequently embodied in the characters, as Rüdiger Imhof observes, with reference to Max's childhood friend, Chloe: "Her willful vagueness tormented and infuriated him, and he had to put up with her caprices, her high-handedness. But it was she who gave him his first experience of the absolute otherness or people."[83] Banville has always been fascinated by the sense of otherness generated by the indifferent material world and this finds appropriate expression in the self-contained disinterestedness of art that characterizes his work. This sense of distance between the creative mind and the world is, according to Denis Donoghue, a quality that resides at the center of genuine artistic activity: "Autonomy, disinterestedness, and impersonality are the values to be recognized."[84] The disinterestedness of art is, in effect, a mirror of the world's essential indifference. So, when Max, near the close of his account, again reminds us of the "great world's shrugs of indifference," Banville is alerting us to both the odd sense of dislocation that one feels in the face of the world and the peculiar, mirrored, otherness that works of art possess, a point emphasized by Susanne Langer in her discussion of the arts in general:

> Every real work of art has a tendency to appear thus dissociated from its mundane environment. The most immediate impression it creates is one of "otherness" from reality—the impression of an illusion enfolding the thing, action, statement, or flow of sound that constitutes the work.[85]

Otherness, she argues, has been variously articulated as "'strangeness,' 'semblance,' 'illusion,' 'transparency,' 'autonomy,' and 'self-sufficiency.'"[86] Banville has frequently claimed that the world's strangeness, and his characters' puzzlement in

INTRODUCTION

the face of it, best defines his work.[87] Thus, the strangeness of the storyworlds is relationally (rather than representationally) connected to the world from which it was originally derived. It also appears clear, especially with a self-contained author like Banville, that the fictional world doesn't have a natural counterpoint in social reality beyond a limited surface signposting or, as Linda Hutcheon claims, with respect to the possible autonomous nature of fictional worlds: "In literature words create worlds; they are not necessarily counters, however adequate, to any extraordinary reality. In that very fact lays their aesthetic validity and their ontological status."[88]

In the face of an indifferent material reality, Banville's fictional universes are always characterized by a sense of the autonomous, or the inherent glow of the artificial, and not simply on the level of narratorial description. In fact, the sense of the artificial is always self-reflexively proclaimed in the fictions and generates a body of work that is a nuanced contemporary exemplary of the self-conscious mode. This narrative mode became a key constituent feature in his work from the outset, ranging from the relatively predictable metafictional devices that one finds in "The Possessed" (1970) and *Nightspawn*,[89] like the destabilizing, intrusive narrator and the parody of stock genres, to the sophisticated use of the metaphor of the house that one finds in many novels, from *Birchwood* onward. The particular application of this mode becomes a central feature of Banville's aesthetic. The self-conscious mode, of course, implicitly acknowledges the limits of traditional realism, but this was simply a point of departure in Banville's work. Ultimately, one can discern a sophisticated entwined pattern between Banville's artistic observations and his self-consciously artificial plots. He never relinquishes plot to the degree that Beckett does in his fiction and yet radically reimagines its function, which is perpetually at the service of his art. Banville's work can thus be interpreted as a progressive engagement with the significance of the imagining consciousness and each stage in his development as a novelist involves formal and imaginative variants of this investigation.

The profound sense of otherness that characterizes Banville's artificial storyworlds is affected via a variety of key narrative strategies. From the outset, for example, his fictions are richly patterned intertextual composites that engender a deep resonance in the work; on the level of plot there is always a sense of allusory doubling that hints at other fictive worlds shimmering just out of view. Similarly, Banville's characters continually reappear in slightly modified guises throughout his work. For example, a devilish interloper repeatedly appears, initially as the red-haired Michael in *Birchwood*, and as a sequence of other figures in *Nightspawn* (Julian Kyd), *Doctor Copernicus* (Andreas), *Mefisto* (Felix), *Ghosts* (Felix), *Athena* (Francie), *The Sea* (Carlo Grace), *The Infinities* (Benny Grace), and *The Blue Guitar* (Freddie Hyland).[90] Many of Banville's narrators too resemble each other and have similar obsessions. This produces a powerful sense of events being perpetually revisited—or, as Morrow in *Athena* declares: "She is the perfect illustration of Adorno's dictum that 'In their relation to empirical reality works of art recall the theologumenon [sic] that in a state of redemption everything will be just as it is and yet wholly different'" (105). It is in this sense that Banville's fictional contexts are revised, rearranged, and reconceptualized. In addition, there are a series of metaphorical patterns that extend throughout the body of work, including the topographical space of the house, the missing twin or "other" aspect of his own self, and the clown-figure or Pierrot. All such elements serve a variety of self-reflexive purposes and ensure that the primary representative mode is continuously unhinged by the presence of a concurrent, alternate, world that is powerfully present, if embedded beneath the primary plot. This doesn't simply deflate the authority of the primary plot, it generates a series of haunted presences, or worlds that are perpetually out of reach. The creation of this metaphorical spectral world ultimately acts as a figurative indication of Banville's sense of the relationship between art and the world.

Throughout his work Banville erects an evocative sequence of metaphoric parallels to generate a complex literary-aesthetic discourse within his fictions. While notionally this is similar to the overt self-reflexive mode adopted by authors of metafictional texts like Flann O'Brien's *At-Swim-Two-Birds* and Italo Calvino's *If on a winter's night a traveler*, respectively, Banville's method also implicitly rejects the disruptive aesthetic that defined the metafictional novel. Instead, an ostensibly viable plot—however scant—almost always remains in place as a supporting mechanism for the aesthetic discourse that is embedded in the intellectual pursuit of scientific, historical, philosophical, and aesthetic truths in the novels. For instance, Copernicus's account of his process diagnoses the problem with his own scientific system in terms akin to the limits of mimetic fiction which, in turn, self-reflexively reveals Banville's artistic endeavours: "You imagine my book is a kind of mirror in which the real world is reflected; but you are mistaken, you must realise that. In order to build such a mirror, I should need to be able to perceive the whole world, in its entirety and its essence" (*DC*, 219). The overtly plausible plotted worlds that are outlined in the historical novels (*Doctor Copernicus* and *Kepler*[91]) underpin an extension of the discourse one first encounters in *Birchwood*; a distinct

INTRODUCTION

metaphoric parallel between science and art is maintained throughout, allowing Banville to self-reflexively engage with his own art form in terms that echo the creative dimensions of scientific inquiry. But this is just one of several ways that Banville's artistic fictions are representative of a unique kind of fiction. After the science tetralogy his work grows increasingly more innovative in the ways that it articulates an aesthetic discourse.

In the following chapters, Banville's development of an extended discourse about art, and about his own evolving aesthetic, will be traced via the major developmental stages of his career. All of the major works will be investigated within the context of this centrally significant movement, focussing both on pivotal individual novels and on several clusters of novels that speak more closely to each other's development. While there is significant treatment of the science tetralogy in chapter 1, the emphasis lies primarily on the metaphorical significance of science for Banville's aesthetic trajectory. In any event, the four science novels have been attended to in great detail in earlier years by Imhof and McMinn, and thereafter by Berensmeyer. Furthermore, this work doesn't explicitly deal with *The Untouchable*,[92] primarily because it doesn't represent a key developmental moment in Banville, nor is it nominally part of one of the important groupings of novels; its integrated value is thus not compelling to Banville's overall development. Furthermore, in many respects it explicitly revisits several tropes and technical treatments of art that had earlier been employed. For example, as Victoria Stewart points out, *The Untouchable* "fits into the category of historiographic fiction"[93] that had been used in novels like *Doctor Copernicus* and *Kepler*, and "the imaginative trajectory for the narrative is the same" as all of his other novels, in Eibhear Walsh's view.[94] Furthermore, the deployment of the fake painting as a doubled emblem of authenticity/inauthenticity is also used extensively in *Ghosts* and *Athena*.

Initially, chapter 1 will trace the evolution of Banville's aesthetic by focusing on some artistically self-conscious developmental stages in the literary fiction, including the trope of the house, the progression beyond the limits of metafiction, and the experimentation with science. This chapter is bookended by considerations of two key novels, *Birchwood* and *Mefisto*, illustrating the manner in which certain Banville novels represent key developmental moments. *The Book of Evidence* is another such key moment in Banville's progressive trajectory and forms the central focus of attention in chapter 2. The direct confrontation with the meaning of the imagination, as expressed via a metaphorical system based on the visual arts in the Frames Trilogy—*The Book of Evidence, Ghosts, Athena*—dominates all aspects of the trilogy. Each of the three novels seeks to respond to Freddy Montgomery's primary failing in the first installment, his "failure of imagination" (*BoE*, 215). Chapter 2 demonstrates the manner in which Banville's aesthetic process seeks to integrate some of the narrative processes of the visual arts that will later become central to his mature work. Chapter 3 is the only chapter that is devoted to a single novel, primarily because, as I will argue, *The Sea* is Banville's most accomplished work due to the manner in which it seamlessly merges his metaphorical system with a plot that shimmers in its own doubleness throughout. This chapter will address Banville's folding of Pierre Bonnard's aesthetic approaches into his own narrative frame, using paintings in a more nuanced and extensive way than ever previously. *The Sea* was published midway through what has become known as the Cleave Trilogy, which is the subject of chapter 4. The three Cleave novels—*Eclipse, Shroud* (2002), and *Ancient Light*—directly or otherwise, feature Alex Cleave, Cass Cleave, and Axel Vander, in different contexts and time frames, and always in slightly adjusted relations to each other. Rather than deploy another variation of a self-reflexive metaphorical system, many of the artistic implications arise from the emphasis on acting, impersonation and a general confusion of self that accompanies such issues. The influence of Heinrich von Kleist is also very clear in the trilogy, particularly because Alex Cleave was an actor whose career faltered while performing the lead in Kleist's *Amphitryon*. Chapter 5 more fully addresses the immense influence of Kleist in Banville, both in the novels, particularly *The Infinities*, and the three adaptations of Kleist's plays. Kleist's poetics were based on a philosophy of controlled confusion and it is very clear that Banville integrates a certain degree of Kleistean thought into his own aesthetic.

In 2006, somewhat appropriately for an artist who has long worked at developing doubled narrative systems, and in which everything appears the same, and yet different, Banville invented a pen name, Benjamin Black, and initiated a sequence of crime novels, most of which feature the figure of Quirke, a pathologist who doubles as an unofficial investigator.[95] My primary focus is on the Quirke novels, which offer a representative indicator of Black's significance for Banville's overall oeuvre. Chapter 6 considers the relationship between Banville and Black and maps the manner in which the sometimes austere artistic principles of Banville seep into Black, and how the art-motivated novels inform the crime novels. Rather than see this as a radically new departure, this chapter will argue that the Black novels are another variation in Banville's artistic odyssey.

INTRODUCTION

Schopenhauer argues that if a writer is worth reading, "his merit rises just in proportion as he owes little to his [subject] matter" and justifies his position by highlighting that "the three great tragedians of Greece, for example, all worked at the same subject-matter."[96] The following chapters will demonstrate that Banville constructs an elaborate fictive universe in which each subsequent novel, or installment in the Banville pantheon, repeatedly circles around the same essential problems of being, with respect to the strangeness of human existence. Familiar but disorientated characters are repeatedly assembled in variants of the same landscape in order to generate an increasingly complex discourse about the relationship between artistic process and being. Subject matter is of significance only to facilitate the elaboration of this discourse and offers little by way of direct engagement with material reality. As I will demonstrate hereafter, this does not represent a gesture of withdrawal, or a refusal to engage with social reality, but rather a carefully calibrated judgment that is deemed necessary to fabricate a very special kind of artistic surface. Ortega y Gasset likens this "surface" to a quality of transparency in artistic works, to which he suggests most readers fail to "adjust their attention" sufficiently and who instead focus on the "human reality which the work of art refers to."[97] His ultimate aim is to "see no human realities there, but only artistic transparencies, pure essences."[98]

Banville's textual worlds are themselves self-consciously aware of their own "essences," of their status as art objects, and they repeatedly deflate and subvert any authentic content or meaning with a variety of metafictional strategies. As such they contain an overt awareness of a particular aesthetic tradition embedded within the fictional scenarios and at key moments in all of the novels this tradition is revealed, as in the closing stages of *The Infinities*:

> This is the mortal world. It is a world where nothing is lost, where all is accounted for while yet the mystery of things is preserved; a world where they may live, however briefly, however tenuously, in the failing evening of the self, solitary and at the same time together somehow here in this place, dying as they may be and yet fixed forever in a luminous, unending instant.[99]

The "luminous unending instant" in which "the mystery of things" is preserved is, ultimately, the central aim of Banville's work rather than an openly discursive mode. What Gasset refers to as the "transparencies" or "the essences" is directly linked to the formal, elegant, arrangement of material substances. And this too is directly linked to Sontag's resistance to the process of heavy-handed interpretive practice—like Gasset she views "transparence" as the "highest, most liberating value in art" and claims that this quality is akin to "experiencing the luminousness of the thing in itself, of things being what they are."[100] For Banville, and for so many aesthetic philosophers and critics, the aim of the work of art is to illuminate aspects of being rather than to simply mimic the world and its content. Faced with the kind of art that resists representational forms, as is clearly the case with Banville, Sontag advises that the "function of criticism should be to show *how it is what it is*, even *that it is what it is*, rather than to show *what it means*."[101] In the following chapters, the present author endeavors to show *how it is what it is*.

Notes

1. John Banville, *The Blue Guitar* (New York: Alfred A. Knopf, 2015), 29.
2. Banville, *Birchwood* (London: Panther Books, 1984).
3. "Fully Booked: Q & A with John Banville," interview with Travis Elborough, *Picador*, June 29, 2012. http://www.picador.com/blog/june-2012/fully-booked-q-a-with-john-banville (accessed October 31, 2016).
4. See interviews with Schwall, Friberg, and Haughton, in particular for Banville's recurring observations about the art and beauty, with reference to his own work. Hedwig Schwall, "An Interview with John Banville," *European English Messenger* 6, no. 1 (1997): 16; Hedda Friberg, "John Banville and Derek Hand in Conversation," *Irish University Review* 36, no. 1 (2006): 200–215; Hugh Haughton and Bryan Radley, "An Interview with John Banville," *Modernism/Modernity* 18, no. 4 (November 2011): 868.
5. Schwall, "An Interview with John Banville," 16.
6. Banville engages in lengthy discussion in interviews with Elborough and Schwall about the difference, as he sees it, between "meaning" and "significance." Elborough, "Fully Booked;" Schwall, "An Interview with John Banville."
7. Schwall, "An Interview with John Banville," 15.
8. Elborough, "Fully Booked."
9. Friberg, "John Banville and Derek Hand in Conversation," 200–215.
10. Gordon Graham, *Philosophy of the Arts: An Introduction to Aesthetics* (New York: Routledge, 2007), 142.
11. Ibid., 144.
12. Ibid., 148.
13. Ibid.
14. Ibid., 145.
15. Ibid., 146.

INTRODUCTION

16. Michelle B. Timmerman, "15 Questions with John Banville," *The Harvard Crimson* (February 26, 2010), http://www.thecrimson.com/article/2010/2/26/fm-jb-think-work/?page=single (accessed October 31, 2016).
17. Friberg, "Banville and Hand," 201.
18. Haughton and Radley, "An Interview with John Banville," 868.
19. Elborough, "Fully Booked."
20. Banville, *The Sea* (London: Picador, 2005).
21. Belinda McKeon, "John Banville: The Art of Fiction No. 200," interview with John Banville, *The Paris Review*, no. 188, Spring 2009, http://www.theparisreview.org/interviews/5907/the-art-of-fiction-no-200-john-banville (accessed October 31, 2016).
22. John Banville, *Eclipse* (London: Picador, 2000).
23. "Oblique Dreamer: Interview with John Banville," with *The Observer*, *The Guardian*, 17 September 2000, https://www.theguardian.com/books/2000/sep/17/fiction.johnbanville (accessed October 31, 2016).
24. Elborough, "Fully Booked."
25. Banville, *Time Pieces: A Dublin Memoir* (Dublin: Hachette Books, 2016); *The Newton Letter: An Interlude* (London: Panther Books, 1984), 3; *The Broken Jug: After Heinrich von Kleist* (Oldcastle: Gallery Press, 1994); *The Book of Evidence* (London: Secker & Warburg, 1989).
26. Banville, *Ancient Light* (London: Viking Penguin, 2012).
27. "Oblique Dreamer: Interview with John Banville."
28. Ibid.
29. Haughton and Radley, "Interview with John Banville," 867.
30. McKeon, "John Banville: The Art of Fiction."
31. Schwall, "An Interview with John Banville," 119.
32. Etienne Gilson, *Form and Substance in the Arts*, trans. Salvator Attanasio (Illinois: Dalkey Archive Press, 2001), 225.
33. Noël Carroll, "Identifying Art," in *Aesthetics: A Comprehensive Anthology*, ed. Steven M. Cahn and Aaron Meskin (Oxford: Blackwell Publishing, 2008), 451.
34. Milan Kundera, *The Art of the Novel*, trans. Linda Asher (New York: Perennial Classics, 2003), 15–16.
35. Ibid., 122–23.
36. McKeon, "John Banville: The Art of Fiction."
37. John Banville, "The Personae of Summer," in *Irish Writers and Their Creative Processes*, ed. Jacqueline Genet and Wynne Hellegouarc'h (Gerrards Cross: Colin Smythe Ltd., 1996), 119.
38. Henry James, *The Art of Criticism: Henry James on the Theory and the Practice of Fiction*, ed. William Veeder and Susan M. Griffin (Chicago: Chicago University Press, 1986), 290.
39. Ibid., 291.
40. Schwall, "Interview with John Banville," 19.
41. Banville's work repeatedly references Nabokov. For example, as early as *Birchwood*, he borrows the eponymous title of Nabokov's *Ada* as the name of one of the twins. And in *Mefisto*, there is a reference to "*die ewige Wiederkunft*" or Nietzsche's Eternal

INTRODUCTION

Recurrence—the novel partially repeats the same events in different forms in the novel, so Nietzsche philosophically accounts for the formal arrangement in the novel. Furthermore, the entire deconstruction of moral reasoning in *The Book of Evidence* is directly derived from Nietzsche's *Beyond Good and Evil*, trans. R. J. Hollingdale (Harmondsworth: Penguin, 1974).

42. Vladimir Nabokov, *Strong Opinions* (New York: Vintage, 1990), 118.
43. Ibid.
44. Ibid.
45. Kundera, "Art of the Novel," 15.
46. Italo Calvino, "Lightness," *Six Memos for the New Millennium* (New York: Vintage, 1993), 4.
47. Banville, "The Personae of Summer," 119.
48. Banville made this claim immediately after winning the Man Booker prize for *The Sea* in 2005, and later confirmed his position in an interview with Belinda McKeon for the *Paris Review*: "But I did also mean what I said. Whether *The Sea* is a successful work of art is not for me to say, but a work of art is what I set out to make." As recently as 2012, in a review of Banville's novel, *Ancient Light*, Joan Acocella, again reminds her readers of his post-Booker win claim, linking it to his "legendary arrogance." McKeon, "John Banville: The Art of Fiction"; Joan Acocella, "Doubling Down: John Banville's Complicated Lives," *The New Yorker (*October 8, 2012) http://www.newyorker.com/magazine/2012/10/08/doubling-down (accessed 31 August, 2016).
49. Peter Lamarque, *The Philosophy of Literature* (Oxford: Blackwell, 2009), 12–14.
50. Gilson, "Forms and Substances," 37.
51. Ibid., 34.
52. Frank Kermode, *The Sense of an Ending: Studies in the Theory of Fiction* (New York: Oxford University Press, 2000), 128.
53. Ibid., 131.
54. Graham, "Philosophy of the Arts," 140.
55. Lamarque, "Philosophy of Literature," 15.
56. Etienne Gilson, *The Arts of the Beautiful* (Illinois: Dalkey Archive Press, 2000), 132.
57. McKeon, "John Banville: The Art of Fiction."
58. Gilson, "Arts of the Beautiful," 75.
59. Graham, "Philosophy of the Arts," 146.
60. Schwall, "Interview with John Banville," 15.
61. Kundera, "Art of the Novel," 122.
62. Joseph McMinn, *The Supreme Fictions of John Banville* (Manchester: Manchester University Press, 1999), 2.
63. Derek Hand, *John Banville: Exploring Fictions* (Dublin: The Liffey Press, 2002), 113.
64. Ruth Frehner, "The Dark One and the Fair: John Banville's Historians of the Imagination and their Gender Stereotypes," *BELLS: Barcelona English Language and Literature Series* 11 (2000): 51–64.
65. Ibid., 53.

INTRODUCTION

66. Elke D'Hoker, "Portrait of the Other as a Woman with Gloves: Ethical Perspectives in John Banville's The Book of Evidence," *Critique* 44, no. 1 (Fall 2002): 31–32.
67. Patricia Coughlan, "Banville, the Feminine, and the Scenes of Eros," *Irish University Review* 36, no. 1 (Spring-Summer, 2006): 82–83.
68. Ibid., 85.
69. Ibid., 97.
70. Anja Müller, "'You Have Been Framed': The Function of Ekphrasis for the Representation of Women in John Banville's Trilogy (The Book of Evidence, Ghosts, Athena)," *Studies in the Novel* 36, no. 2 (Summer 2004): 199.
71. Banville, *Ghosts* (London: Secker & Warburg, 1993).
72. Banville, *Athena* (London: Secker & Warburg, 1995).
73. Ibid., 198.
74. Carol Dell'Amico, "John Banville and Benjamin Black: The *Mundo*, Crime, Women," *Éire-Ireland* 49, no. 1 & 2 (Spring-Summer 2014): 109.
75. Ibid., 111.
76. Banville, *Shroud* (London: Picador, 2002).
77. Banville, *The Infinities* (London: Picador, 2009).
78. Ibid., 112–13.
79. Haughton and Radley, "Interview with John Banville," 857.
80. "Q & A with Benjamin Black," *Crimespree Magazine*, January 27, 2016. http://crimespreemag.com/qa-with-benjamin-black/ (accessed July 31, 2016).
81. Susan Sontag, *Against Interpretation and Other Essays* (New York: Picador, 1966), 5.
82. Ibid.
83. Ibid., 175.
84. Denis Donoghue, *Speaking of Beauty* (New Haven: Yale University Press, 2003), 81.
85. Susanne K. Langer, *Feeling and Form: A Theory of Art* (New York: Charles Scribner's Sons, 1953), 45–46.
86. Ibid.
87. For example, Friberg, "Banville and Hand," 206.
88. Linda Hutcheon, *Narcissistic Narrative: The Metafictional Paradox* (Waterloo: Wilfred Laurier University Press, 1980), 102–3.
89. Banville, *Nightspawn* (London: Secker & Warburg, 1971).
90. Banville, *Doctor Copernicus* (London: Panther Books, 1984); *Mefisto* (New Hampshire: David R. Godine, 1989).
91. Banville, *Kepler* (London: Panther Books, 1985).
92. Banville, *The Untouchable* (London: Picador, 1997).
93. Victoria Stewart, "'I May Have Miscalled Everything.' John Banville's *The Untouchable*," *English* 52 (Autumn 2003), 238.
94. Eibhear Walsh, "'A Lout's Game': Espionage, Irishness, and Sexuality in *The Untouchable*," *Irish University Review* 36, no. 1 (Spring-Summer, 2006), 109.

95. There are two notable exceptions that do not feature Quirke: *The Lemur* (2008), and the Raymond Chandler title *The Black-Eyed Blonde* (2014). See chapter 6 for more detailed information.

96. Arthur Schopenhauer, *The Essays of Arthur Schopenhauer: The Art of Literature*, trans. Bailey Saunders (United Kingdom: Dodo Press, 2013), 5.

97. José Ortega y Gas, *The Dehumanization of Art, and Other Writings on Art and Culture* (New York: Doubleday Anchor Books, 1956), 42.

98. Ibid., 43.

99. Banville, *The Infinities*, 300. The significance of this self-conscious moment is also confirmed by virtue of Banville having rephrased and reinvented a near-identical moment from the novel *Ghosts* written more than fifteen years earlier:

> This is the golden world. The painter has gathered his little group and set them down in this wind-tossed glade, in this delicate, artificial light, and painted them as angels and clowns. It is a world where nothing is lost, where all is accounted for while yet the mystery of things is preserved; a world where they may live, however briefly, however tenuously, in the failing evening of the self . . . in a luminous, unending instant. (*Ghosts*, 231)

100. Sontag, "Against Interpretation," 13.

101. Ibid., 14.

1

The Early Evolution of an Aesthetic

From *Long Lankin* to *Mefisto*

BANVILLE'S WORK HAS ALWAYS ENGAGED with art in progressively intricate and nuanced ways. In his early fictions this is primarily expressed via the deployment of metafictional self-reflexive devices and the use of subtle patterns of metaphors that generate a figurative doubling of expression. Early works like *Long Lankin*,[1] *Nightspawn*, and *Birchwood* feature standard self-referential commentary as part of their narratorial fabric—as when Gabriel Godkin openly assures us that he is "inventing" (*BW,* 21)—and, as the work progresses, the deployment of the self-conscious mode is radically extended.

With specific emphasis on *Long Lankin*, *Nightspawn*, and *Birchwood*, this chapter will initially illustrate how Banville's early fictions were already engaged in an artistic discourse with their own condition as artifices and thereafter with the tetralogy of science novels—*Doctor Copernicus* (1976), *Kepler* (1981), *The Newton Letter* (1982), and *Mefisto* (1986)—how a sophisticated metaphorical inquiry, ostensibly rooted in scientific and historical systems, was constructed. While most critics have noticed that his work engages the problem and meaning of art, this essay will argue that the first three texts are primarily constructed around patterns of key *motifs* that serve as vital intimations of the author's aesthetic fascinations, and that they are each fundamentally concerned, above all else, with the possibilities and processes of literary art forms. These three works of fiction may be read as extended metafictional commentaries on their own making, on the meaning of art and, ultimately, as direct critiques of the meaning and possibility of what is frequently termed postmodern fiction; in order to effect this extended discourse, Banville establishes a series of metaphorical patterns including, silence, the topographical space of the house (in *Birchwood* merged with the ancestral home—or Irish Big House), the twin, the lost sister, the lost brother—or red-haired outsider—the circus (and/or clown-figure), and astronomy. All of these motifs are evident in *Long Lankin*, several are developed further in *Nightspawn* and *Birchwood*, and thereafter extend throughout Banville's work in general. They frequently

CHAPTER 1

act as focal points around which the dominant issues revolve, culminating, via a metaphorical commentary, in a radical reassessment of postmodern self-reflexive fiction. *Birchwood*, in particular, firmly establishes the direction that Banville's future work takes.

Banville's early works are best understood in the context of the primary narrative techniques of metafiction, or fiction that reflects on "its own framing and assumptions."[2] For example, the novella that accompanies the original version of *Long Lankin*,[3] "The Possessed," features a writer-narrator whose observations about his own writing initiate the self-reflexive mode that Banville was to use throughout his career. Similarly, both *Nightspawn* and *Birchwood*, in significantly different ways, owe much to metafiction, in terms of compositional artistic design, and all four novels of the science tetralogy draw attention to their own statuses as works of creative process. Metafiction typically draws attention to the fictive and textual nature of its own form via an overt self-conscious voice but it also frequently reveals its own fictionality by virtue of the use of anachronistic details or quotations, by placing projected worlds in confrontation, or what Brian McHale calls "worlds-in-collision,"[4] and by the extensive use of intertextual elements—in effect rendering the work itself a purely textual event. More extreme variations include the dizzying use of embedded worlds-within-worlds—or Chinese-box fiction (or Babushka dolls fiction)—the use of disorienting variations on the *mise-en-abyme* device, and Borgesian forking-paths fictions. While metafictional tendencies are evident in a wide range of literary texts, from Shakespeare's *The Tempest* to Sterne's *Tristram Shandy*, and Joyce's *Ulysses*, the use of these features in postmodern writing tends to subvert the text's own authority. In Banville's early work one can discern a persistent use of the metafictional mode that is intended to undermine its own authority as a center of meaning, but also to continually alert his readers to the status of his works as artifices.

The nine stories in *Long Lankin* thematically revolve around the attainment of freedom, the collapse of relationships and a general diminishing of happiness. However, Rüdiger Imhof has noticed the "artistry"[5] of the stories. In addition, Kersti Tarien Powell notes how the writer-figure Ben White's awareness of the stars and a circus anticipates Banville's later fiction,[6] and Joseph McMinn emphasizes that the "two figures of imaginative escapism, literary astronomer and circus entertainer, provide Banville with important metaphors for much of his subsequent fiction . . . knowing that they could be of greater imaginative use at a later stage of his design."[7] More emphatically, perhaps, John Kenny astutely claims that "Banville's first two books, in their apparent move away from obviously Irish concerns, can be read as a kind of aesthetic autobiography."[8] Similarly, while the apparent realism of the short stories partially recalls Joyce's *Dubliners*, a subtle extended commentary on the process of writing is also evident. For example, in "Nightwind," Mor is cast in a Beckettesque role in terms of the symbolically charged terminology used to describe him: "He shuffled down the corridor, trying the handles of the blind white doors. From one room there came sounds, a cry, a soft phase of laughter, and in the silence they seemed a glimpse of the closed, secret worlds he would never enter" (*LL*, 58). The story repeatedly alludes to communicative difficulties and to the problem of gaining access to material reality, echoing the problem of artistic silence about which Banville has frequently spoken: "All right, silence is fine; but what do you do if you have a voice and it won't stay still? First of all, in my case at least, one has to use that voice to speak about that voice; one has to build up a base which is nearest to the honesty of silence and begin from there."[9] The stories reveal a perpetual concern with the communicative process and images of corridors and blind white doors, echoing Beckett and several other metafictional authors, extend throughout Banville's early work. For example, Beckett's *The Unnamable* conceives a room "low of ceiling, thick of wall, why low, why thick, I don't know,"[10] while Robbe-Grillet's unnamed narrator in *Topology of Phantom City*, reveals his spatial claustrophobia in similar terms: "faced with the row of closed doors, down the endless empty corridor, unalterably neat and clean."[11] The architectural motif of rooms and corridors acts as a symbolic gesture of resistance to overt narrative representation akin to what one frequently encounters in postmodern fictional worlds. The qualities of silence and emptiness or—more precisely—the presence of the inarticulate is a central resonant metaphor in postmodern fiction, as explored most thoroughly in Ihab Hassan's *The Dismemberment of Orpheus: Toward a Postmodern Literature* and George Steiner's *Language and Silence*. Inaccessible rooms, empty corridors, closed doors, and sparse houses comprise the central architectural frame in many postmodern fictions and the various heroes must eventually confront the hidden centres of silence, which is precisely the case in Banville's work from the outset.

Banville also establishes a firm connection between writing and life in *Long Lankin*'s "A Death." Stephen reveals to Alice, his estranged lover, "Oh yes I was going to write a book. A love story. The story of Stephen and Alice who thought that love would last forever. And when they found it wouldn't or at least that it changed so much that they couldn't recognise it anymore the blow was too heavy" (33). Stephen is both confounded by the fluid nature of living and also anticipates Banville's later artistic incarnations when alluding to

CHAPTER 1

Kant's thing-in-itself: "The things around him as he looked at them began to seem unreal in their extreme reality. Everything he touched gave to his fingers the very essence of itself" (35). Echoing the opening childhood observations of Copernicus in *Doctor Copernicus*,[12] and Stephen's namesake in *A Portrait of the Artist as Young Man*, Banville's obsessive concern with the discordance between reality and appearance is already evident.

Throughout all of his work, Banville's overt plots are deeply intertwined with parallel, or metaphorical, statements of artistic process and in both the science tetralogy and the Frames Trilogy, quite precise appropriations of plotted elements acquire artistic significance. In the early stories the commentary on art, writing, and realism is more subtle. For example, in "The Visit," the contrast between reality and fantasy is repeatedly emphasized while the young girl impatiently awaits the return of her long-absent father. In the interim she meets Rainbird, a clown-like figure who shows her his tricks, with the result that she no longer desires to meet her all-too-real father when he actually appears; this, in effect, emphasizes the contrasting attractions of enchantment and material reality. Thereafter, the novella, "The Possessed," which forms the final section of *Long Lankin*, reveals Banville's artistic focus far more explicitly than the short stories, from the opening epigraph from Gide's *The Immoralist*[13] to Ben White's final artistic prediction at the close of the novella. Ben is the Long Lankin figure who seeks the metaphorical blood he believes will release him from his past, although Banville's efforts to assign symbolic intent to the novella struggle to achieve metaphorical clarity. In addition, there are many direct efforts in "The Possessed" to integrate artistic and philosophical speculation into the narrative, as with Wolf's defense of his lifestyle: "Yes my world is false. I agree, But for all that there's honesty . . . you see my fine friend we have the courage to admit all the lies you believe in . . . we never imagine our falseness to be anything but false and that's the secret" (125). Wolf's words are a forceful self-reflexive statement in favor of a purely fictionalized mode of being.

In spite of its clear weaknesses, confirmed by the author's decision to excise it from the revised 1984 version, the novella represents a valuable declaration of intent, if not artistic achievement. The allegorically charged focus on the achievement of freedom in the text tends to be overwrought but is nevertheless a gesture of liberation from mimetic writing, particularly when Ben indicates at the close of the novel that he may join a circus or write a book about the stars after he departs. The circus motif has, of course, particular resonance in Banville's work, as usefully elaborated on by Kenny,[14] while the reference to the stars anticipates the novels about Copernicus and Kepler. Furthermore, at the close of the novella, Ben "went through the gates on to the road, there to start on his long journey home" (*LL*, 189), explicitly inviting us to enter his next fictional storyworld—Banville's first novel—*Nightspawn*, which the author describes as "a dosshouse perhaps, full of lice and madmen."[15] This is the same house that one always encounters in Banville, the house of fiction that Ben White tells us is "full of dead souls" (144), and in which Ben and Flora grew up, "a rambling old house buried in the country near the sea" (183), and that which later acquires central significance in *Birchwood*, *The Newton Letter*, and many other novels thereafter.

Nightspawn is an answer to the question posed at the end of *Long Lankin*: what does one do with the freedom achieved after artistically moving beyond realism? Banville's first novel is a parody of the suspense thriller genre, in which the writer-narrator Ben narrates a story of intrigue, abortive revolution, murder, betrayal, and love, with a supporting cast of stereotypical characters: a political revolutionary, an alcoholic, a corrupt general, a powerful, interfering businessman, and Helena—a mesmerizing variant of Helen of Troy. The novel is also an intertextual collage suffused with parodic echoes of Dostoevsky's *Notes from Underground*,[16] and features a self-reflexive Nabokovian riddle,[17] suggesting Banville's early association with that master of textual gimmickry and fictional games. Furthermore Benjamin S. White is an anagram of an individual who never actually appears in the novel, James H. Twinbein, while the novel also toys with chess imagery, echoing Nabokov's fascination with the game, particularly in *The Defense*, in which Luzhin's obsession with chess gradually replaces the world of reality.[18] The names White (and Weiss), Black and Knight, and multiple other references, ultimately infer that the characters are akin to pieces in a game controlled by a skilled player.

Banville has claimed that *Nightspawn* is "an inside-out novel,"[19] suggesting that it betrays the conventions of realism by exposing its workings, and the novel repeatedly exhibits overt metafictional narrative strategies in an effort to deflate any real sense of its own sincerity: "On the pavement, Julian, Helena and Knight lay snapping and kicking, clawing at each other in agony, wallowing in blood. . . . Something was wrong with this farce. . . . No creatures writhed on the ground" (*NS*, 212). The characters are largely intertextual borrowings, any efforts to explain the plot are thwarted, and the novel finishes without resolution; any chance of clarity evaporates on the dying lips of Colonel Sesosteris while the love story between Ben and Helena is a confused, self-generated hoax. Ben is a marionette figure, cobbled together

CHAPTER 1

from various stock figures; exiled writer, spy, and gangster. He imagines himself to be a cunning murderer in a landscape which perpetually confounds him, on an island which increasingly appears to be a self-contained imagined ontology. His island, he complains, "torments" him, it is "arid and irretrievably dead," "forsaken" (11), and "barren" (34), while his brain is "a bright blank void" (12). This empty canvas is waiting to be filled and Julian's arrival, with "majestic aplomb," initiates the process of engendering an imaginary universe, which is conflated with healing throughout: "I am talking about the healing of wounds. I am talking about art" (198–99). Ben needs to heal the wounds that he incurred during the later stages of "The Possessed," although the melodramatic tone serves to undermine the sincerity of such an aim, and it is more useful to interpret his claims as self-conscious parody and artistic commentary. For example, Ben's story of Cain is loaded with broader artistic significance in the context of Banville's coded set of signals. He tells Helena that Cain built a house with his bare hands but, on the advice of an old man, demolished it, after which he stole a boat, sailed to an island, and attempted to build something from sand (46–47). The departure from the house in turn results in his journey to a strange island full of "fanged and flesh devouring beasts . . . slouching through the undergrowth" (48). Mirroring Ben's own journey from the house of games in "The Possessed," to this island of stock figures, the story of Cain acts as a parallel echo of the Ben's journey from realism to the kind of formless freedom indicated in the epigraph to "The Possessed" (*LL*, 99), from Gide's *The Immoralist*. *Nightspawn* then becomes both a demonstration of, and commentary on, playful anti-realist fiction, echoing the metafictional style of novels like John Barth's *The Sot-Weed Factor* (1960) and Nabokov's *Pale Fire* (1962), near contemporaries of *Nightspawn*. As Ben White lurches to a close, he openly admits to the sham that the novel has been: "Why go on? There is nothing more to say. There never was anything to say" (*NS*, 198). But he also admits that he "cannot stop, cannot face that suffocating void which will engulf me as I set down the last word," (198) echoing the close to Beckett's *The Unnamable*. Aesthetically, *Nightspawn* is highly derivative, mirroring many of the devices of his metafictional near-contemporaries and, like them, it ultimately propels itself into near-erasure and expires in halting aphasia. It was a crucial developmental stage for Banville, and the subsequent novel was to be a major transformative moment. *Nightspawn* is Banville's only pure metafictional text, whose intention is to erase its own claims to validity, but *Birchwood*, more innovatively, seeks to map out a range of new aesthetic possibilities.

Unlike with *Nightspawn*, the interrogative mode in *Birchwood* is absorbed more fluidly into the fabric of the telling, rendering the novel much more convincing both as a fiction and as a treatise on the creative act, despite its disruptive aesthetic. Parodying the big-house genre, Gabriel's father is a philanderer and a wastrel, his mother drifts into insanity, and his grandparents perish in unlikely ways. Similarly, characters from other fictions stalk the pages of *Birchwood*; Granny Godkin's death by instantaneous combustion is borrowed from Dickens's *Bleak House*, there is a Nabokovian Ada and a Shakespearian Prospero who fails to appear. Gabriel begins his search for an imaginary sister "in silence," cunningly, echoing Stephen in *A Portrait* while part I of *Birchwood*, "The Book of the Dead," alludes to the books of verses placed with the ancient Egyptian dead for assistance in the afterworld; and Michael and Gabriel intertextually echo the names of the archangels. *Birchwood* is an elaborate pastiche, composed of other works, which have been transplanted into Gabriel's empty "white landscape" (*BW*, 172). Several figures from Banville's previous works reappear, and many of the characters from *Birchwood*, were in turn to make appearances in the later work. Rainbird is not only literally borrowed from *Long Lankin*'s "The Visit," he also relates a story to the circus people of being knocked from his bicycle by a girl, an explicit echo of the earlier short story, and a tale that intrigues Gabriel because he is, after all, searching for a girl. The girl in "The Visit" also resembles Flora from "Summer Voices," the focus of Ben White's attention in "The Possessed." The pattern of male protagonist seeking to resolve his problems by finding, or rediscovering, a female, often a sister, is thus fully established in *Birchwood* and the significance of the lost, murdered, or absent girl and/or twin becomes central to many of Banville's novels henceforth. So too with the red-haired Michael who, similar to corresponding figures in *Nightspawn* (Julian Kyd), *Doctor Copernicus* (Andreas), *Mefisto* (Felix), *Ghosts* (Felix), *Athena* (Francie), and *The Sea* (Carlo Grace), acts as a scornful provocative voice aimed at destabilizing the male lead.

On a generic level, *Birchwood* experiments with the big-house form by creating a deeply self-reflexive document and parodically uses this most politicized of forms to create a text that takes great liberties with historical and social actualities. Brian Donnelly's description of Gabriel Godkin as a "portrait of the crazed imagination bred of incest and ancestral insanity"[20] recognizes the literal surface role that the primary character is occupying but essentially neglects his more central function as parodic representation of the hero in a quest-adventure story. Vera Kreilkamp, alternatively, suggests that the novel,

CHAPTER 1

although a "fulfilment of the tradition as well as a parody and subversion of it," transforms "a literary symbol of political and economic loss into a haunting image of the failure of memory and the inaccessibility of the past,"[21] and thus positions an epistemological concern at the heart of the novel, rather than a strictly historical or political one. Historical reference thus becomes literary metaphor and metaphor turns back on itself in self-parody, not just in terms of the big house but as the metaphorical expression of human knowledge and communication. In *Birchwood*, the big house is effectively a metonym for the social-realist novel and illustrates some of the reasons for the author's (and Gabriel's) departure from this kind of text/world. Gabriel tells us that Birchwood is his father's "baroque madhouse," rather than his own (*BW*, 15), and throughout the novel repeatedly comments on how the house, and its "inmates" were "disintegrating" (69), "diminished" (79), "dying" (85), and full of "emptiness and echo" (73). The value of the *topos* of the house to him is that he could "knock" from its walls, "the bright reverberations of fantasy" (34), and it is "suffused with summer and silence, another world" (29). Ultimately Gabriel leaves the house because of a book, *The Something Twins*, a story about "Gabriel and Rose" (48), which sounds remarkably like *Birchwood* itself, and represents Banville's first embedded mirrored narrative. Similarly, all the events that take place in the first section are rendered unstable when Gabriel announces his departure from the house:

> I had all day been playing all the parts in a non-stop show, Rosie was right there, did she but know it, I had been Granny Godkin exploding, Nockter falling, the telephonist hooting, Rosie fleeing, [old] Gabriel struggling with his ague, and now I was tired of it all, they would have to play their own parts without me, for I was retiring from the boards. (*BW*, 82)

Gabriel Godkin is presented not just as an artist figure, but as one who is keenly aware of his own fictionality. Furthermore, his close ontological proximity to his creator, Banville, is firmly registered when he identifies himself by the "fake" near-anagrammatic name Johan Livelb. In this ambivalent fictional sense Gabriel is antecedent to Copernicus, Kepler, Freddie, Cleave, Oliver et al., with there being little real character variation between many of the leading male protagonists, except in terms of how they diversely mark out the landscape for artistic self-commentary.

Gabriel's abandonment of the big house and subsequent joining of the circus invites us to read the text as metaphorical commentary on his progression as an artist figure, in turn a commentary on Banville's own artistic shift. The novel reflects a more nuanced position than simply an abandonment of the mimetic principle; the central section, which recounts Gabriel's adventure with the circus, extends the inherent literary-artistic debate and while the beauty of the circus performances initially enchants him, the "essence of these fickle things joined with something more, a sense of strange and infinite possibilities" (125). He thereafter grows increasingly disenchanted: "we played with exaggeration as a means of keeping reality at bay" (144) and reveals that his laughter, like that of the others, "made no sound at all" (107), while the "collapsible kingdom" sells "shoddy dreams" (108). The circus, finally, is "a game we played, enchanters and enchanted . . . a game that meant nothing, was a wisp of smoke" (117). While Joseph McMinn has noted that everything "about the circus family is deliberately unreal—the theatrical names, the exotic costumes"[22] and Derek Hand has commented that "the magic of the Circus, its make-believe improvisation and ramshackle coherence only truly coming together in performance, becomes a means of understanding art and the act of writing,"[23] it is possible to further extend such observations. The circus metaphor has a particular resonance for metafiction, specifically the kind of self-conscious metafiction that Banville has experimented with in *Nightspawn* and Gabriel's journey with Silas's (and the invisible Prospero's) circus also acts as an extended commentary on the attractions and ultimate limits of the self-referential fantasy world. As Gabriel wryly observes, "so we played with exaggeration as a means of keeping reality at bay. It did not work. Reality was hunger, and there was no gainsaying that" (144). Gabriel's observation may be read as a critique of metafiction, or fiction that perpetually undermines its own capacity to speak, and that refutes material existence. Between *Birchwood* and *Nightspawn*, there is a marked difference in this respect primarily because the earlier novel was ultimately framed within the limits of the metafictional form. With *Birchwood*, alternatively, Banville manages to incorporate the epistemological difficulties associated with language, memory, and perception that one finds in the major metafictional texts and integrates them as constituent parts of a coherent self-sustaining fiction. As McMinn has discerned, "only briefly in *Nightspawn* does Banville create and hold a compelling fiction of this sense of human sadness in the face of Nature's remote beauty,"[24] while he acknowledges this to be a significant reason for the comparative success of *Birchwood*. What transpires is that *Birchwood* manages to more successfully integrate a self-reflexive artistic commentary in its fictional landscape, however allusory and self-evidently fictional it may be.

CHAPTER 1

Part II exemplifies the focus of this autotelic enterprise in several ways. The central significance of Prospero to the circus is registered not by his presence but by Silas's citing of his words. In having Silas, the ring-master, quote Prospero the magician—"'Gentles, gentles, our revels now are ended . . .'" (116)—Banville intertextually summons Shakespeare's master artist-figure, orchestrator of the greatest of imaginary island revels and, in doing so, illustrates the extent to which his allegiance lies with artist-figures who too produce intricately wrought landscapes. More significant still is what this association with Prospero represents when one recalls that, in *The Tempest*, Prospero proceeds as follows: "These our actors/As I foretold you, were all spirits and/Are melted into air, into thin air; And, like the baseless fabric of this vision."[25] The ontological status of the events and characters in Gabriel's universe are hence intertextually erased as textual subjects but not before the significance of his later self-association ("I became my Prospero and yours") with Shakespeare's magician becomes apparent. Gabriel's conclusive comment on the circus also reveals the actual quest for his imaginary lost sister to be little more than a diversion: "I travelled, but I did not travel far" (157), and his return to the house is the first clear indication of Banville's intended direction as an artist. One can read the whole central section as an *intratextual* commentary on Banville's own previous work, with the search for a lost sister/female figure and the theme of incest alluding to *Long Lankin* ("Summer Voices" and "The Possessed") and *Nightspawn*, and the adventure with the circus suggestive of the overt metafictional devices that define *Nightspawn*'s narrative form. *Birchwood* then would appear to be a self-referential summary of his earliest fictional journeys, a kind of aesthetic taking stock. Imhof acknowledges that Banville's Gabriel's "narrative discourse . . . represents a supreme effort at testing . . . various art forms,"[26] and suggests that the *Air and Angels* section is primarily a quest romance—which it most certainly is. I would also argue, however, that imbuing his plots with a parallel set of motifs that engender artistic discourse is a method to which Banville repeatedly returns throughout his career and *Birchwood* is an early, highly accomplished, indicator of the emergence of this crafted pattern in his work. Thus the circus elements offer very fertile, and appropriate, metaphorical materials to construct a critique of the self-conscious metafictional subgenre, and Gabriel's ultimate dissatisfaction with it is clearly sounded: "We did find a way to neutralize the truth if not quite banish it, and that was by inventing taller stories than the tallest the lowland could produce. One day, however, the trick backfired" (144). Banville's desire to somehow align reality and imagination is evident here and he signals his departure from the glittery but empty fictional form with which he had briefly experimented in *Nightspawn*.

Banville's ambivalent attitude to conventional narrative models is exemplified in *Birchwood*. For example, Gabriel here explains his desire to retain the adventure quest: "I knew too that my quest, mocked and laughed at, was fantasy, but I clung to it fiercely, unwilling to betray myself, for if I could not be a knight errant I would not be anything" (118). So too with his reaction upon returning to his ancestral home: "My broken kingdom all was changed and yet was as it always was" (165). This apparent paradox is revisited several times in the latter stages of the novel in an effort to reveal Banville's reconstructed aesthetic, which revolves around a retreat from metafiction and a partial retention of some of the formal characteristics of realism, but the nature of the relationship with realism, symbolized by the house, or house of fiction, is fundamentally altered:

> Perhaps I shall leave here. Where would I go? Is that why they all fought so hard for Birchwood, because there is nowhere else for them to be? Outside is destruction and decay. I do not speak the language of this wild country. I shall stay here, alone, and live a life different from any the house has ever known. (174)

The house comes to symbolize not just the big-house genre but realist fiction in general and outside the formal structures of conventional storytelling is destruction and decay; this artistic declaration promises a return to traditional forms, if not traditional methods. Gabriel's assurance that he will "stay in this house and [. . .] live a life different from any the house has ever known" is, according to Banville, the "only direct statement I've ever made in any book."[27] The significance of the metaphor of the house, from this point, becomes central to Banville's aesthetic self-reflexive commentary. While such statements offer a coherent indication of the author's experimental zeal a whole new aesthetic, a new house, needs to be invented, a point that Gabriel alludes to when he explicitly presents himself as an artist figure, and kin to all of Banville's artist-creator figures: "Now the white landscape was empty. Perhaps it is better thus, I said, and added, faintly, I might find some other creatures to inhabit it. And I did, and so I became my own Prospero, and yours" (172). The extended metaphor of the house is registered as the foremost motif in the landscape of Banville's emerging fictional world. Gabriel "worked on the house, cleared out the attic, boarded the windows" (174), and spends his days "watching the sky, the lake, the enormous sea. This world" (175). The metaphor of the house

CHAPTER 1

thereafter extends throughout Banville's work, particularly in *The Newton Letter*, *Mefisto*, *The Book of Evidence*, *Ghosts*, *Eclipse*, *The Sea*, *The Infinities*, *Ancient Light*, and *The Blue Guitar*, always serving as a means to discuss the framing significance of the novel form itself. Here is Max, from *The Sea*, for example, attempting to fit an imagined model of the house upon the material reality that lies before him:

> I found that the model of the house in my head, try as it would to accommodate itself to the original, kept coming up against a stubborn resistance. Everything was slightly out of scale, all angles slightly out of true [. . .] I experienced a sense almost of panic as the real, the crassly complacent real, took hold of the things I thought I remembered and shook them into its own shape. Something precious was dissolving and pouring away between my fingers. (156–57)

The house, originally derived from Henry James's metaphor for the novel form's creative possibilities, assumes similar figurative significance for Banville's creative process; throughout his work the house is one of the key self-referential ways that characters overtly speak of the fictive universes in which they discover themselves. In fact, the pattern of perpetually renegotiating the meaning and shape of the motif of the house perpetually acts as overt self-referential commentary in Banville's work. Almost thirty years later, in *Eclipse*, Cleave concludes *his* installment in the Banvillean pantheon by alluding to the house in telling terms: "Yes, I shall give her the house. I hope that she will live here. I hope she will let me visit her. . . . I have all kinds of wild ideas, mad projects. We might fix up the place between us, she and I" (*E*, 213). The house again is registered as a central motif and Cleave, like Gabriel, is a self-reflexive counterpoint to Banville the artist.

The residual impact of the metaphor of the house is felt throughout Banville's work, although several politically inclined critics seize upon the "Irishness" of the motif as a means of seeking a direct connection with Irish history. For example, Mika Momoo argues that the big-house motif in the novels borrows at least some of its significance from the political history from which it is borrowed: "The Big House novel has traditionally dealt with problems of legitimacy in terms of who is the lawful owner of the house, or has the right to inherit the land. In *Birchwood*, Banville asks these questions, too, but in a more self-referential way: who is the legitimate, authorial narrator of the story?"[28] While not without some critical merit, observations of this kind betray a tendency to imbue the social and historical with more significance than can be ultimately justified. Throughout the novel, Gabriel repeatedly points to the doubling of inference with respect to the house, which becomes a consistent allegorical motif that resonates with the creative activity of the writer *every* time it is mentioned. For example, Gabriel, our retrospective narrator, prepares to tell his tale at the beginning of the novel by revealing, "I have begun to work on the house. Not that it is in need of repair, no. I swept away the broken glass, dead flowers, the other unnameable things" (11). Echoing the Beckettian sundering of language from the objects that they designate, Gabriel implicitly conveys the nature of his linguistic condition from the outset, and continually registers connections between his aesthetic-philosophical motivations and the architecture of the house, initially with respect to the Kantian thing-in-itself: "Still it eluded me, that thing-in-itself, and it was not until I ventured into the attics and the cellars, my favourite haunts, the forgotten corners, that the past at last blossomed in the present" (13). Similarly, Banville's confrontation with the postmodern motif of silence repeatedly finds expression in the context of the house: "a hollow horn of silence sounded throughout the house" (25), and: "The house seemed huge, hollow, all emptiness and echo" (73), while Gabriel expresses his creative possibilities as follows: "What were these paltry things compared to Birchwood, out of whose weeping walls I could knock the bright reverberations of fantasy" (34).

Embedded within the metaphorical house of fiction it is also possible to discern a sense of the author's aspirations for his newly imagined edifice, or form: "Often now, late at night, or working in the house on rainy days, I feel something soft and persistent pressing in on me, and with sadness and joy I welcome back this scene, or others like it, suffused with summer and silence, another world" (29). The desire to locate that other world, or imaginary ontology, is a feature of all of Banville's work, even if it takes significantly different emphasis in the later works. In *Birchwood*, Gabriel's self-generated task is linked to the essential difficulty of creating a harmony that might somehow acknowledge the presence of the world. The "harmony of the season mocks" (175) Gabriel and he acknowledges once again that art is a poor, but crucial, imitation of the world in which he finds himself:

> I began to write, as a means of finding them [people/characters] again, and thought that at last I had discovered a form which would contain and order all my losses. I was wrong. There is no form, no order, only echoes and coincidences, sleight of hand, dark laughter. I accept it. (174)

CHAPTER 1

In this we are granted an overt indication of the logic of Banville's aesthetic arrangement of his fictional ontologies which nevertheless retain the surface layers of plotted action.

Birchwood represents a key developmental moment in Banville's catalogue of novels, primarily because it contains the seeds of the more focused treatments of art that thereafter recur. Apart from the overt declaration of the artificial nature of the text via self-reflexive commentary, the assembling of stock characters, the anachronistic details, and highly allusive textual landscapes, it was also already evident that he was intent on developing a double-layered fusion of fictional plot and self-conscious artistic progress-statement. Rather than mimicking the example of pure *avant-garde* experimentation, it was evident that the nominal retention of plot was part of a narrative response to the formal cul de sac that postmodernism, arguably, had created for the novel form. Although the plot is essentially a parody of the big-house novel fused with an adventure tale, and populated by a variety of stock characters, as detailed by Imhof and McMinn in their early studies of Banville (Imhof 1989; McMinn 1991, 1999[29]), an explicit artistic statement was also woven into the fabric of the unlikely tale, particularly with respect to its author's fascination with a self-consciously nonrepresentational poetics, or the purely invented landscape, the "silence and harmony" that he finds in the "second silent world which exists, independent, ordered by unknown laws" (*BW*, 21). Unlike the merely subversive anti-realist impulses that one finds in *Nightspawn*, Gabriel has a perpetual sense of the harmony and order that lingers beneath, or beyond, the philosophical systems that he is already toying with, and despite the chaos of the world there persists the faint promise of beauty and completeness—qualities that assume central significance in Banville's varied quests in later novels:

> Listen, listen, if I know my world, which is doubtful, but if I do, I know it is chaotic, mean and vicious, with laws cast in the wrong moulds, a fair conception gone awry, in short an awful place, and yet, and yet a place capable of glory in those rare moments when a little light breaks forth, and something is not explained, not forgiven, but merely illuminated. (*BW*, 33)

The merely "illuminated" is a central—perhaps most important—aspiration of art. This proposition lies at the heart of Banville's work and all of the novels feature an elaborate discourse on the nature and possibilities of art. Far from seeking to engage with a poetics of representation, Banville's fictional storyworlds are governed by different principles. Gordon Graham offers aesthetic clarification of this kind of impulse: "We must think of works of art as being *brought* to experience rather than being *drawn* from it . . . a novel is not to be thought of as providing us with a faithful reflection of experience or a skillful summary of it, but as obliging us to view some aspect of experience through an image which allows us to attain an illuminating perspective upon it."[30] In Banville's terms, this aspiration is emphatically expressed: "All—all!—art attempts to do is to quicken the sense of life, to make vivid for the reader the mysterious predicament of being alive for a brief span in this exquisite and terrible world."[31]

Banville's direct engagement with art, initially in *Long Lankin*, *Nightspawn*, and *Birchwood*, extends throughout his work in ever-increasingly more subtle and complex ways. For example, the use of the direct self-reflexive voice in *Birchwood* is still evident in *The Book of Evidence*, fifteen years later, in which Freddie's account, like Banville's, is contained in *his* book of evidence, which he ultimately informs us is just another of his (their) "official fictions" (*BoE*, 220). In the intervening years, in the four novels that engage with science, Banville retains, but diversifies, the self-reflexive mode in several ways. While deliberately focused on the creative aspects of their protagonists, *Doctor Copernicus* and *Kepler* are simultaneously allegories for Banville's artistic process, and therefore extend the deep self-reflexive resonance that we find in the earlier works. Allegory possesses a certain doubleness of intention, and simultaneously projects competing fictional modes. It also alerts one to the polysemic qualities of words, which are central constituent parts of the form, and acknowledges, as Maureen Quilligan clarifies, "the fact that language can signify many things at once."[32] Furthermore, allegory contains both literal and concealed meanings, as well as a complex negotiated relationship between these modes. That it can be read literally is certainly part of the reason for the appeal of the form—and may perhaps explain Banville's reluctance to completely dispense with plot/character—but it is also clear that the connecting anchoring-moments invite and prioritize a richer interpretation. Brian McHale extends this logic beyond a literal/allegorical opposition, particularly in the context of postmodernist fiction, and suggests that "allegory projects a world and erases it in the same gesture, inducing a flicker between presence and absence of this world, between topological reality and 'literal' reality—literal in the *literal* sense of 'words on the page.' For what this flicker foregrounds above all else is the textuality of the text."[33] Read in this context, Banville's two historical novels continually remind us of their own inherent textuality which, in turn, reminds us of the extended artistic conversation that flickers in and out of view. Our attention, of course, is also continually drawn to the ways in which the polysemic words on the

CHAPTER 1

page generate this flickering. Furthermore, David Lodge considers allegory to be "another technique of defamiliarization,"[34] a quality that alerts one to the inherent fictionality of the text. Hence the enhancement of the self-reflexive mode operates on several levels—via the primary allegorical level and by an implicit display of the intense fictionality of the surface of the plot, a feature that is maintained throughout these two novels.

Banville's science tetralogy, which was later marketed as the Revolutions Trilogy, is based upon the classical Greek tetralogy of three tragedies and a satire. *The Newton Letter* is Banville's satire, what he calls an exercise in "sending myself up."[35] The first two parts to the tetralogy, *Doctor Copernicus* and *Kepler*, which Linda Hutcheon views to be prime examples of historiographic metafictions,[36] initially appear to represent a radical shift in direction, notwithstanding the parodic historical reconstruction one encounters earlier in *Birchwood*. The two science-focused novels initially appear to be far more serious reconstructions of the intellectual pursuits and private dramas of their two famous scientists, Nicholas Copernicus and Johannes Kepler, but artistically they advance similar discourses to those of the other novels; the implications of language, the treachery of memory and the hazards of locating a fixed version of truth when one evaluates the world, are all familiar Banvillean artistic problems. As one grows to expect in later years, it is already evident that the content of the works, the historical subject matter, is of little direct significance. Banville has openly declared as much with respect to the *Doctor Copernicus* and *Kepler*: "science, history and mathematics are no more important to those books than the *Odyssey* is to *Ulysses*."[37] Nonetheless, Banville is also on record arguing for a closer correspondence between science and art: "My thesis is that modern science, particularly physics, in being forced, under pressure of its own advances, to acknowledge that the truths it offers are true not in an absolute but in a poetic sense, that its laws are contingent, that its facts are a kind of metaphor" (40). Perhaps more crucial are his views on the fundamental nature of what science seeks to achieve:

> Science keeps uncovering more and more secrets, keeps getting closer and closer to . . . well, to *something*, in the same way that computations in the infinitesimal calculus keep approaching nearer and nearer to infinity without ever getting there. Progress must be progress *toward* something, surely, some final end to the quest for knowledge? But to my mind the world has no meaning. It simply is. Leibnitz's thrilling question, "Why is there something rather than nothing?" is significant not because an answer to it is possible, but

because out of the blind, boiling chaos that is the world, a species should have emerged that is capable of posing such a question.[38]

This has clear significance for Banville's aspirations as an artist. Far from attempting to generate fictions that offer a sense of meaning in the world, the artist simply illuminates certain aspects of lived experience. In this sense, modern physics too illuminates that which it seeks to interrogate and new patterns and models continually emerge, but the question of a fixed meaning is challenged.

Because many earlier Banville critics, particularly Imhof, McMinn, and Berensmeyer, have closely dealt with the specifics of science in their treatments of the tetralogy, and worked through the development of Banville's interests in science more generally, there is little value in again revisiting this aspect of Banville's work. Furthermore, for this study the value of science lies primarily in its metaphoric potential, particularly with respect to the notion of scientific inquiry as a creative pursuit. For example, Copernicus explains his scientific process during a key epiphanic moment, initiating an artistic fascination that arguably dominates all of Banville's work: "No: astronomy was but the knife. What he was after was the deeper, the deepest thing: the kernel, the essence, the true" (*DC*, 90). The distinction between the analytical process and truth parallels the linguistic relation to the world, as expressed by the prelinguistic Copernicus as a child: "At first it had no name. It was the thing itself, the vivid thing. It was his friend" (*DC*, 13). Echoing Stephen Dedalus's opening encounters with language in *A Portrait of the Artist as a Young Man*, and the Kantian thing-in-itself, Copernicus expresses one of the essential tensions that lie at the heart of literary art: the distinction between objective reality and linguistic signs. The early works had in fact initiated an exploration of the creative silence that is encountered as one turns away from the demands of verisimilitude, and *Doctor Copernicus* and *Kepler* are primarily extensions of this process of exploration. Copernicus's account diagnoses the problem with respect to his own scientific system in terms akin to the limits of referential fiction which, in turn, self-reflexively indicates Banville's artistic endeavors: "You imagine my book is a kind of mirror in which the real world is reflected; but you are mistaken, you must realise that. In order to build such a mirror, I should need to be able to perceive the whole world, in its entirety and its essence" (*DC*, 219). The overtly plausible plotted worlds that Banville outlines in the historical novels thus underpin an extension of the discourse one encounters in *Birchwood*; a distinct metaphoric parallel between science and art is maintained

CHAPTER 1

throughout, allowing Banville to self-reflexively engage with his own art form. Although Lysaght acknowledges that Copernicus's "epistemological dilemma" is "a paradigm of Banville's own artistic predicament" (84) he also oddly insists that "self-conscious commentary upon the shortcomings and failings of the act of writing is scarcely in evidence."[39] The surface plausibility of the historical novels appears to motivate such a reading but the metaphorical correspondences between art and science are explicitly obvious in almost every aspect of Copernicus's creative impulses, so much so that Mark O'Connell asserts that Banville's "metafictional strategy in Doctor Copernicus is to surreptitiously write about writing whilst appearing to write about science. There are passages in which it is difficult to avoid the suspicion that Banville is engaging in a kind of covert auto-representation."[40] The correspondences primarily operate in the context of descriptions of Copernicus's scientific or creative challenges. For example, Copernicus, aware that Ptolemy's theory of planetary motion is flawed, seeks to find the truth but ultimately his model of the universe too flounders; while it "saves the phenomena" it does not locate the truth for which he yearns. What is finally foregrounded is the difference between truth and the epistemological systems that are employed to locate it:

> There is no need to search for truth. We know it already, before we ever think of setting out on our quests . . . we *are* the truth. The world, and ourselves, this is the truth. There is no other, or, if there is, it is of use to us only as an ideal, that brings us a little comfort, a little consolation, now and then. (*DC*, 252)

The distinction between actuality, the thing-in-itself, and the epistemological process is foregrounded, just as it had been in the earlier *Birchwood*, and in the sense that such statements have direct ramifications for the act of writing and the ordering of reality in text.

Banville's Kepler, in the subsequent novel, seeks a mathematical truth for Copernicus's belief that the sun is the pivotal point of the universe, and believes the "verification of the theory," to be no more than "mere hackwork" (*K*, 96). The fictional Kepler's aim is to mathematically map the motion of the planets and to thus discover the error in the Copernican system. With the flawed information available to Kepler, his theory appears to work but, as with Copernicus, it ultimately fails and he finally grows to understand the real significance of his life's work: "We must take it all on trust. That's the secret. How simple! He smiled. It was not a mere book that was thus thrown away, but the foundation of a life's work. It seemed not to matter" (*K*, 185).

Like Copernicus, Kepler discovers that his attempts to discover truth are self-sustaining fictions which fail to transfix reality—which is both a commentary on scientific process, and on the aspirations of art.

One of the constituent components of Banville's artistic process throughout his work is a dramatization of his various creator-figures' failures to imaginatively engage with material existence and Kepler's mathematical fictions are similarly mirrored in the frequent misreadings of his life. Of his stepdaughter, the reticent Regina, and forerunner of many of Banville's symbolic female-figures, he claims; "There was in her an air of completeness, of being, for herself, a precise sufficiency" (*K*, 18). But, later, he appears puzzled by the tone of her previous letter: "This is not your tone of voice, which I remember with tenderness and love, this is not how you would speak to me, if the choice were yours. I can only believe that these words were dictated to you" (*K*, 131). Kepler's ultimate understanding of the gap between reality and the fictions he weaves is central to Banville self-reflexive enterprise. The novel concludes with the astronomer having lost interest in the "work of his intellect" (*K*, 184), echoing Banville's own abandonment of the historical form, which he has claimed was a "wrong direction"[41] and, despite the differences between the two novels, there is a sense that the narrative experiment is somewhat repetitive.

The allegorical form or the doubling of artistic intent, in the historical novels is formulated on several levels, most literally in the explicit factual details of Kepler's life and work, which directly parallel those of Banville. *Kepler*, for example, repeatedly references the astronomer's struggle with the orbit of Mars: "And seventeen months were to become seven years before the thing was done" (*K*, 74). The reference to seven years, which recurs several times in the text, is a reminder that Banville too invested seven years writing the two historical novels, while the depiction of Kepler as a man who has lost interest in scientific discovery anticipates Banville's own rejection of the scientific-historical fiction genre. *The Newton Letter* also later explicitly refers to this: "Seven years I gave to it—seven years . . . shall I say I lost faith in the primacy of the text" (*NL*, 9).

Furthermore, both novels are initially framed by explicit epigraphs which are directly concerned with the creative process and are written by writers whose work, like Banville's, can be viewed as process-focused. The epigraph to *Doctor Copernicus* is taken from Wallace Stevens's *Notes Toward a Supreme Fiction*,[42] whose self-referential analytical poetics advise a return to a kind of prelapsarian intellectual ignorance or prelinguistic vision, in order to rediscover the essence of

CHAPTER 1

life and create what Stevens calls "a supreme fiction." For Stevens, it is the first impression that constitutes truth before it is deformed by our knowledge systems. The first truth, Stevens suggests, can be presented through a special form of fiction which might salvage the "inconceivable idea of the sun."[43] Stevens's poetics, coupled with the poetic imperatives of Rainer Maria Rilke, who's *Duino Elegies* provides the epigraph to *Kepler*,[44] offers a clear indication of Banville's aesthetic logic at this formative stage of his career. Rilke's "The Ninth Elegy" offers an emphatic declaration of poetic intent:

> Tell him *things*. He will stand more astonished: as you did beside
> the roper in Rome or the potter in Egypt.[45]

Rilke foregrounds the artistic telling and the elevation of humble things to a level capable of astonishing the Gods and, like Stevens, uses the poetic form itself as a declaration of poetic possibility—essentially a self-reflexive process-statement. Banville has offered a fusion of the Rilke and Stevens quotations as a declaration of one of the key attributes of art:

> Together the Rilke and Stevens quotations create a synthesis which is the very core of art . . . of the tension between the desire to take things into ourselves by saying them, by praising them to the Angels and the impossibility finally of making the world our own, that poetry springs, and that other poetry which some of us disguise by not justifying the right hand margin of our books. Hence the note of solitude, of stoic despair, which great art always sounds.[46]

In the space between the immense desire to say the world, to impose our complex systems of order, and the impossibility of that happening, art emerges, he suggests—and his historical scientists exemplify this in precisely the same way that his own novels do.

Kepler's misconstrual of many aspects of his life echoes Banville's acknowledgment of the deep tension that underpins the artistic encounter with material reality, and elevates a central creative feature to the centre of his aesthetic. Similarly, Copernicus emphasizes the essential gap between the imagining mind and the actuality of "real" people:

> At first he knew them to be hallucinations, but then he realized that the matter was deeper than that: they were real enough, as real as anything can be that is not of oneself, that is of the outside, for had he not always believed that others are not known but invented, that the world consists solely of oneself while all else is phantom, necessarily. (*DC*, 241)

As Imhof suggests, with respect to *Kepler*, "the mind of man stamps his own interpretation on the world."[47] However, this is far more than mere solipsism; Banville's response suggests an imaginative transfiguration of reality into artistic form, the creation of a "kind of superreality"[48] that is imbued with the formal, synthetic, norms of art. Generated from the imagining mind, this superreality acts as an artistic response to the apparent failure of art to represent the precise details of life—although implicit in this process is the rationale that art is simply not meant to represent reality in such a mirror-like fashion.

Banville's historical novels can thus be viewed as self-conscious demonstrations of the progressive failing of art—progressive in that only by demonstrating the failings of the desire to tell can one gain insight into the nature of the sophisticated fictions that we weave. A mapping of the two astronomers' essentially creative processes—and both of these novels are ultimately concerned with this aspect of the two heroes' histories—offered him a suitable comparative structure within which his ongoing investigation into the possibilities of literary art could be further explored. The potent parallels are repeatedly teased out throughout both novels, as with the following revelatory moment in *Kepler*:

> And why had this annunciation been made to him, what heaven-hurled angel had whispered in his ear? He marvelled at the process, how a part of his mind had worked away in secret and in silence while the rest of him swilled and capered and lusted after poxed whores. (*K*, 73)

Both *Doctor Copernicus* and *Kepler* are primarily occupied with the creative processes of their protagonists and it is precisely in this respect that they most closely resemble artists, with practically every reference to their intellectual process having simultaneous allegorical significance for the processes of art, as when Copernicus seeks to explain some basic scientific principles to Rheticus: "'You think that to see is to perceive, but listen, listen, *seeing is not perception!* Why will no one realize that?'" (219–20). Similarly, the depictions of their searches for scientific truth—or more precisely the demonstration of the failures of such searches—("My book is not science – it is a dream. I am not even sure if science is possible" [220])—mirrors the impossibility of truly knowing reality in literary fiction. However, the demonstration of the failure of representative forms of art is also a ruse of sorts, because readers of Banville know very well that prior to *Doctor Copernicus* mimesis was already undermined as an aesthetic position. So the novels do not discover the limits of representation,

CHAPTER 1

they simply demonstrate the veracity of these limits and assert the fictionality of all narrative systems.

The true shift for Banville is formal, in that *Doctor Copernicus* and *Kepler* more closely align with the historical novel form than any of his previous works. Of course, the historical novels are themselves *faux* historical novels because in several ways, including anachronistic quotations from modern scientists (Einstein, Arthur Eddington, Max Planck) and writers (Kierkegaard, Kafka, Wallace Stevens) and the use of a subversive, allegorical, self-reflexive narrative voice, they are self-evidently fictive accounts that refuse to offer a straight telling of historically verifiable events, even if there is a factual skeleton used in both. Furthermore, there is an absurdly overwrought structural form employed in *Kepler*, which Mark O'Connell likens to a giant acrostic: "Banville has also constructed the novel so that the first letters of each of its 50 chapters spell out the names of four central figures in the history of science: Johannes Kepler, Tycho Brahe, Galileo Galileus and Isaac Newton."[49] In addition, the manner in which Banville's Kepler is obsessed with the structure of his endeavors openly echoes the structural design of the novel to such a degree that the different denotative elements in the allegory practically coalesce. In a letter to Hans Georg Herwart von Hohenburg, Kepler explains his plan for his projected book, which he will divide into five parts that "correspond to the five planetary intervals, while the number of chapters in each part will be based upon the signifying quantities of each of the five regular or Platonic solids which, according to my *Mysterium*, may be fitted into these intervals" (96). Banville titles each of the chapters after five of Kepler's books and bases each chapter on one of the five regular solids; Kepler wrongly believed that the five regular solids (the cube, the tetrahedron, the dodecahedron, the icosahedron and the octahedron) could be inserted between the orbits of the planets and, as many critics have pointed out,[50] Banville offers special emphasis to this theory.

Despite the embedded metafictional tropes and the obvious allegorical framing, both novels, unlike *Birchwood*, are not as explicitly subversive as their immediate predecessor. Banville's artistic promise at the close of *Birchwood*, offered via the extended metaphor of the house, clearly indicates that he will live in the house but that he will "live a life different from any the house has ever known," because outside the formal structures of established fictional genres lies "destruction and decay" (174). The two historical novels nominally satisfy the generic norms of fictional history but simultaneously enlarge its artistic possibilities. Already one can observe the fact that Banville's novels are innovations on the historical novel genre because the true subject of their formal games is the process of their own art. Banville has always effectively decoded his own texts while enacting a self-reflexive discourse about the nature of fiction and art or, as Derek Hand has claimed, his work, taken as a whole, is "an open-ended dialogue about art, about its worth and functions in the modern world."[51]

Part III of the tetralogy, *The Newton Letter*, returns to the first person narration of *Birchwood* and relates a tale of its unnamed historian's intellectual crisis, via the form of a letter of resignation to the muse of history, Clio. The narrator has abandoned his attempt to write a history of Isaac Newton after having retreated to a lodge adjacent to "Fern House," a run-down big house, where he had hoped to complete his work. The abortive historical attempt evolves into his account of a failed endeavor to read reality and the novel thus becomes a document of his doubled crisis; it echoes the doubling of intellectual endeavor and artistic process of the two historical novels, although in a less stratified manner, since the metaphorical parallel of science is of far less significance in *The Newton Letter*, with Lysaght suggesting that it marks a "return to the question of narrative practice itself."[52] Banville, for example, teases his readers in the short novella: the historian indicates that he has worked on his history of Newton for seven years, the length of time that Banville devoted to writing *Doctor Copernicus* and *Kepler*, and has now abandoned history as a pursuit. More significant is the overt manner in which the Newton historian acknowledges his misreading of the events that unfold before him, again echoing the essentially fluid nature of our engagements with material reality. This is emphasized via the manner in which the narrator's subjective imagination invents the people he encounters. For example, his sexual relationship with Ottilie is initially contrasted with his feelings for Charlotte, his "passion of the mind" (*NL*, 53), but he later imaginatively fuses both to create a third name, Charlottilie, intertextually alluding to Humbert's elevation of word-play above meaningful referential discourse in Nabokov's *Lolita*.[53] The novel clearly seeks to emphasize the distinction between reality and the fictive patterns woven in the mind, again simultaneously registering the importance of the primary level of plot while also expressing the novel's self-conscious relationship with material reality. The novel is both *about* something (a man misreading material reality) and also, in a more significant sense, it *is* simultaneously a work of art that playfully echoes the problems of its protagonists in its own fictional form.

The unnamed historian, though not a scientist like Copernicus or Kepler, is continually presented as a creator in *The Newton Letter*. While his

CHAPTER 1

role as a failed historian is significant, it is in his inability to forge a meaningful relationship between his intellectual systems and the world that he serves as an effective guide to Banville's aesthetic development and contributes to the emerging debate related to the relationship between text (or knowledge system) and the world. Echoing Kepler, he initially retreats from his intellectual pursuits because the immediacy of the world profoundly distracts him: "Shall I say, I've lost faith in the primacy of the text? Real people keep getting in the way now, objects, landscapes even. Everything ramifies" (*NL*, 9). This, however, is somewhat misleading because the narrator in turn manages to completely misconstrue the "real" world that has so distracted him. Banville's historian is depicted as a detached academic who constructs a series of elaborate fictions that reinforce the by-now familiar position that reality is shaped by our imagining minds.

In *The Newton Letter* Banville shifts his emphasis away from the systematic mathematical designs of great scientists and focuses instead on the apparent primacy of social reality as a way to illustrate that the subjects of our intellectual imaginings are forever conditioned by the perceiving eye. Joseph McMinn interprets the narrator's confusion as derived from the conceptual habits of his scholarly work: "The very system which man has developed in order to explain and duplicate reality, ends up making him feel like a total stranger to that reality,"[54] while John Kenny prefers to place an emphasis on the political implications of misreading that "reality" in the context of Catholic and Protestant relations with the Big House,"[55] a slightly reductive interpretation of his problems because the historian's misinterpretations extend far beyond the Big House. He is continually frustrated by the fluid nature of external reality and by his inability to apply significance to real objects by means of his defining systems: "I had bought guide books to trees and birds, but I couldn't get the hang of them. The illustrations would not match up with the real specimens before me" (*NL*, 13). Realizing that his methods fail, like those of Kepler and Copernicus, he considers his life: "I was like a man living underground who, coming up for air is dazzled by the light and cannot find the way back into his bolthole. I trudge back and forth over the familiar ground, muttering. I am lost" (90). This is a variation of the house-of-fiction motif, in that the bolthole is suggestive of a kind of safe-zone, outside of which is confusion and chaos. The significance for Banville's development lies in his response to the narrator's crisis; having stepped out of the familiar, the recognizable literary house of fiction—the historical novel—he must now relearn to assign significance and generate order. Faced with an absence of fixed systematic understanding, or adequate methods, the historian is compelled to recalibrate his imaginative sense of being and it is in his account of the fluid, fictive world that he comes closest to a genuine understanding of it.

As with the two historical novels, Banville formulates his tale of intellectual crisis within an elaborate intertextual frame, indicating a second layer of creative design built into the novel. This is particularly significant because the allusions point to several sources that are themselves engaged with the nature of the creative process, self-reflexively acting, in effect, as critical commentary. For example, the Newton historian's invoking words, "Tell her something, tell her a fact, a fragment from the big world, a coloured stone, a bit of clouded green glass," (*NL*, 83) echo Rilke's invocation in the "Ninth Elegy" to "Tell him things" until "it lives in our hands and eyes."[56] Although Banville repeatedly affirms the artificiality of art in his work he always retains a belief in the power of art to *signify* something for life. While our constructions (literary, artistic, and scientific) cannot provide replicas of life they can speak of what Rilke refers to as a "Supernumerous existence"[57] or, as reframed by the historian: "I am pregnant myself in a way. Supernumerous existence wells up in my heart" (*NL*, 90). Allusions of this kind imbue the novel with a self-reflexive quality and draw one's attention to the aestheticized surface of the world of the text, while certain instances that masquerade as scenic description also manage to alert us to the essential separateness of certain perceived moments: "It was a notion of a time out of time, of this summer as a self-contained unit separate from the time of the ordinary world" (*NL*, 58). Such moments of supernumerous existence can be aesthetically rescued, or forged, from time and space. *The Newton Letter* seeks to merge life and art into that fluid "one meaning" pursued by Rilke, and simultaneously declares this intention in multiple ways.

Like the earlier *Birchwood*, *The Newton Letter* constructs its house of fiction both literally and figuratively in the shadow of the big house. Fern House is "the kind of place where you picture a mad stepdaughter locked up in the attic" (*NL*, 11), parodically alluding to several big-house novels, including *Birchwood*, while the narrator also defines his immediate context via a series of well-trodden allusions to other fictions. For example, he tells us of Ottilie's romantic vision of her parents: "In her fantasy they were a kind of Scott and Zelda, beautiful and doomed" (*NL*, 36), alerting us to the fact that the subject of his fictional misreadings is herself prone to imposing fictional tropes on her own existence. In this fashion one can discern a layering upon layering of fictive modes, which also finds rich expression in Banville's use of

CHAPTER 1

Newton's second letter—a fiction—which is partially borrowed from Hugo Von Hofmannstahl's *Ein Brief*, or *The Letter of Lord Chandos*. Hofmannstahl's *Ein Brief* too is a confessional letter and relates its author's plight in trying to designate a reality from the words which man has created, expressly in order to know or describe life. As with Banville's historian, Hoffmanstahl's narrator is isolated from life because his systems fail, and he claims that he can no longer formulate ideas and use language: "I have lost completely the ability to think or to speak of anything coherently" (73), and finally suggests that, "neither in the coming year nor in the following nor in all the years of this my life shall I write a book, whether in English or in Latin" (79), although John Pilling suggests that it is still ultimately a document of a "crisis conquered,"[58] in part because of Lord Chandos's suggestion that he may one day be able to think and write in a "language none of whose words is known to me, a language in which inanimate things speak to me and wherein I may one day have to justify myself before an unknown judge" (79). This mirrors Banville's historian's renunciation of language, or text, and his loss of faith in his intellectual systems, as well as his fear that he too will one day again lie in the ruins of failed systems. However, like Lord Chandos, he has created a fiction of process, albeit ultimately of a special kind of failure. Imhof sees *Ein Brief* as one of the earliest expressions of "the artistic predicament of the twentieth century artist,"[59] and as such it corresponds to many other intertextual presences in Banville that too seek to aesthetically respond to artistic crises.

The Newton Letter can be viewed as an intermediary text in many respects; it aesthetically mirrors Banville's resignation from the historical novel form, satirizing the efforts of its own narrator-historian who, like Banville via *Doctor Copernicus* and Kepler had sought to write (on one level) the history of a great scientist. It simultaneously generates the initiation of an artistic form that would be more fully realized in the final part of the tetralogy, *Mefisto*. I contend that *Mefisto* is a more aesthetically significant novel although *The Newton Letter* has proven to be an attractive proposition with some Irish critics (Kenny, Hand) because of its overt use of the big-house genre, and the Irish setting is more clearly outlined, unlike with the nightmarish surface texture that defines *Mefisto*.

Mefisto retains many of the ideas explored elsewhere in the tetralogy but, as Banville claims, it "reformulates them."[60] Most obviously, it too seeks to engage with the troubled problem of transforming reality into the forms of art or, more precisely, to the challenge of how to respond to the immediacy of the world when fixed forms have been removed. *Mefisto* self-reflexively acknowledges its own condition as text from the outset, while ostensibly discussing mathematics: "I could go on. I shall go on. I too have my equations, my symmetries, and will insist on them" (3–4), playfully alluding to the closing lines of Beckett's *The Unnamable* to concretize the literary emphasis. The parallel between the novelist's activity and that of the mathematician is maintained throughout, although in the latter half of the novel the self-referential voice more fully engages with a literary-imaginative focus:

> Have I tied up all the ends? Even an invented world has its rules, tedious, absurd perhaps, but not to be gainsaid. . . . More than once I have turned in the street at the sight of a flash of red hair, a face slyly smiling among the faceless ones. Is it my imagination? Was it ever anything else? (*M*, 234)

Banville saw *Mefisto* as a major shift in emphasis, indicating that he was "striking out into new territory."[61] The departure from the historical novel, already largely evident in *The Newton Letter*, is complete with *Mefisto* and the scientific subject matter of the novel is now embedded in a relatively contemporary, if unspecific, Irish setting. *Mefisto* also ambitiously rewrites *Birchwood* by revisiting the big-house genre in a significant manner; it retains the name Gabriel, features the purely invented worlds of its earlier counterpart, and peoples the strange plot with a series of self-evidently fictional characters. Unlike Gabriel Godkin, however, Gabriel Swan is a child mathematical prodigy, one whom Banville claims "is more of an 'artist,' whatever that may be, than a 'scientist,' whatever that may be."[62] He is befriended by the Mephistophelian Felix—henceforth a recurring presence in Banville's fictive universe, as I have illustrated elsewhere[63]—and his followers Dr. Kasperl and Sophie, whose ancestral home, Ashburn he frequently visited. After a house fire at Ashburn, the physically deformed Gabriel stalks the streets of Dublin in part II and relates a strange tale in what is effectively a distorted mirror image of part I of the novel, and he grows conscious of a fundamental transfiguration in self: "But I was different. I was someone else, someone I knew and didn't know. I had stepped into the mirror" (*M*, 132).

By employing a doubling of literary and mathematical references the novel repeatedly emphasizes the notion of a hidden order. Gabriel admits, for example, that when he encounters Sophie after a period of separation he realizes: "She had so throbbed in my imagination that now when I confronted the real she, it was as if I had just parted from her more dazzling double" (*M*, 68). The gap between imagination and material reality is again asserted. In order

CHAPTER 1

to express the essential difference between these two ontological zones *Mefisto* is constructed as a series of symmetrical images, allusions, and narrative structures. Part I of *Mefisto*, entitled "Marionettes," for example, is a counterpoint to part II, "Angels." The key to the code of Banville's symmetry can be found in a combination of two of his early literary influences, Rilke and Heinrich von Kleist.[64] Kleist's *The Puppet Theatre* makes a crucial distinction between the artificial elegance of the puppet (or marionette) and the movements of real dancers which are compromised by the "affectation," the self-consciousness of being human.[65] Furthermore, Erich Heller's comparison of Kleist and Rilke further explains the distinction between Marionettes and Angels:

> Kleist has devoted his beautiful philosophical dialogue *On the Marionette Theatre*, where a dancer, a ballet master, is seeking out the perfect model of graceful movement, goes back beyond the child, even beyond the sphere of organic nature, to the mechanical contraption of the marionette; for in its absolute and unconscious obedience to natural laws, the laws of weight and counterweight, the marionette displays in its motions a grace that is wholly unaffected—unaffected, that is, by even the slightest trace of self-consciousness, a grace that is not obtainable by any man or woman: "Only a god could, in this respect, be its equal.". . . But the ultimate and at last real show will be enacted only when the Angel—Rilke's embodiment of "the fullness of being"—will hold in his hands the wires of the puppet.[66]

Kleist's and Rilke's aspirations correspond to Banville's symmetrical patterns in *Mefisto*, with the title of part II, "Angels," implying a desire to elevate the second part of the novel to the status of Rilke's Angels, or "fullness of being"—to somehow recondition the movement of the puppet characters of part I in the context of a newly imagined ontological frame.

The two sections of *Mefisto* also echo each other in terms of the deployment of the motif of the lost or other self, or what Gabriel names "a momentous absence": "A connecting cord remained, which parturition and even death had not broken, along which by subtle tugs and thrums I sensed what was not there [. . .] It seemed to me I was not all my own, that I was being shared" (*M*, 17–18). Similarly, the names of the Gemini twins, Castor and Pollux, are used, respectively, to identify Gabriel in the two sections and, in part II, it is suggested that he evolves into an other, deeper self: "This was the place I had never been before, which I had not known existed. I was inside me" (*M*, 124). Several of the other characters also have symmetrical counterparts in part II;

most notably Kasperl and Sophie are reimagined as the palindromic Kosok, and Adele.

Of course, being a novel ostensibly concerned with the implications of science, *Mefisto* also avails of mathematical and scientific exemplum to register a sense of the essential duality of existence or, as Imhof argues in the context of the atomist world view:

> The Greek atomists held that behind the bewildering, complex appearance of the forms of matter there lay a structure of atoms—indivisible particles—obeying simple laws which enable us to explain and correlate the experience of our senses. Chance is the completion and manifestation of necessity, of order of a specific kind. This is to say that beneath the surface of apparently contingent, or chance, events there always is hidden a deeper necessity.[67]

Chance, Gabriel tells at the outset of his tale, "was in the beginning" (*M*, 3), before his mathematical systems had interceded but, ultimately, he concludes the novel having abandoned a strict systematic mode of being: "It will be different this time, I think it will be different. I won't do as I used to, in the old days. No. In future, I will leave things, I will try to leave things, to chance" (234). But chance does not mean arbitrary in Banville's fiction. J. G. Hibben tells us that chance "may be defined as a complex of causal elements, in which indefinitely many combinations are possible, and each combination yields a distinct result."[68] Banville's refutation of the primary significance of causation simultaneously asserts the significance of "chance" as a major defining component in the world's order:

> However, as we know very well if we think about it for a moment, there is no such thing as an event and no such thing as a cause; there is only, as Nietzsche points out, a continuum. Causation, then, is no more and no less than what physicists would call a thought experiment . . . a thing invented by men in order to explain and, therefore, make habitable a chaotic, hostile and impassive world. I foresee a time, not at all far off, when physics will produce a new theory of reality. In the new schema, chance will play a large, perhaps central part.[69]

While in the same interview Banville concedes that chance is a difficult thing to define,[70] there is an acceptance of a complex, inaccessible order beneath, or despite, the systems that we typically use as analytical gestures. For Banville, Heisenberg's principle in indeterminacy[71] reinforces the notion that all methods

CHAPTER 1

of scientific investigation are doomed to failure, primarily because they inevitably leave the imprint of their own systems on the object being analyzed. He summarizes Heisenberg's principle in the following manner: "Heisenberg's principle in indeterminacy [. . .] put simply, says that we cannot investigate darkness by bathing it in light—a seemingly innocent observation, but one which, in the world of atomic physics has enormous consequences."[72] Banville's attempts to generate dual fictional zones reflect his sense of a distinction between an inner imaginative order and the complexity of external reality:

> Inside us, however, somewhere in our head or heart, there exists another version, a separate reality which has shape and significance, which we think of as some sort of truth, and which is endowed with a beginning, a middle and an end. It is the desire to see this inward reality made manifest in the world that gives rise to what Wallace Stevens calls our "rage for order!" Amid disintegration we yearn for synthesis. Religion used to attempt the task. Now in a secular age we must look elsewhere for a "supreme fiction."[73]

Mefisto can thus be seen as an attempt to articulate, in his terms, a supreme fiction that both acknowledges the presence of external reality and simultaneously reveals the transfiguration of that presence in aesthetic form. Similarly, the thing-in-itself, or truth, that so fascinated Copernicus, is also acknowledged as a haunting presence that remains beyond the reach of man's intellectual systems but may be alluded to via the frames of art. A certain exterior order may exist but it cannot be isolated or defined. It simply exists without meaning, without utterance, to be known but not said; in one extraordinary moment near the close of *Mefisto*, Gabriel ventures into this essentially unknowable space, into the pure essence of himself:

> And it seemed to me that somehow I had always been here, and somehow would remain here always, among Mammy's things, with her little unrelenting eyes fixed on me. She signified something, no, she signified nothing. She had no meaning. She was simply there. And would be there, waiting in that fetid little room, forever. (*M*, 230)

Recalling the pattern of images related to the house that first emerged in *Birchwood*, Banville avails of the suggestive tropes of fiction to articulate a sense of the mute essence, which is untouchable and meaningless to our interrogative rationality. She simply is. Our systems of analysis are confounded and merely send back empty echoes of themselves.

THE EARLY EVOLUTION OF AN AESTHETIC

Gabriel's transformation, from adhering to a specific system to seeking a less programmatic method, self-consciously mirrors Banville's artistic development in terms of his movement from the quasi-historical novel form to a more direct engagement with the world of experience, despite the inherent difficulties that such an enterprise entails. In part II of the novel "Angels," after he has stepped into a different ontological plane, everything takes on new significance for Gabriel. In part I his belief in fixed harmony had persevered, and he had viewed the world primarily in terms of numbers but in part II the erratic world crowds in on his systems and he realizes that his defining methodology will no longer suffice: "A panic of disconnected numbers buzzed in my head. Grass, trees, railings, the road" (*M*, 139). In Gabriel's new vision of life, the things themselves are of central significance as they shake away from their signifying agents: "Things crowded in, the mere things themselves. One drop of water plus one drop of water will not make two drops, but one. Two oranges and two apples do not make four of some new synthesis but remain stubbornly themselves" (*M*, 233). The mathematical model, of course, is again simply a metaphor for all systems with which one attempts to coerce reality into order, so Gabriel's discovery of another way to respond to the world corresponds with Banville's self-conscious movement away from a rigid formal approach:

> From the start the world had been for me an immense formula. Press hard enough upon anything, a cloud . . . and it would unfurl its secret, intricate equations. But what was different now was that it was no longer numbers that lay at the heart of things. Numbers, I saw at last, were only a method, a way of doing. The thing itself would be more subtle, more certain, even, than the manner of its finding. (*M*, 185)

Mefisto greatly differs from the relatively programmatic approach used by Banville in all of his previous works. Novels like *Nightspawn* and *Birchwood*, despite their respective degrees of accomplishment are both instantly recognizable as overt metafictional novels, and even though all four science novels are, as Kenny observes, "above all else analogies for the artistic process,"[74] there are marked differences between them. The two historical novels offer metafictional variations on the historical novel form, and the quasi-realist *The Newton Letter*, while generically related to *Birchwood*, is far less fantastical that the early Big House parody. But *Mefisto* achieves a level of strangeness, in the best possible sense of the word, and a level of formal unpredictability and ambition that was genuinely new for Banville, something that he has frequently alluded to:

CHAPTER 1

> *Mefisto* was a big shift for me. I began to write in a different way. I began to trust my instincts, to lose control, deliberately. It was exciting and it was frightening. The writer who wrote *Mefisto* was a writer in deep trouble. He didn't know what he was doing. He was striking out into new territory—new for him, at least.[75]

This remains a crucial development in Banville, in the direction of what might be considered a pure art form. *Mefisto* incorporates the illusory nature of human perception as a constituent part of its narrative rather than as its subject matter as was the case—via the astronomers—in *Doctor Copernicus* and *Kepler*. As such it is not a representation of reality but it *relates* to reality. After *Mefisto*, even acknowledging the surface-level plotted nature of some novels like *The Book of Evidence* and *The Untouchable*, his work evolved in a direction where the content primarily becomes the subject of its own self-reflexive investigations. The books increasingly place art at their plotted centers freeing Banville from the overt metaphorical parallels that had defined much of the early work. Nevertheless, as we shall see, even in the trilogy of art novels, *The Book of Evidence*, *Ghosts*, and *Athena*, the narrative strategy of employing a metaphorical parallel to some degree extends to the way that Banville uses the visual arts, even if the deployment of the strategy is rendered in a more textually integrated fashion.

Notes

1. Banville, *Long Lankin* (London: Secker & Warburg, 1970).
2. David Herman, Manfred Jahn, and Marie-Laure Ryan, *Routledge Encyclopedia of Narrative Theory* (London: Routledge, 2008), 301.
3. Banville's *Long Lankin* was originally published in 1970, followed by a revised edition in 1984. Banville excluded the novella, "The Possessed," and the story "Persona" from the revised edition.
4. Brian McHale, *Postmodernist Fiction* (London: Routledge, 2003), 69.
5. Rüdiger Imhof, *John Banville: A Critical Introduction* (Dublin: Wolfhound Press, 1997), 26.
6. Kersti Tarien Powell, "Trying to Catch Long Lankin by His Arm: The Evolution of John Banville's *Long Lankin*," *Irish University Review* 31, no. 2 (Autumn-Winter, 2001), 399.
7. Joseph McMinn, *The Supreme Fictions of John Banville* (Manchester: Manchester University Press, 1999), 22.
8. John Kenny, *John Banville* (Dublin: Irish Academic Press, 2009), 41.

9. Imhof, *Critical Introduction*, 42.
10. Samuel Beckett, *The Beckett Trilogy: Molloy, Malone Dies, The Unnamable* (London: Picador, 1979), 373.
11. Alain Robbe-Grillet, *Topology of Phantom City*, trans. J. A. Underwood (London: John Calder, 1978), 142.
12. John Banville, *Doctor Copernicus* (London: Panther Books, 1984). The novel opens with the following lines: "At first it had no name. It was the thing itself, the vivid thing. It was his friend. On windy days it danced, demented, waving wild arms, or in the silence of evening drowsed and dreamed, swaying in the blue, the goldeny air" (13).
13. André Gide, *The Immoralist* (Harmondsworth: Penguin, 1983).
14. Kenny, *John Banville*, 69.
15. Rüdiger Imhof, "My Readers, That Small Band, Deserve a Rest," *Irish University Review* 11, no. 1 (Spring 1981): 6.
16. The opening to *Notes from Underground* is parodied in Ben's opening to *Nightspawn*: "I am a sick man, I am a spiteful man. I think my life is diseased. Only a flood of spleen now could cauterise my wounds" (7). Dostoevsky's more solemn opening novel reads as follows: "I am a sick man . . . I am a hungry man. I am an unattractive man. I think there is something wrong with my liver." Fyodor Dostoevsky, *Notes from Underground/The Double*, trans. Jessie Coulson (Harmondsworth: Penguin, 1980).
17. Vladimir Nabokov, *Despair* (Harmondsworth: Penguin, 1987), 51.

Nabokov's riddle reads: "Guess: my first is that sound, my second is an exclamation, my third will be prefixed to me when I am no more; and the whole is my ruin."

Banville's riddle reads: "One word, three syllables. The first is a wager. The second is a fish. The third is one third less than everything, and the whole is my theme. What is it?" (*NS*, 51).
18. Vladimir Nabokov, *The Defense* (New York: Vintage, 1990).
19. Imhof, "My Readers," 6.
20. Brian Donnelly, "The Big House in the Recent Irish Novel," *Studies* 254 (Summer 1975): 134.
21. Vera Kreilkamp, *The Anglo-Irish Novel and the Big House* (Syracuse: Syracuse University Press, 1998), 249.
22. McMinn, *Supreme Fictions*, 38.
23. Derek Hand, *John Banville: Exploring Fictions* (Dublin: The Liffey Press, 2002), 32.
24. McMinn, *Supreme Fictions*, 31.
25. William Shakespeare, *The Tempest* (New York: Signet/Penguin, 1982), 103.
26. Rüdiger Imhof, *The Modern Irish Novel: Irish Novelists after 1945* (Dublin: Wolfhound Press, 2002), 49.
27. Hedwig Schwall, "An Interview with John Banville," *European English Messenger* 6, no. 1 (1997): 13–19.
28. Mika Momoo, "Only Echoes and Coincidences: Textual Authority in John Banville's *Birchwood*," *Journal of Irish Studies* 22 (2007): 46.
29. Rüdiger Imhof, *John Banville: A Critical Introduction* (Dublin: Wolfhound Press, 1989); Joseph McMinn, *John Banville: A Critical Study* (Dublin: Gill and Macmillan, 1991); McMinn, *Supreme Fictions*.

CHAPTER 1

30. Gordon Graham, *Philosophy of the Arts: An Introduction to Aesthetics* (New York: Routledge, 2007), 144.
31. "Fully Booked: Q & A with John Banville," interview by Travis Elborough, *Picador*, June 29, 2012. http://www.picador.com/blog/june-2012/fully-booked-q-a-with-john-banville (accessed October 31, 2016).
32. Maureen Quilligan, *The Language of Allegory: Defining the Genre* (Ithaca and London: Cornell University Press, 1979), 26.
33. Brian McHale, *Postmodernist Fiction* (London: Routledge, 2003), 145–46.
34. David Lodge, *The Art of Fiction* (Harmondsworth: Penguin 1992), 144.
35. John Banville, "Out of Chaos Comes Order," interview with Ciaran Carty, *The Sunday Tribune* (14 September 1989): 18.
36. Linda Hutcheon, *A Poetics of Postmodernism: History, Theory, Fiction* (London: Routledge, 1988), 113.
37. John McKenna, "Rage for Order," in *Dublin* (13 November 1986): 17.
38. John Banville, "Beauty, Charm, and Strangeness: Science as Metaphor," *Science* 281, no. 5373 (3 July 1998): 40.
39. Sean Lysaght, "Banville's Tetralogy: The Limits of Mimesis," *Irish University Review* 21, no. 1 (Spring-Summer 1991): 83.
40. Mark O'Connell, *John Banville's Narcissistic Fictions* (London: Palgrave Macmillan, 2013): 149.
41. Banville has expressed some regret about the two historical fictions: "There are people who tell me they think *Doctor Copernicus* and *Kepler* were my best books, but I feel now that in those novels I took a wrong direction, that I should have done something else." Belinda McKeon, "John Banville: The Art of Fiction No. 200," *The Paris Review*, no. 188, Spring 2009, http://www.theparisreview.org/interviews/5907/the-art-of-fiction-no-200–john-banville (accessed October 31, 2016).
42. The epigraph to *Doctor Copernicus*, taken from Stevens's *Notes Toward a Supreme Fiction*, is as follows:

> You must become an ignorant man again
> And see the sun again with an ignorant eye
> And see it clearly in the idea of it.

43. Wallace Stevens, *The Collected Poems of Wallace Stevens* (London: Faber and Faber, 1984), 380.
44. The epigraph to *Kepler*, taken from Rilke's *Duino Elegies*, is as follows:

> Preise dem Engel die Welt. . . .
> (Praise this world to the Angel)
> (London: Panther Books, 1985).

45. Rainer Maria Rilke, *Selected Poems*, trans. J. B. Leishman, ed. A. Alvarez (Harmondsworth: Penguin, 1978), 65.
46. John Banville, "A Talk," *Irish University Review* 11, no. 1 (Spring, 1981): 16.
47. Imhof, "My Readers," 70–71.

48. "Novelists on the Novel: Ronan Sheehan talks to John Banville and Francis Stuart," interview with Ronan Sheehan, *The Crane Bag* 3, no. 1 (1979): 84.
49. O'Connell, *Narcissistic Fictions*, 155.
50. Hand, *Exploring Fictions*, 97; Imhof, *Critical Introduction*, 129.
51. Hand, *Exploring Fictions*, 71.
52. Lysaght, "Banville's Tetralogy," 92.
53. In *Lolita*, Humbert Humbert, variously, refers to Lolita as Lotte, Lolita, Lottelita, and Lolitchen (Harmondsworth: Penguin 1988), 76.
54. Joseph McMinn, "An Exalted Naming: The Poetical Fictions of John Banville," *The Canadian Journal of Irish Studies* 14, no. 1 (July 1988): 23.
55. Kenny, *John Banville*, 78.
56. Rilke, *Selected Poems*, 64.
57. Rilke, *Selected Poems*, 65.
58. John Pilling, *An Introduction to Fifty Modern European Poets* (London: Pan Books, 1982), 90.
59. Imhof, *Critical Introduction*, 145.
60. Rüdiger Imhof, "Swan's Way, or Goethe, Einstein, Banville—The Eternal Recurrence," *Etudes Irlandaises* 12 (December 1987): 113–29.
61. McKeon, "Art of Fiction."
62. Rüdiger Imhof, "Questions and Answers with John Banville," *Irish Literary Supplement* (Spring 1987): 13.
63. Neil Murphy, "From *Long Lankin* to *Birchwood*: The Genesis of John Banville's Architectural Space," *Irish University Review* 36, no. 1 (Spring-Summer 2006): 9–24.
64. Banville's fascination with Kleist is evident in his "The Helpless Laughter of a Tragedian," *The Irish Times*, 3 December 1988: W9, as well as in the multiple references to Kleist that one finds throughout his work, most explicitly in *Eclipse* and *The Infinities*. In addition, Banville has adapted three of Kleist's dramas, *The Broken Jug: After Kleist* (Oldcastle: Gallery Press, 1994); *God's Gift: a version of Amphitryon* by Heinrich von Kleist (Oldcastle: Gallery Press, 2001); and *Love in the Wars: A version of Penthesilea* (Oldcastle: Gallery Press, 2005).
65. Heinrich von Kleist, "The Puppet Theatre," *Selected Writings*, ed. and trans. David Constantine (Cambridge: Hackett Publishing Company, 2004): 413. In German, Über *das Marionettentheater*, *The Puppet Theatre* is also sometimes translated as *On the Marionette Theatre*.
66. Erich Heller, *The Poet's Self and the Poem: Essays on Goethe, Nietzsche, Rilke and Thomas Mann* (London: Athlone Press, University of London, 1976): 47–48.
67. Imhof, *Critical Introduction*, 159.
68. Ibid., 159.
69. James P. Myers, *Writing Irish: Selected Interviews with Writers from the Irish Literary Supplement* (Syracuse, NY: Syracuse University Press, 1999), 69–70.
70. Ibid.
71. Writing of Heisenberg's uncertainty principle, Fritjof Capra raises an interesting issue: "It is important to realize . . . that this limitation is not caused by the imperfection of our measuring techniques, but is a limitation of principle. If we decide to measure

CHAPTER 1

the particle's position precisely, the particle simply does not have a well-defined momentum, and vice versa." Fritjof Capra, *The Tao of Physics: An Exploration of the Parallels Between Modern Physics and Eastern Mysticism*, 3rd edition (Boston: Shambhala, 1991), 158.

72. John Banville, "Physics and Fictions: Order from Chaos," *The New York Times Book Review* (21 April 1985): 41–42.

73. Banville, "Physics and Fictions," 41.

74. Kenny, *John Banville*, 89.

75. McKeon, "Art of Fiction."

2

The Frames Trilogy

The Book of Evidence, *Ghosts*, and *Athena*

THE TRILOGY OF NOVELS that Freddie Montgomery narrates—*The Book of Evidence* (1989), *Ghosts* (1993), and *Athena* (1995)—reflects an increasingly significant focus on the visual arts in John Banville's work. This emphasis represents an abandonment of the more systematic metaphor of science that had framed the tetralogy and also registers a more direct engagement with the significance of literature as art and with the obsessive gaze that characterizes Banville's highly visual universes. The three novels are each constructed around paintings, forgeries, a failure of imagination, and desperate acts by the respective narrators to recover ontological significance by intense imaginative efforts. Together they represent the point at which Banville elected to make imagination itself the central plotted preoccupation of his fictions, and while the focus on paintings also acts as a self-conscious metaphorical parallel in these novels, similar to the way science was previously used, the figurative system offers a more direct correlation with the subject and substance of art. Freddie's understanding, in *The Book of Evidence*, that a "failure of imagination is [his] real crime, the one that made the others possible," is the central defining claim that informs the artistic motivation for the entire trilogy (215). The crime in *The Book of Evidence*, the murder of Josie Bell, is more metaphorical than literal, of course, speaking primarily to the enormous difficulty of fully apprehending the rich texture of the world after fixed intellectual systems have been abandoned. Mirroring the general developmental trajectory of Banville's work, Freddie, like his creator, has abandoned science and exists instead in "a pure, timeless space," that is no longer constrained by intellectual or moral systems (17). The narrator's abandonment of science self-reflexively corresponds to Banville's progression beyond the science-focused metaphorical systems of the tetralogy into a method that is more closely derived from an essentially artistic response to existence. Extending the intention of Gabriel Swan at the close of *Mefisto* (1986), to henceforth work toward a more immediate response to the world—Freddie is overtly presented as having relinquished the scientific method that had initially sustained him: "Better say I took up sci-

CHAPTER 2

ence in order to make the lack of certainty more manageable. Here was a way, I thought, of erecting a solid structure on the very sands that were everywhere, always, shifting under me" (*BoE,* 18). After his subsequent abandonment of science, he initially fails to adequately compensate for the absence of a systematic method, resulting ultimately in the gratuitous killing of Josie Bell. Freddie gains self-understanding after realizing that he could kill Josie "because for [him] she was not alive" (215), and realizes that the imagination is life-giving while its absence nullifies existence.

The central motif throughout the trilogy is thus the value of the imaginative act, and its capacity to offer a viable aestheticized approximation of the other. The overt plotted schemas in the three novels also serve, more importantly, as near-seamless fulcrums for a multitextured self-reflexive discourse on the nature of artistic process, the ontological status of the imagined storyworlds, and the relationship between art and being. Banville similarly alerts us to the near autobiographical relevance of art by teasingly alluding to his own role as writer throughout the trilogy: "So see me at play there just as in the days of my glowing if not quite gilded youth when it pleased me to pretend to be a scholar. Then it was science, now it is art" (*A,* 80). Such observations also point to more complex and comprehensive self-reflexive inquiries into the significance of art.

The turn from science to art in the trilogy signifies the emergence of a new and prominent "frame of reference,"[1] as Anja Müller has it, which operates on several distinct levels. Firstly, an avalanche of references to the visual arts generates a highly particularized surface texture to the fictive world, as when Freddie observes at one point that living in California, "amid those gentle paintbox colours, under that dome of flawless blue, was like living in another world, a place out of a story book" (*BoE,* 67). Similarly, Anna Behrens is like one of "Klimt's gem-encrusted lovers" (*BoE,* 85), while in *Athena* the trees are described as "Van Gogh trees" (35), and Aunt Corky has a "Rouault face"[2] (33). Similarly, scenes from nature are frequently rendered in the context of works of art, both real and invented:

> Wonderful prospect from this lofty crest, the near green and the far blue and that strip of ash-white beach holding up an enormity of sea and sky, the whole scene clear and delicate, like something by Vaublin himself, a background to one of his celebrated *pèlerinages* or a delicate *fête galante.* (*G,* 30)

On this occasion another layer of significance is knitted into the fabric of the fictional world because the painter, Jean Vaublin, is a fiction whose name is a near-anagram of John Banville; hence a Banville landscape is effectively compared to a Banville landscape within the primary ontological level of the novel's plot. However, it is clear that Vaublin is simultaneously a fictional variation on Jean-Antoine Watteau, as many critics such as Imhof, Hand, and Kenny have observed,[3] and the painting, *Le Monde d'or*, with which he is credited, is in fact a reconstruction of at least two Watteau paintings, *Gilles* (1718–1719) (See Cover Image) and *L'Embarquement pour Cythère* (1717) (See Figure 1). The narrative significance of Banville's deployment of both real and fake paintings in each of the three novels will be considered later in this chapter.

The rendering of an artistic surface to Freddie's world is engendered in several other crucial ways, as is the self-reflexive awareness of that surface among several of the leading characters. At one point in *Ghosts*, for example, Freddie even makes a direct appeal to Banville, his creator, to grant him life: "Oh, if you are really there, bright brother, in your more real reality, think of me, turn all your stern attentions on me, even for an instant, and make *me* real, too" (181), and *Athena* is written as a love letter to art in which the doubling of creative intent, of both Freddie and Banville, is perpetually evident. As a result, *Athena* extends the limits of Banville's self-referential experiment even further, in some respects. Furthermore, on a purely descriptive level, many of the characters are self-evidently synthetic, invented figures, who correspond far more closely to a constructed world than to empirical reality. For example, a bystander is described as a "clockwork man" in *The Book of Evidence*, while passengers on a train are propped up, gazing blankly, like manikins (126), and Licht is referred to as a marionette in *Ghosts* (4). Similarly, Sophie crumples "sideways like a puppet, all arms and knees" (*G*, 10), Felix makes Freddie think of a ventriloquist's dummy" (*G*, 12), and Morden raises a glass to his lips "in dry dumbshow" in *Athena* (14). Such assignations proliferate in all three novels to such a degree that the "hastily painted backdrops" (*BoE*, 114) that characterize the representations of the landscape, are populated by characters who are self-evidently imagined figures, akin to the marionettes that Banville alludes to, via Kleist, in his earlier work.

The sense of the world as being intensely other to empirical reality too is repeatedly emphasised in these three novels. While in early works like *Birchwood* (1973), *The Newton Letter* (1982), and *Mefisto* (1986) there is a powerful sense of the otherness of the fictional worlds and a perpetual reminder of the characters' incapacity to attain a coherent sense of the thing-in-itself, the trilogy encodes many of the characters with an awareness of the fictionalized nature of their surroundings. For example, they experience a powerful sense

CHAPTER 2

of the strangeness of their existence, exhibiting a consciousness of their roles both as invented humans and as characters reconstituted from other fictions. Terms like strange, or strangeness, have a profound significance for Banville's work because he repeatedly associates them with a rarefied quality of art. So, when we are informed that the daylight is "strange" at the beginning of *The Book of Evidence*, one is immediately alerted to the fact that the prison that Freddie is nominally describing may, in fact, refer to something other than a literal prison. In the immediate aftermath of Josie's murder, for instance, he explains his sense of extreme dislocation in terms of *strangeness*, the newly transfigured world begins to echo the principle of a world transformed via artistic consciousness: "What did I feel? Remorse, grief, a terrible—no no no, I won't lie. I can't remember feeling anything, except that sense of strangeness, of being in a place I knew but did not recognise" (119). This pattern is even more emphatic in *Ghosts*, in which Flora speaks of the world, and her place in it, as being strange almost every time she speaks, particularly in the early stages of the novel when she struggles to establish a sense of where she is and yet has strong sense that she has been there before (5), as do several of the other characters. Furthermore, the world that the characters inhabit is repeatedly referred to as strange: "Everything is strange at that hour, stranger than usual, I mean: the world looks as I imagine it will look after I am dead, wide and empty and streaked with long shadows, shocked somehow and not quite solid, all odd-angled and shifting facades" (29).

Banville's frequent association of strangeness with art is telling here,[4] and in all of his novels hereafter, because the landscape that the characters inhabit may be conceived of as a work of art that possesses all the strangeness of a transformed (and enhanced) world. This is in turn connected with the principle that all lived experience is necessarily transformed in one's reception of it, as when Freddie muses on the oddness of the world: "The wind in the chimneys, the gulls, all that: the strangeness of things. The strangeness of being here, of being anywhere" (*G*, 207). The association of strangeness with art, within the novels, is frequently registered, particularly in terms of overt connections between hitherto mentioned synthetic character-types. For example, in *Athena*, the elusive, half-visible figure A. is observed by Freddie (who has changed his name to Morrow) in a manner which suggests that his conception of her is directly antagonistic to any mode of realist representation and instead seeks to alert one to her purely imagined non-referential status:

> She would take a deep breath, drawing back her shoulders and lifting her head, carefully keeping her glance from straying in the direction of the spyhole; her movements were at once stiff and graceful, and touched with a strange unhuman pathos, like those of a skillfully manipulated marionette. (*A*, 156)

The "strange unhuman pathos" may be said to be the precise quality that Banville seeks to place at the heart of his straw characters, not in the sense of them being mere scarecrows but in that their power lies precisely in their non-human qualities—as with Kleist's celebration of the unself-conscious gracefulness of his marionettes.

The generation of a literary world that is explicitly "other" to material reality is, of course, also facilitated by populating the storyworlds with overtly fictionalized figures. When we first encounter Freddie in *The Book of Evidence*, his first person narrative reveals an almost compulsive translation of all events into a sequence of filmic and stereotypical clichés; he himself is "Jean-Jacques the cultured killer" (5) while Randolph, Paco, and Senior Aguirre are all stiffly typecast as villains in his fantasy island existence. His wife Daphne is repeatedly reinvented via the lens of Greek myth and various other surface images, while she and Anna Behrens in their United States phase are reduced to eroticized variations of Daisy and Jordan from *The Great Gatsby*. Freddie's interpretive consciousness reduces everything to type, to mere role, as he is unable to move beyond the imposition of preconceived models. This sense is further enhanced by the narrator's repeated suspicion that the world in which he exists is but one dimension of a dual universe. Early in *The Book of Evidence*, for example, Freddie intimates that his landscape feels like a transfiguration of primary reality:

> I felt vaguely as if something momentous had happened, as if in the blink of an eye everything around me had been whipped away and replaced instantly with an exact replica, perfect in every detail, down to the last dust-mote. I walked on, into this substitute world, tactfully keeping a blank expression, and seemed to hear a disembodied held breath being let go in relief that the difficult trick had worked yet again. (*BoE*, 43)

Such moments in Banville's work serve to render the plotted landscapes multi-dimensional, while perpetually acknowledging the inevitability, perhaps even desirability, of different "levels of reality," to avail of Calvino's term.[5] Many years later, in *The Infinities* (2009), Old Adam is presented as a great scientist

CHAPTER 2

who had conducted work on his theory of many-worlds, but as early as *Ghosts*, the narrator textually plays with the same theory: "For is it not possible that somewhere in this crystalline multiplicity of worlds, in this infinite, mirrored regression, there is a place where the dead have not died, and I am innocent?" (*G*, 172–73).

Although Freddie's yearning may here simply be considered a wished-for reconstruction of his imaginative failings in *The Book of Evidence*, it is also clear that he registers a complex series of fictional dimensions to the primary world, in which the spatial texture of the fiction assumes many aspects. The repeated emphasis on painterly vocabulary and elevated perspectives on both mundane and significant moments in the plots of the novels are also significant. In *The Book of Evidence*, for instance, Freddie, aware of the curious living presence of the garden, imagines himself framed in the window—momentarily a figure perceived by the other:

> I pressed my forehead against the window-pane, and shivered at the clammy, cold touch of the glass. . . . It seemed to me the garden was watching me, in its stealthy, tightlipped way, or that it was at least somehow aware of me, framed here in the window, wringing my hands, a stricken starer-out. (*BoE*, 54)

Similarly, in the sequence that immediately precedes the killing of Josie, he unexpectedly comes across her in the hallway of Whitewater house, framed against the open french window, effectively depicting her, momentarily, as a figure in a painting, with "one knee flexed and one hand lifted" (79), as though a still within the frame. This instant occurs immediately after Freddie has encountered the painting of the woman for which he will eventually commit his major crime, effectively conflating the two women within fixed, exclusionary frames. Josie closes the scene by disappearing back into the French window. Such moments proliferate throughout these three novels, with scene after scene seeking to both maintain the semblance of a primary narrative plot but simultaneously reaching toward multiple levels of ontological presence, imbuing the text with a nebulous, nonstatic surface but also registering on all levels, the potency of imagined variations on a fixed materiality.

The three novels' overt plots are compromised by the presence of an army of marionette figures, intertextual references, parallel visual arts landscapes that overlay the primary ontological fictional levels, and a constant sense of the world itself as already othered, all contributing to the notion of a multilayered ontology. Furthermore, the novels themselves act as extensions, or installments, of Banville's overall model of the fictional universe as a house of fiction. All three novels repeatedly evoke a parallel discourse rooted in the trope of the house. Henry James's influence on Banville is again clear. Holly Blackford interprets the house, or James's metaphor for "consciousness and perception,"[6] as expressed in *The Portrait of a Lady* (1880–1881) as follows: "Between those four walls she had lived ever since; they were to surround her for the rest of her life. It was the house of darkness, the house of dumbness, the house of suffocation."[7] Banville firmly establishes the metaphor of the house in *Birchwood* in order to self-reflexively offer extended discourse on his own house of fiction—although his usage, unlike that of James, is more aesthetic than psychological. Throughout the art trilogy, the house metaphor is extended to mirror certain aspects of Banville's own fictional transformation in each work. In *The Book of Evidence*, for example, it is used to knit the fictional landscape to previous renditions of the metaphor, as when Freddie recalls his own youthful desires to be an architect, or masterbuilder who would create an extraordinary edifice:

> Indeed, when I was young I saw myself as a masterbuilder who would one day assemble a marvelous edifice around myself, a kind of grand pavilion, airy and light, which would contain me utterly and yet wherein I would be free. Look, they would say, distinguishing this eminence from afar, look how sound it is, how solid: it's him all right, yes, no doubt about it, the man himself. Meantime, however, unhoused, I felt at once exposed and invisible. How shall I describe it, this sense of myself as something without weight, without moorings, a floating phantom? (16)

As is so frequently the case with Banville's heroes, at the outset of their journeys they find themselves cast adrift afresh, homeless, or about to return to the house. When Freddie returns to the family home after his empty sojourn among the Mediterranean islands, he discovers a rotting house (45). Ultimately he is disinherited and forced to fend for himself outside of the containable fictional universe of the house, which is perfectly in keeping with Freddie's loss of certainty, morality, and social belonging. Unsurprisingly, when we encounter him next, in *Ghosts*, much emphasis is placed on the architecture of the island house that he shares with Professor Kreutznaer and Licht:

> The house. It is large and of another age. It stands on a green rise, built of wood and stone, tall, narrow, ungainly, each storey seeming to lean in a different direction. Long ago it was painted red but

CHAPTER 2

> the years and the salt winds have turned it to a light shade of pink. The roof is steep with high chimneys and gay scalloping under the eaves. The delicate octagonal turret with the weathervane on top is a surprise, people see its slender panes flashing from afar and say, Ah! and smile. On the first floor there is a balcony that runs along all four sides, with french windows giving on to it, where no doubt before the day is done someone will stand, with her hand in her hair, gazing off in sunlight. Below the balcony the front porch is a deep, dim hollow, and the front door has two broad panels of ruby glass and a tarnished brass knocker in the shape of a lion's paw. Details, details: pile them on. The windows are blank. (*G*, 7–8)

The interpolation of the house with art, and with Freddie's own presence as figure in the aestheticized landscape, is also evident in his association of these elements on several occasions, as when he admits, "I live here in this lambent, salt-washed world, in these faded rooms, amid this stillness. And it lives in me" (*G*, 8). He further emphasizes the interpenetration of his self and the house as follows: "I think to myself: *My life is a ruin, an abandoned house, a derelict place*" (*G*, 54). The overt declaration of the house as derelict echoes the abandoned houses in *Birchwood* and *Mefisto*, a feature that appears to be a necessity in order for the process of fictional rejuvenation to occur. In this, the house acts as an explicit self-conscious, coded expression of the aims of the novels themselves, a point that is emphasized in conjunction with Freddie's allusion to another classical fable of creative endeavor, *Frankenstein*: "The house, the Professor, the work on Vaublin, all this represented for me the last outpost at the border; beyond were the fiery, waterless wastes where no man or even monster could survive" (*G*, 216).

The plot of *Athena* is also interpenetrated with an extended parallel to the house but the particular emphasis in the final installment of the trilogy is on the interior space, the walls, rooms, and corridors, in direct conversation with the novel's overt commentary on art. The "secret white room," for example, that lies both at the core of the novel, and of the derelict house on Rue Street, is associated throughout with the achievement, however temporary, of something akin to pure aesthetic appropriation, or the construction of "a marvelous edifice" (*A*, 2). Reminiscent of the still, silent white rooms and corridors of Beckett's topographical landscapes,[8] Freddie (or Morrow), locates a center of meaning amidst the derelict rooms and corridors of the house, and explicitly associates this centered space with "the familiar otherwhere of art":

> In the first days in that secret room I was happier than I can remember ever having been before, astray in the familiar otherwhere

of art. Astray, yes, and yet somehow at the same time more keenly aware of things and of myself, than in any other of the periods of my life that have printed themselves with particular significance on my memory. (*A*, 81)

Not only does he establish a narrative connection between the metaphorical house and art, he also conveys a powerful sense of an ontological other within the terms of the novel's primary plot. The house, self-conscious metaphor for the process of writing itself, acts as a locus for an alternative communion with an imaginative apprehension of reality, and this imagined zone, so closely related to the thing-in-itself that all of Banville's previous heroes sought, lost, or wished to recover, is almost literalized via the emphatic association with the potent house imagery:

> It was like suddenly breaking through to a different version of reality, a new and hitherto undreamed-of dimension of a familiar world. It was like—yes, it was like what they seem to mean when they talk of love. To place one of these extraordinary artefacts before me on the little table in the white room and go to work on it with my tweezers and my magnifying glass was to be given license to enter the innermost secret places of a sacred object. (*A*, 83)

The deployment of the metaphor of the house throughout the trilogy acts as a powerful narrative tool to facilitate Banville's version of the self-conscious mode. It permits him to retain the nominal primary reality in which characters stalk the streets of recognizably real landscapes, but mirroring this ontological level throughout is a constant reminder of the multifariousness of the real, with everything being echoed through the self-conscious, self-evidently aestheticized universe. These novels continually foreground elements that take us beyond a simplified notion of represented reality, in an ultimately cohesive gesture that seeks an apprehension of what we take to be real.

For Banville, there is a fundamental difference between meaning and significance and this position is echoed in the very forms of fiction themselves. In *The Book of Evidence*, for example, Freddie repeatedly insists that his own factual commentaries about the painting, or even his imagined reconstruction of the woman being painted, don't "mean" anything (104, 108)—a point that is clarified in *Ghosts*, when he considers the figures in the painting at the center of this novel, Vaublin's *Le monde d'or*:

> What does it mean, what are they doing, these enigmatic figures frozen forever on the point of departure, what is this atmosphere

CHAPTER 2

> of portentousness without apparent portent? There is no meaning, of course, only a profound and inexplicable significance; why is that not enough for me? Art imitates nature not by mimesis but by achieving for itself a natural objectivity, I of all people should know that. (95)

Freddie's position here directly corresponds to Banville's in several interviews, in which he distinguishes between what he names "translatable" content and significance,[9] and emphatically rejects the possibility of mimesis. What he seeks hereafter is the construction of works of art in which everything internally ramifies. Everything refers ultimately to itself as a work of art, or as an ontology that is other to the real.

Several Banville critics have acknowledged the central significance of paintings in the trilogy, although their precise interpretive emphases have greatly varied. Elke D'Hoker, for instance, views Banville's general shift in the trilogy of novels to illustrate a movement from "an epistemological perspective to more overt ethical concerns," and "a more focused investigation of the ethical consequences of our necessarily subjective representations."[10] D'Hoker's Levinasian reading of Freddie's response to both the imagined backstory of the painting in *The Book of Evidence* and the corresponding failure to imagine Josie ultimately argues that Freddie's imaginative gestures are acts of destructive appropriation. Similarly, Mark O'Connell, partially in agreement with D'Hoker, argues that Freddie's engagement with art is "deeply narcissistic,"[11] while John Kenny views *The Book of Evidence* to be "the most forceful of Banville's moral narratives"[12] (*JB* 123). While these readings offer compelling interpretative strategies and within the context of their own critical modes meaningfully address the central issues that Banville raises, there remains the sense that the central aesthetic questions raised by the presence of the paintings, and their corresponding aestheticized female figures (Josie, Flora, A.), may be in danger of getting lost in the rhetorical sweep of the ethical imperatives raised. Banville's integration of paintings, and the narrative-imaginative issues that they register, serve particular functions in each of the three novels. However, the tendency to excavate their meanings from a purely ethical perspective inflates the value of the critical context above that of the texts and deflects attention from the aesthetic significance of the self-conscious conversations that the novels essentially are. This is not to suggest an absence of ethically sensitive issues; after all, Banville conceded more than a decade after the publication of *The Book of Evidence* that the novel was, in many ways, about Ireland because it was about the "failure of imagination and the failure to imagine other people into existence," with particular reference to the horrors of the Omagh bombing in 1998.[13] Nonetheless, the failure of imagination that Freddie embodies is primarily relevant in the earlier part of the novel and it is an imaginative lack that the novel seeks to remedy by virtue of its deployment of an extended discourse on the significance of art thereafter.

The painting, *Portrait of a Woman with Gloves*, around which the primary plot rotates, and from which the artistic significance of the novel radiates has according to Imhof, been attributed to "Vermeer, de Groot, and Valentiner." The painting, however, is Willem Drost's "Portrait of a Woman" (Figure 2).[14] The painting serves as a segue to several other narrative elements in the novel, with the figure of the female acting as the primary transitional pivot. Arguably one can include the various female characters in this, including Freddie's wife, Daphne, Anna Behrens, Joanne, and Josie Bell, because they each act as focal points for Freddie's imaginative gestures. This is itself a pattern that has invited further critical consideration of gender-specific representations in Banville's fiction, as outlined in the Introduction. Furthermore, Daphne, Freddie's "our lady of the laurels" (7), or his "abstracted Maya" (8–9) is repeatedly described in terms of her similarity with figures from Greek myth (Daphne and Apollo, or the Goddess Maia), while he admires her "abstracted air" (7) and her "absent" gaze (8)—in every sense this represents an essential turning away from her, a removal of agency, and a failing to reach beyond the membrane of his subjectivising consciousness. It is only after the murder, late in the novel, that he—tellingly—gains some vague sense of who she is. When he informed Daphne that he intended to plead guilty her reaction astonishes him: "Daphne, when I told her, burst into tears at once. . . . How little I knew, how little I understood. I sat and gazed at her, aghast, my mouth open. I could not speak. How was it possible, that I could not have seen that behind her reticence there was all this passion, this pain?" (216). In this, Daphne echoes the other women in the novel, or rather, Freddie's inability to "see" them and he repeats a tendency that he has exhibited throughout—although one can argue that his inability to see also extends to male figures like Senor Aguirre and Randolph, both of whom he conceives of only in stereotypical terms.

The contiguity of the woman in the painting (and the imagined scenario of her being painted) and Josie Bell is the primary locus of significance in the novel. Our first encounter with the painting, after all, is practically conflated with our initial meeting with Josie. Having first encountered the *Portrait of a Woman with Gloves* in a "long, high, narrow, many-windowed room," reminiscent of Henry James's apertures, etc., in golden air, "suffused

CHAPTER 2

with the heavy soft light of evening," Freddie felt as though he "had stepped straight into the eighteenth century" (77). His reaction is significant: "I stood there for what seemed a long time, and gradually a kind of embarrassment took hold of me, a hot, shamefaced awareness of myself, as if somehow I, this soiled sack of flesh, were the one who was being scrutinized, with careful cold attention" (79). The impersonal power of art is here suggested, an aspect that grows increasingly significant throughout the trilogy. More significant at this juncture, however, is the manner in which Josie's appearance is textually conflated with the figure in the painting:

> It was not just the woman's painted stare that watched me. Everything in the picture, that brooch, those gloves, the flocculent darkness at her back, every spot on the canvas was an eye fixed on me unblinkingly. I retreated a pace, faintly aghast. The silence was fraying at the edges. I heard cows lowing, a car starting up. I remembered the taxi, and turned to go. A maid was standing in the open French window. She must have come in just then and seen me there and started back in alarm. (*BoE*, 79)

Blending the viewing of the painting with Josie initiates a sequence of crucial interweavings of the two figures. For example, the next time that Freddie views the painting, on the day of the theft and murder, a similar conflation occurs with Josie entering the room precisely at the moment that he is stealing the painting:

> So I struggled up, moaning and sniveling, and grasped the picture in my arms and staggered with it blindly, nose to nose, in the direction of the French window. Those eyes were staring into mine, I almost blushed. And then—how shall I express it—then somehow I sensed, behind that stare, another presence, watching me. I stopped, and lowered the picture, and there she was, standing in the open window, just as she had stood the day before, wide-eyed, with one hand raised. (*BoE*, 110)

In an almost exact reprise of the first encounter, the two women again merge, with Josie holding exactly the same pose, framed against the French windows, almost a figure in a painting herself—which, in a sense, she is. The narrative overlay that is achieved by this contiguity impels one to compare Freddie's descriptions of both women in two scenes—the imagined life that Freddie conjures for the girl in the painting, and the scene in which he ends Josie's life. Inevitably, the two scenes are recounted sequentially in the novel.

In Freddie's imagined life of the girl, there is a concurrent description of the artist that also offers valuable insight to the process of painting. Much is made of the artist's apparent disinterest, and of the "impersonal intensity" that he employs (107), echoing the cold detachment that Freddie had earlier noticed in the painting itself and reminiscent of the modernist artistic imperative that one encounters in Eliot and Joyce.[15] The sense of detached intensity is ultimately mirrored in the woman's reaction to seeing the painting of herself: "She had expected it would be like looking in a mirror, but this is someone she does not recognize, and yet knows. The words come unbidden into her head: Now I know how to die. She puts on her glove, and signals to her maid" (108). The suggestion of death, and her maid's presence, foreshadows what is about to occur in the immediately preceding pages: the killing of Josie Bell.

Several critics have suggested that Freddie fails to see the girl until it is too late, just before he kills her, arguing that his claims that he had never before "felt another's presence so immediately and with such raw force," and that he saw her as "somehow radiant" (113), represent genuine aesthetic acknowledgment of her presence. Elke D'Hoker argues that Freddie "clearly sees the maid in the moment before he kills her"[16] and Tony E. Jackson, agrees, suggesting that "[o]nly as Freddie is about to take the maid's life does he see her life as it really is."[17] However, it is possible to offer an alternative interpretation to Freddie's claim, particularly in the context of a comparative analysis with the imagined life of the girl in the painting. In addition to viewing the imagined life as a literal act of appropriation by Freddie, as D'Hoker does,[18] it is also possible to view the account as the articulation of an artistic credo that registers a case for impersonality as a genuine artistic aim, a familiar modernist position. Of course, the account is literally a subjective emanation from Freddie in the novel, but Banville's habitual tendency to allow layers of artistic reality to ramify and echo each other permits one to interpret the account as a coded explanation of what is required of the artist when he/she seeks to reflect the alterity of their subject. Thus, the behavior of the fictional artist is more crucially significant than offering an itemized list of Freddie's considerable failings.

If we can move beyond character analysis when evaluating Freddie's role, we may be able to consider the significant illustrative role of the artist's impersonality. Conversely, Freddie's encounter with Josie is redolent with subjectivity, with overpersonalization. He immediately feels that everything is so unfair, he is embarrassed and full of rage. He imagines that he is able to see

CHAPTER 2

"clean through her head"—hardly an overt sign of being able to see her "as she truly is," as he claims. Similarly, while he insists that he feels her presence, he both fails to actually describe her with any great clarity and persists with the habit he has repeatedly exhibited throughout the novel, up to this point—he embalms her in clichés: she is, "wide-eyed, like a rebuked child," (112) they are like "a married couple having a fight," (113) while he himself is "an old lion roaring at the whip and chair" (111). Furthermore, Freddie later reveals what he views to be his essential sin:

> [T]hat I *never* imagined her vividly enough, that I never made her be there sufficiently, that I did not make her live. Yes, that failure of imagination is my real crime, the one that made the others possible. What I told that policeman is true—I killed her because I could kill her, and I could kill her because for me she was not alive. (Italics my emphasis: 215)

The stark admission of his failure to see her does not support the suggestion that he truly saw her immediately before the murder. Similarly, reflecting on the murder he casually merges the first time he saw her "in the open French window with the blue and gold of summer at her back," with the moment when he "hit her again and again," admitting that on both occasions there had "been no more of her there, for me, than there was in the newspaper stories" (215). It is far more likely that Freddie's momentary claim that he witnessed her radiance were as willfully inaccurate as his belief that he knew his wife and his repeated miscomprehensions about people throughout the period before the murder. From the outset, everything is reduced to simple cliché; people, his time in prison, conceptions of himself (he is, variously, Billy Bunter, Jean Jacques the cultured killer, a mummy, an exotic animal, a character from *Waiting for Godot* gazing at a single tree from the bars of his cell). This tendency recurs with great frequency until the death of Josie, after which Freddie's tendency to view everyone and everything through the lens of loose intertextual references greatly recedes. In this, Freddie has been a poor artist, one who substitutes the necessary imaginative intensity of the painter of the girl with lazy clichéd attributions. Thereafter, in part II, the lazy, inherited, intertextual web imposes itself much less on his consciousness. It is notable that Daphne, Joanne, Josie Bell, are then all partially revealed to him.

The painting in *The Book of Evidence* mirrors the artwork-in process that is the novel itself. Or, as Canon-Roger suggests, "In *The Book of Evidence*, in his own way John Banville both shows a verbal picture in the making and provides the means of a satiric interpretation for it."[19] The role that the painting plays in the plot, Freddie's ekphrasis, and the fictional account of the painting of the girl, within the novel's fictional storyworld, all effect a metaphorical hall-of-mirrors in which a complex self-reflexive commentary on the limits and possibilities of art are played out, including reflections on the role of imagination, the possibility of representation, and an aesthetics of impersonality. Furthermore, the painting affects the temporal sequence that shapes the novel by introducing some of the quality of stillness that is so frequently associated with the still-life paintings of artists like Vermeer. This extends beyond the ekphrastic moments. On several occasions after the death of Josie, Freddie's (and Banville's) immediate surroundings seem suspended in instances of aesthetic apprehension: "Everything sparkled in the rinsed sea-air. The sunlight had a flickering, hallucinatory quality, and I felt I was seeing somehow into the very process of it, catching the photons themselves in flight" (191). The fusion and mirroring of different ontological levels in the novel represents an attempt to move beyond representational and temporally sequential narrative forms. Absorbing the spatial stillness of paintings into the narrative frame of the novel initiates a process that dominates the trilogy, as well as novels like *The Untouchable* (1997), *The Sea* (2005), and *The Blue Guitar* (2015), all of which have paintings at their narrative centers. This stillness is akin to what Stephen Cheeke refers to as the "for ever now" quality of visual images in his explication of the way complex form intersects with a sense of "art's eternity":

> Aesthetic patterning and form, not merely in the sense of high technical competence, but also in the sense (and the two are indivisible) of complex intelligibility, promise a marvelous and perhaps mystical intersection of the timeless and the temporal or chronologically linear.[20]

In many respects, Banville's interweaving of the visual and the verbal, of the multiple interconnected narrative levels, also aspires to a similar merging of the temporal sequence that one usually finds in prose fiction.

The interweaving of the visual and verbal textual levels in *The Book of Evidence* offers a telling, if ultimately preliminary, indication of the formal possibilities offered by a narrative integration of paintings and literature. These possibilities are more advanced in *Ghosts*, in which Freddie has been released from prison and appears to be living on an island as an assistant to Professor Kreutznaer, an expert on the work of the fictional painter, Jean Vaublin. *Ghosts* extends the narrative possibilities of the verbal-visual interaction in a far more

CHAPTER 2

comprehensive manner than its immediate predecessor. Its primary narrative frame is predicated on at least two paintings by the eighteenth-century French artist, Jean Antoine Watteau, *Gilles* (Cover Image) and *L'Embarquement pour Cythére* (Figure 1), while a third, *Le pélerinage a l'isle de Cythère*, also has a presence in the novel. Freddie explicitly alludes to Watteau's "*pélerinages* or a delicate *fête galante*" (G, 30) and to "Cythera" on several occasions (G, 31, 216), attributing them to Vaublin. *Le monde d'or*, the Jean Vaublin painting that dominates the narrative fabric of *Ghosts* is, to a substantial degree, an amalgam of the three Watteau paintings which in turn reflect the surface action of Banville's novel. The interweaving of Vaublin, Watteau, and Banville is potently conveyed via the way in which the paintings and the novel reflect and echo each other. Furthermore, the characters that seep from the novel into the imagined painting are also appropriated from other Banville novels. Flora is reborn from "Summer Voices" and "The Possessed," from *Long Lankin*, Sophie and Felix return from *Mefisto*, and all seem to remember the strange world from their previous incarnations.

Freddie, who himself occupies a curious ontological position in the novel, initially stands aloof, observing the characters as they orientate themselves to their new, if familiar, landscape: "I think of them like the figures in one of Vaublin's twilit landscapes, placed here and there in isolation about the scene, each figure somehow the source of its own illumination, aglow in the midst of shadows, still and speechless, not dead and yet not alive either, waiting perhaps to be brought to some kind of life" (G, 82). They *are*, after all, characters in a Vaublin/Banville landscape with both fictional and real images overlapping, bleeding into one another until distinction between them gradually blurs. The same is true of the novel's elaborate pictorial descriptions: "And then one day, a day much like any other in that turning season between spring's breathless imminences and the first, gold flourishings of summer, I would look out the window and see that little band of castaways toiling up the road to the house and a door would open into another world" (221). The castaways, inversions of their mirrored counterparts in the paintings(s), act as pivots between worlds, as the novel continues to permit its surfaces to reflect all of the narrative levels.

Even the consciousness of the characters appears to slip and slide between fictional levels, partially aware but largely puzzled at the nonstatic nature of their world which ultimately acts as a commentary on the nature of being and how one rationalizes different levels of perception and consciousness. Flora even dreams, at one point, of the golden world (mirroring *Le monde d'or*):

> Flora is dreaming of the golden world.
> Worlds within worlds. They bleed into each other. I am at once here and there, then and now, as if by magic. I think of the stillness that lives in the depths of mirrors. It is not our world that is reflected there. It is another place entirely, another universe, cunningly made to mimic ours. Anything is possible there; even the dead may come back to life. Flaws develop in the glass, patches of silvering fall away and reveal the inhabitants of that parallel, inverted world going about their lives all unawares. (*G*, 55)

Flora's dream articulates the integrated moving surface that is the ontological frame of the fiction, while also offering self-reflexive commentary on the manner in which the novel is both itself and other simultaneously—both novel and painting. This process also finds expression in numerous other ways in the novel, as when she notices a color reproduction of *Le monde d'or* in the bedroom which features "a sort of clown dressed in white standing up with his arms hanging, and people behind him walking off down a hill to where a ship was waiting, and at the left a smirking man astride a donkey" (46). The bridge between her own world and that of the painting is further enhanced a few pages later when she looks at Felix and realizes that behind "his shoulder, like another version of him in miniature in a far-off mirror, the man on the donkey in the picture grinned at her gloatingly" (49). Felix is the harlequin in the painting, while Freddie himself is identified as Gilles, the Pierrot, and the other characters appear to be among those waiting to reboard the ship, as indeed they finally do in the novel.

Despite the persistent parallels, echoes, and contiguities, a key difference between painting and prose fiction remains. As G. E. Lessing influentially argued, in the eighteenth century, painting and literature (for Lessing, poetry) "make use of entirely different means or symbols—the first, namely of form and color in space, the second of articulated sounds in time."[21] Paintings are associated with stillness or spatiality, while a sense of temporality and movement usually informs literary fiction. There is little doubt that Banville seeks to absorb some of the painterly quality of stasis into his work, particularly since many of his preferred distinctly non-avant garde visual artists are firmly associated with still lifes. Even in *The Book of Evidence* there are moments when Freddie switches to the present tense in the midst of the past tense ("Am I still handcuffed?" 201), illustrating temporal and spatial slippages between what is being told and the narrator's role as literal observer of his own tale.

CHAPTER 2

The narratorial shift is far more emphatically rendered in *Ghosts*, in part because the interrelationship between the different planes of existence (Watteau's paintings, *Le monde d'or*, and the novel *Ghosts* in the process of writing about itself) are more fully integrated. The beginning of the novel is related by Freddie in the present tense, followed by frequent switches to the past tense. This pattern is repeated throughout the novel, with Freddie's narrative focal point hovering above some of the unfolding events in the present tense, even if much of the novel is related via the past tense. The impact of this is twofold. Firstly, Freddie's present-tense observations about the characters reveal that he occupies, at the beginning of the novel at least, a different ontological level to the others, as he stands outside the characters and offers his observations of the scene before him, much like one would do with a painting:

> There is an old boy in a boater, a pretty young woman, called Flora, of course, and a blonde woman in a black skirt and a black leather jacket with a camera slung over her shoulder. Also an assortment of children: three, to be precise. And a thin, lithe, sallow man with bad teeth and hair dyed black and a darkly watchful eye. His name is Felix. (*G*, 5)

His apparently prior awareness of the characters indicates that his level of comprehension of their existence exceeds that of Licht who appears far less clear of their significance. Secondly, the persistent use of the present tense, coupled with the manner in which Freddie observes the figures in his landscape, facilitate the insertion of a series of still moments that mirror the effects of the visual or, more precisely, "the illusion of movement" or "movement arrested" as Stephen Cheeke has it:[22]

> Outside the window the garden stands aghast in a tangle of trumpeting convolvulus. Nothing happens, nothing will happen, yet everything is poised, waiting, a chair in the corner crouching with its arms braced, the coiled fronds of a fern, that copper pot with the streaming sunspot on its rim. (*G*, 40)

Such tableaux-style moments proliferate in the novel, echoing the stillness that one finds in Vaublin's *Le monde d'or*, which is also both a reflection of, and a model for, the novel—the "illusion of movement" is realized when the temporal sequence of narrative fiction allows the stasis to flow.

The painting itself, to which Banville devotes a detailed ekphrastic section late in the novel (225–31), heavily focuses on the figure of the Pierrot in the painting *Gilles* who, we are assured, "stands before us like our own reflection distorted in a mirror, known yet strange" (225), reminding us again of the hall of correspondences that the novel is. The painting is a partial reflection of the novel, and vice versa, while *Gilles* mirrors Freddie, both in terms of his pure fictionality ("has he dropped from the sky or risen from the underworld?" [225]) and as an overt articulation of a key characteristic of Banville's art: "His sole purpose, it would appear, is to be painted; he is wholly pose; we feel ourselves to be the spectators at a melancholy comedy. See how strangely he fits into his costume; he seems not so much to be wearing it as standing behind it, like a cut-out paper doll" (*G*, 228). The pure artificiality of *Gilles* can be viewed as a counterpoint to Banville's own aesthetic disinclination to offer realist representation and, as such, the Watteau/Vaublin aesthetic is a fitting model to intersect with his own fictional world. Furthermore, the painting serves to add further emphasis to Banville's long-established practice of self-reflexive commentary via the use of metaphoric parallels. In this instance, the ekphrastic commentary is extended to offer insight into the storyworld that the characters themselves inhabit and, furthermore, to offer self-reflexive commentary on the textual frame itself:

> This is the golden world. The painter has gathered his little group and set them down in this wind-tossed glade, in this delicate, artificial light, and painted them as angels and as clowns. It is a world where nothing is lost, where all is accounted for while yet the mystery of things is preserved; a world where they may live, however briefly, however tenuously, in the failing evening of the self, solitary and at the same time together somehow here in this place, dying as they may be and yet fixed forever in a luminous, unending instant. (*G*, 225–31)

Banville's aesthetic enterprise, and the central parallel significance of the painting within the novel, is rendered clear in these lines and the relevance of the ekphrasis is again shown to be vital to his narrative aesthetic. Whether seeking to momentarily evade the temporal sequence of the textual plot, or forging a series of parallel, self-reflexive commentaries, the significance of the painting in *Ghosts* is immense. It also makes a far-reaching contribution to the extraordinary, complex, multifaceted hall of mirrors that we encounter in this novel. Mirroring the pure artificiality of Watteau's commedia dell'arte, while simultaneously textually echoing the fictive spaces that we encounter elsewhere in Banville, *Ghosts* represents one of Banville's most accomplished narrative experiments. Everything echoes everything else in this tempestuous island with its "deep, formless song that seemed to rise out of the earth itself" (6).

Banville's use of ekphrasis in *Ghosts* has extensive implications. Not only does he offer an ekphrastic meditation on a painting, as is commonly the case in literary texts like Browning's "Eurydice to Orpheus" (1868), responding to Leighton's *Orpheus and Eurydice* (1864), he also folds the static narrative of the painting into the sequential narrative of the novel. The painting is allowed to spatially move beyond the frames of its fixed image while the narrative fiction, alternatively, seeks to adopt some of the stillness of the image within its own movement; it suspends time to emphasize the resonating stillnesses in particular moments in the plot. Furthermore, the presence of the painting offers Banville another metaphoric zone within which he may self-consciously articulate his extended observations about art, representation, and the nature of the fictional form. In this *Ghosts* both confirms and extends the central compulsions which have always lain at the heart of the work. For example, the overt evaluation of the value of Vaublin's *Le monde d'or* that Freddie offers is simultaneously a commentary on both Watteau's paintings and Banville's novel:

> There is a mystery here, not only in *Le monde d'or*, that last and most enigmatic of his masterpieces, but throughout his work; something is missing, something is deliberately not being said. Yet I think it is this very reticence that lends his pictures their peculiar power. He is the painter of absences, of endings. His scenes all seem to hover on the point of vanishing. (*G*, 35–36)

That he was drawn to Watteau's work is significant, echoing, as it does, some of the above observations, as well as resonating with Banville's own aesthetic. One of Watteau's first biographers, the Comte de Caylus observed that "His compositions have no subject. They express none of the conflicts of the passions and are consequentially deprived of one of the most affecting characteristics, that is, action."[23] Similarly, Bryson has suggested that Watteau's paintings are "essentially subjectless,"[24] a point echoed in Banville's repeated suggestions in his fiction he has "nothing to say. I have no statements to make, I have no messages to deliver. I simply want to re-create the world as I see it and to provide delight to readers. No messages."[25] In turn, the reticence, about which Freddie speaks, also suggests a sense of the materiality of things forever suspended beyond one's evaluative methods. Freddie frequently ponders the essential mysteriousness of art, a quality that the novel itself, redolent with the peculiarity of Freddie's own ontological position and the constant reminders of the strangeness of existence, embodies. Or, as Kenny suggests, "Vaublin's masterpiece, *Le monde d'or*, may itself be taken as a painted analogue of the novel in which it appears,"[26] as the following brief ekphrasis illustrates:

> *Le monde d'or* is one of those handful of timeless images that seem to have been hanging forever in the gallery of the mind. There is something mysterious here beyond the inherent mysteriousness of art itself. I look at this picture, I cannot help it, in a spirit of shamefaced interrogation, asking, What does it mean, what are they doing, these enigmatic figures frozen forever on the point of departure, what is this atmosphere of portentousness without apparent portent? There is no meaning, of course, only a profound and inexplicable significance; why is that not enough for me? (*G*, 94–95)

Freddie's observation about the difference between meaning and significance is a commonly expressed Banvillean distinction and alerts one again to the critical risks of trying to excavate meaning from his fictions.

The imaginative challenge that Freddie poses for himself at the close of *The Book of Evidence*, to somehow bring the girl "back to life" (215), is reengaged in *Ghosts*, in which it is suggested that the world is dependent on Freddie's keen eye and imaginative verve to tease it into life. Freddie assumes that he must make amends for his sociopathic deed in *The Book of Evidence* and seeks "to have her live and to live in her, to conjugate in her the verb of being" (*G*, 70), an aspiration that is ultimately proven to be misguided. Rather than take ownership of her, of seeking to "beget her," her authentic self can only be achieved, by detachment—echoing the kind of artistic response that the artist in the imagined life of the girl in the painting had to his subject:

> As I sat with my mouth open and listened to her I felt everyone and everything shiver and shift, falling into vividest forms, detaching themselves from me and my conception of them and changing themselves instead into what they were, no longer figment, no longer mystery, no longer a part of my imagining. (*G*, 147)

Banville's doubling of the world, essentially a variant of the *mise en abyme*, as we have seen, is achieved by interweaving the visual imagery of Watteau's paintings with the primary narrative, where the "mystery of things is preserved" (*G*, 230) the thing-in-itself remains hidden, but is luminously present in the artistic presence that is conjured. The illuminations of art and the paintings of Watteau act both as the surface texture on the aestheticized world and as the central metaphor upon which Banville's observations about the artistic process are based. *Ghosts*, unlike many of Banville's previous novels, is freed

CHAPTER 2

of the scientific, historical, or philosophical systems which gave their plots substance; even the overt engagement with Nietzschean morality in *The Book of Evidence* is now absent. This represents a conscious decision by Banville to extend the limits of his previous artistic parallels and to directly engage with art itself: "I suppose because the language of science is too systematized—I couldn't incorporate any actual scientific discourse in my book because it stood out too much. And I am fascinated by the surface of things, and painting deals with these. Painting is the triumph of looking, of obsessed scrutiny."[27]

The resonant presence of paintings in *The Book of Evidence*, and even more so in *Ghosts*, offered Banville a way to less obtrusively engage with the mysteries of being, of consciousness, and the imaginative apprehension of one's existence—all dominant fascinations in his work. In the first two novels of the trilogy paintings serve quite different narrative functions. Freddie's response, in *The Book of Evidence*, to the anonymous painting is mirrored by his failure to "imagine" the various female figures in the novel, especially Josie Bell, via a series of narrative juxtapositions in which the nature of "obsessed scrutiny" is constantly revisited. The imagined life of the girl also serves as a potent metaphoric parallel. In *Ghosts*, however, the association between the different ontological levels (intertextual, narrative fiction, painting) is far more comprehensively achieved, with the fictional painting at its center. With *Athena*, we partly return to the ekphrastic mode, via a sequence of catalogue-style responses to the seven fictional paintings but the presence of the figure A., a quasi-personified expression of art itself, greatly complicates the novel's engagement with art, as does the fact that the seven paintings are fakes, with an eight, allegedly being real (*A*, 230).

In *Athena*, Morrow's (the Freddie figure) artistic commentaries on the fake paintings are synonymous with a critique of Banville's own work. In addition, the paintings are all attributed to artists whose names are anagrams, or near-anagrams of John Banville or J. Banville, the first being Johann Livelb, Gabriel Godkin's fake stage name in Banville's *Birchwood*. Similarly, all paintings were allegedly painted when each artist was forty-seven to forty-eight years old, Banville's age when he was writing *Athena*. More crucially, as several critics have observed, the subjects of the paintings correspond to various aspects of Banville's work.[28] Mark O'Connell argues that the scenes depicted in the seven entries correspond, via Freddie's confusion, to "the dissolution of his own love affair with A" (174).[29] A., in turn, represents art itself, a point to which I will presently return. John Kenny offers a more specific itemization of the analogous relationship between the paintings and Banville's work, arguing that the commentaries "might be seen to correspond to each of the seven novels Banville had written up to *Athena*; and *Athena* itself, like the one painting that is not given its own critical piece, might be seen as the final, eight work."[30] Of course, both perspectives may also be true in the sense that Banville's characteristic fascinations recur so frequently, in slightly modified forms, it is arguable that the specific detail from each commentary applies both to *Athena* and to Banville's own catalogue of novels. For example, the *Pursuit of Daphne* (1680), by Johann Livelb, is self-depreciatingly described by Freddie as follows: "Here as in so much of Livelb's work the loftiness of the classical theme is sacrificed for the sake of showiness and vulgar effects" (*A*, 19). More emphatically, in *The Rape of Prosperine* (1655) by L. van Hobelijn, Prosperine is depicted as,

> a frail yet striking figure. Intensely realized, seems strangely unconcerned by what is occurring and gazes back over her shoulder, out of the frame, with an air of languid melancholy, caught here as she is between the bright world of the living and the land of the dead, in neither of which she will ever again be wholly at home. (*A*, 42–43)

Reminiscent of so many of Banville's quasi-other worldly female figures she hovers between ontological planes, uncertain of her own status. In several of the other entries, direct observations about what might be perceived to be characteristics of Banville's writing are offered, as with the comments on Giovanni Belli's *Pygmalion* (called *Pygmalion and Galatea*) (1602–1670), in which the artist's work is described as being "marked by the inwardness and isolation of a man who has distanced himself from the known, the familiar, and betrays a hopeless yearning for all that has been lost and abandoned" (75), while in the entry for Job van Hellin's *Syrinx Delivered* (1645), the artist's "coolness of approach" is identified, "a coldness, some critics would say—which sets him apart from the majority of Ruben's pupils" (103), and in a typically convoluted Banvillean intertextual allusion, the subject of Jan Vibell's *Acis and Galatea* (1677) is, we are informed, "reminiscent of the landscapes of Watteau and Vaublin" (*A*, 203). So the art of the anagrammatic Jan Vibbell is reminiscent of both the real Watteau and the fake Vaublin, all of whom resonate with the work of Banville, whose own Freddie makes the observation to begin with. The image-text world of the novel reverberates with a sequence of doublings of works of art, artists, and Banville's extended, elaborate storyworld.

John Kenny also points to a progressive merging of the catalogue pieces with the novel itself, particularly with respect to the presence of A., from the fifth entry onward. A. is directly addressed in the final few entries as "you"

CHAPTER 2

so that the "impersonal third-person critique" now becomes personalized (160), as she gradually emerges from Freddie's yearning to the status of *being* in her own right. Banville has suggested that he wanted A. to be "physically palpable—but not present"[31] and the way that she gradually assumes presence in the paintings suggests the role that art can play in our capacity to realize ourselves. This point is openly articulated in the catalogue entry for L. E. van Ohlbijn's *Capture of Ganymede* (1620), specifically at the point when A. speaks for the first time in the series of ekphrases:

> Those tears: he must have painted them with a brush made of a single sable hair. Remember how I showed them to you through the magnifying glass? Your breath forming on the picture, engreying the surface and then clearing, so that the scene kept fading and coming back as if appearing out of a mountain mist. There was a tiny mole on your cheek that I had not noticed before, with its own single hair. "Why would he bother?" you said. So that one day, my love, you and I would lean with our heads together here like this in the quiet and calm of a rainy afternoon and be for a moment almost ourselves. (*A*, 130–31)

Details like the repetition of the word "hair," respectively, in terms of the painter's brush and A.'s mole, reinforce the persistent connection between art and A. Similarly, the full identification of A. also rests on both the title of the novel, *Athena*, and of the eighth "real" painting, *Birth of Athena* (230). The significance of the association between A., Athena, and art also extends to the presence of a variation on the Greek mythical structure embedded within the fictional frame of the novel. Athena, daughter of Zeus, was born fully formed emerging from the forehead of her father after Hephaestus cracked open Zeus's head to cure him of his headaches. She is, also, variously, the Goddess of wisdom and civilization, war, artisans, and, in Homer's *Odyssey*, she is a skilled deceiver and liar. And if A. is Athena then her father, the Da, the Master of disguises in the novel should be Zeus (*A*, 70). But the mythic frame is not static and turns in on itself. Gangland Dublin is structured by the Godly, A. is no virgin, as Athena was supposed to be, and the Da's cross-dressing is a comic variation on Zeus's mythical disguises. Furthermore, A.'s mother is called "that Pasiphäe of the Plains" in the novel (*A*, 124) but Pasiphäe is the mother of the Minotaur who is Freddie in this novel. Thus, A. mythically speaking, becomes Freddie's sister and their love affair recalls Ben White's and Flora's incest in *The Possessed*. The interlocked intertextual Banvillean world is abundantly apparent.

But, of course, strictly speaking they are not meant to be representations of literal humans. At the close of the novel, Freddie offers commentary on the final painting, *Birth of Athena*:

> Consider these creatures, these people who are not people, these inhabitants of heaven. The god has a headache, his son wields the axe, the girl springs forth with bow and shield. She is walking towards the world. Her owl flies before her. It is twilight. Look at these clouds, this limitless and impenetrable sky. This is what remains. A crease runs athwart it like a bloodless vein. Everything is changed and yet the same. (*A*, 232)

Once again the ekphrasis speaks to both the painting that occupies its direct attention, and to the novel that mirrors it in so many ways, while also aspiring to be a work of art in its own right. The multilayered ontological spatiality of the novel also mimics the relation between the real and the fictional, or between life and art, a quality that gradually evolves to be of major significance in the novels hereafter. This finds expression via Banville continually splitting the events and characters into two fictional levels. In the case of A., we are told: "There is the she who is gone, who is in some southern somewhere, lost to me forever, and then there is this other, who steps out of my head and goes hurrying off along the sunlit pavements to do I don't know what. To live. If I can call it living; and I shall" (233). More directly self-conscious is his reference to, with respect to A., Adorno's distinction between empirical reality and art: "She is the perfect illustration of Adorno's dictum that 'In their relation to empirical reality works of art recall the theologumenon [sic] that in a state of redemption everything will be just as it is and yet wholly different'" (*A*, 105). Banville's fictions have always been the same, and yet different. Morrow's proximity to his subject seems closer now than ever and yet everything too seems the same. But that is precisely Banville's point. The almost overwhelming echoes of other textual models confirm that the activity of artistic creation is, and always has been, a ubiquitous human fascination.

In *Athena*, references to birthing myths abound, including Athena's own mythical birth, A.'s birth, Dr. Frankenstein's imagined misery at the loss of his monster (223), H. G. Wells's *The Island of Dr. Moreau* (from which Morrow's name is derived), and Jekyll and Hyde. As a self-consciously fictional rendition of artistic parturition, *Athena* probes the precise nature of that very process, just like Banville's heroes have always done. The difference with *Athena* is not necessarily that Morrow manages to "create" a woman, but that in the process of trying to imagine her into existence he manages to realize himself. That is

87

what it has always been about, the novel implies. Morrow is then both Dr. Frankenstein and the monster simultaneously, self-reflexively composed, as he is, of shreds of other fictional creations. In addition, several critics have specifically focused on A. as evidence of a possible shift in Banville's representation of, or formation of, women. Anja Müller and Patricia Coughlan both see possible evidence of the emergence of a more credible form of female agency than in previous Banville novels.[32] Coughlan tempers this somewhat by pointing out that even if A. is endowed with agency "it is predominantly figured as sexual and manipulative"—which doesn't exactly register a positive progression.[33]

With *Athena*, the destination is by no means reached, because it can never be. The essence of art remains forever just out of reach, just as A. ultimately disappears in the novel—which may itself be a form of meaningful agency. What remains is an illuminating record of the imagination interrogating itself, or, as Imhof has it: "*Athena* is concerned with imagination imagining itself."[34] Nothing is translatable for Banville nor does "anything have meaning" in the sense that the content of existence is capable of yielding its essences. Thus, art, for Banville, serves the purpose of showing, "the absolute mystery of things. Knowing is having information, understanding is absorbing, internalizing the world."[35] This is a crucial moment in Banville's work, in which he distinguishes between extracting meaning from existence, and simply attending to the mystery of being which, in turn, is closely associated with the process of art itself, an association that he frequently registers in interviews. For example, he asserts that the "world and being in it are such a mystery that the artist stands before it in a trance of bafflement, like an idiot at High Mass."[36] As his work progresses further, in the Cleave novels, and in *The Sea*, *The Infinities*, and *The Blue Guitar*, it grows increasingly evident that the idea of bafflement or confusion becomes even more central to his aesthetic sense and the novels appear more interested in reflecting the confusion of human existence than resolving it, or even illustrating failed attempts to resolve it, as was formerly the case with the earlier work.

The novel that immediately follows the Art trilogy, *The Untouchable*, also positions a fake painting, Poussin's *The Death of Seneca*, at its center. The novel is a historiographic metafiction-cum spy narrative that is based on the life of Anthony Blunt (Victor Maskell in the novel), a Soviet spy and leading art historian who specialized in the work of Nicholas Poussin. Maskell greatly values his "Poussin" painting and repeatedly performs partial ekphrases as a means of facilitating extended discussions on the stoic, to such a degree that the narrative device becomes quite labored and the use of the painting is rarely as well integrated as it is in the trilogy. As Roberta Gefter argues with respect to the Art Trilogy and *The Untouchable*, the novels "are all texts that intentionally revel in the self-reflexive, self-conscious technical narcissism . . . in the textual game," but the manner in which the game is integrated with the artistic form of each novel varies greatly.[37] In *The Untouchable* the painting is primarily used as a means of overtly injecting philosophical observations into the text. Banville's apparent desire to revisit the kind of historical reconstruction that he had earlier deployed in his scientific historical fictions, replete with a convoluted spy plot, doesn't, as a result, achieve the kind of seamless use of the visual arts that one finds several years later in *The Sea*, and thus doesn't represent a progressive artistic development.

Notes

1. Anja Müller, "'You Have Been Framed': The Function of Ekphrasis for the Representation of Women in John Banville's Trilogy (*The Book of Evidence, Ghosts, Athena*)," *Studies in the Novel* 36, no. 2 (Summer 2004): 185–205.
2. Vladimir Nabokov employs an identical metaphorical device in *Lolita*, one of many correspondences between *The Book of Evidence* and Nabokov's novel. For example, Humbert Humbert refers to "Claude Lorrain Clouds" and a "stern El Greco horizon" (152) while Freddie, like Humbert, refers to himself, in mock-elegant tones, as Jean Jacques, the cultured killer (124). Similarly, Banville, like Nabokov, employs the device of direct address to the Jury, uses many overt self-reflexive devices, and too stakes much on the fancy prose style of *his* murderer. Vladimir Nabokov, *Lolita* (New York: Vintage, 1997).
3. Rüdiger Imhof, *John Banville: A Critical Introduction* (Dublin: Wolfhound Press, 1997), 199; Derek Hand, *John Banville: Exploring Fictions* (Dublin: The Liffey Press, 2002), 151; John Kenny, *John Banville* (Dublin: Irish Academic Press, 2009), 165.
4. Banville suggests, in an interview with Derek Hand, for example, that strangeness is "the mark of art." Hedda Friberg, "John Banville and Derek Hand in Conversation," *Irish University Review* 36, no. 1 (2006): 200.
5. Calvino asserts that "Different levels of reality also exist in literature; in fact literature rests precisely on the distinction among various levels, and would be unthinkable without an awareness of this distinction." Italo Calvino, "Levels of Reality in Literature," *The Literature Machine* (London: Secker and Warburg, 1989), 101–121.
6. Holly Virginia Blackford, "Apertures in the House of Fiction: Novel Methods and Child Study, 1870–1910," *Children's Literature Association Quarterly* 32, no. 4 (Winter 2007): 369.
7. Ibid., 360.
8. The metaphorical use of the interiority of houses is repeatedly deployed in Beckett's *Trilogy*. For example, he positions his unnamable in such a space: "The silence, a word

CHAPTER 2

on the silence, in the silence, that's the worst, to speak of silence, then lock me up, lock someone up, that is to say, what is to say, calm, calm, I'm calm, I'm locked up, I'm in something, it's not I, that's all I know, no more about that, that is to say, make a place, a little world, it will be round, this time it will be round, it's not certain, low of ceiling, thick of wall, why low, why thick, I don't know . . ." Samuel Beckett, *The Beckett Trilogy: Molloy, Malone Dies, The Unnamable* (London: Picador, 1979), 373.

9. See especially Hedwig Schwall, "An Interview with John Banville," *European English Messenger* 6, no. 1 (1997): 13–19.

10. Elke D'Hoker, "Portrait of the Other as a Woman with Gloves: Ethical Perspectives in John Banville's *The Book of Evidence*," *Critique* 44, no. 1 (Fall 2002): 23.

11. Mark O'Connell, *John Banville's Narcissistic Fictions* (London: Palgrave Macmillan, 2013), 188.

12. Kenny, *John Banville*, 123.

13. "Oblique Dreamer: Interview with John Banville," *Observer* 17 (September 2000): 15.

14. Imhof, *Critical Introduction*, 256; Willem Drost's "Portrait of a Woman" (1653–1655), is held in the Museum of Fine Arts, the Hungarian National Gallery, in Budapest.

15. T. S. Eliot, for example, suggests that the "progress of an artist is a continual self-sacrifice, a continual extinction of personality" in his "Tradition and the Individual Talent" (*The Norton Anthology of English Literature*, 6th editon, Vol. 2, 2173). Similarly, Stephen, in *A Portrait of the Artist as a Young Man*, contends that the "personality of the artist, at first a cry or a cadence or a mood and then a fluid and lambent narrative, finally refines itself out of existence, impersonalizes itself, so to speak." James Joyce, *A Portrait of the Artist as a Young Man* (Harmondsworth: Penguin, 1992), 233.

16. D'Hoker, "Portrait of the Other," 27.

17. Tony E. Jackson, "Science, Art, and the Shipwreck of Knowledge: The Novels of John Banville," *Contemporary Literature* 38, no. 3 (Autumn, 1997): 520.

18. D'Hoker, "Portrait of the Other," 27.

19. Françoise Canon-Roger, "John Banville's *Imagines* in 'The Book of Evidence,'" *European Journal of English Studies* 4, no. 1 (2000): 25.

20. Stephen Cheeke, *Writing for Art: The Aesthetics of Ekphrasis* (Manchester: Manchester University Press, 2008), 51.

21. G. E. Lessing, *Selected Prose Works of G. E. Lessing*, ed. Edward Bell, trans. E. C. Beasley and Helen Zimmern (London: G. Bell, 1879), 91.

22. Cheeke, *Writing for Art*, 23.

23. John Weretka, "The Guitar, the Musette and Meaning in the *fêtes galantes* of Watteau," *EMAJ: Electronic Melbourne Art Journal*, no. 3 (2008): https://emajartjournal.files.wordpress.com/2012/08/weretka.pdf (accessed April 23, 2016).

24. Norman Bryson, *Word and Image: French Painting of the Ancien Régime* (Cambridge: Cambridge University Press, 1981), 65.

25. "15 Questions with John Banville," interview by Michelle B. Timmerman, *The Harvard Crimson*, February 26, 2010, http://www.thecrimson.com/article/2010/2/26/fm-jb-think-work/ (accessed October 31, 2016).

26. Kenny, *John Banville*, 166.

27. "Master of Paradox: Interview with John Banville," interview by Helen Meany, *The Irish Times* (March 24, 1993): 12.
28. Kenny, *John Banville*, 166; O'Connell, *Narcissistic Fictions*, 171–74.
29. O'Connell, *Narcissistic Fictions*, 174.
30. Kenny, *John Banville*, 166.
31. Schwall, "An Interview with John Banville," 14.
32. Müller, "You Have Been Framed," 199; Patricia Coughlan, "Banville, the Feminine, and the Scenes of Eros," *Irish University Review* 36, no. 1 (Spring-Summer, 2006): 86.
33. Coughlan, "Banville, the Feminine," 97.
34. Rüdiger Imhof, "John Banville's *Athena*: A Love Letter to Art," *Asylum Arts Review* 1, no. 1 (Autumn 1995b): 27.
35. Schwall, "An Interview with John Banville," 15.
36. John Banville, "The Personae of Summer," in *Irish Writers and Their Creative Processes*, ed. Jacqueline Genet and Wynne Hellegouarc'h (Gerrards Cross: Colin Smythe Ltd., 1996), 119.
37. Roberta Gefter-Wondrich, "Postmodern Love, Postmodern Death and God-like Authors in Irish Fiction: The Case of John Banville," *BELLS: Barcelona English Language and Literature Series*, ed. Mireia Aragay and Jaqueline A. Hurtley (Barcelona: PPU, 2000–2011), 86.

3

Brushstrokes of Memory

The Sea

JOHN BANVILLE'S *THE SEA* (2005) OCCUPIES the focus of our attention in this chapter, the only single novel that is afforded such close scrutiny. There are several reasons for this, one of which is what initially appears to be a fundamental aesthetic shift away from the purely invented landscapes of most of the previous novels to at least a nominal accommodation of Banville's own personal history. Many critics have observed this shift, with Kenny suggesting that *The Sea* is more "human"[1] than Banville's previous work and Mark O'Connell pointing to the connection between Banville's observations about his childhood in Wexford and the novel. In Banville's memories of Wexford there is "a boy, like Myles Grace, with webbed toes," a dairyman to whom the young writer went to collect milk, like Max does in the novel, and an acknowledgment of the class distinctions between the different kinds of holiday homes in the seaside resort, an awareness that Max too inherits.[2] In fact, Banville has openly acknowledged that the novel uses elements from his childhood in several interviews.[3] However, one also needs to proceed with caution with respect to the extent to which the autobiographical elements genuinely modify the approach because many familiar complex artistic patterns are woven into *The Sea*, arguably to an even more ambitious level than elsewhere. Banville himself pointedly insists, with respect to his relationship with the character Max, that

> there is something of me and my history in Max—there has to be, since I am the only material I have to work with. . . . I have no interest in writing about my "trajectory"—indeed, although it may seem paradoxical in the light of the foregoing, I have no interest in writing about myself at all. True art is always impersonal.[4]

Banville's somewhat predictable refutation of any hint of personalization of the work, however, is more closely related to his disavowal of literary fiction that seeks to map overt meaning, personal development, or extended psychological analysis of a life. The presence of incidents from his own past at the very least

CHAPTER 3

aesthetically infuses his highly fictionalized world with notional gateways to material reality if not, of course, material reality itself. The sophisticated, self-conscious artistic motivations and complex artistic form nevertheless remain the novel's most overt, accomplished achievements. Or, as Kenny, observes, with respect to this potential tension: "It is perhaps Banville's overarching achievement here to retain his uncompromising commitment to a technically perfected art while writing a meditation on childhood and age."[5] This chapter will illustrate several ways in which Banville achieves such a "technically perfected art," while ultimately demonstrating how this, in turn, serves to accommodate and accentuate a meditation on childhood, age, and the nature of being.

The Sea is Banville's most technically accomplished work and is an exemplum of the artistic ambition that lies at the center of all of his work. In this, the most refined expression of the kind of fiction that Banville writes, much of the power of the novel resides in the seamless construction of a sophisticated, multilayered literary, mythic, and artistic form, in addition to its poetic use of language, its philosophical range, and its nuanced engagement with his other fictions. Furthermore, the novel employs a variety of narrative strategies that imaginatively speak to the way that time asserts itself in non-linear fashion, wavelike, via memory, and these strategies create a resonant textual layering throughout that seamlessly allows time to slip and slide between the three distinct time zones featured in the novel (Max's childhood, the period of his wife's illness, and his life in "The Cedars" after her death). In the novel, time repeats, not literally, but via the ghostly presences that proliferate our imaginations; it imagines rather than recovers the past, and this is the pathway to a kind of reclamation, it is suggested. *The Sea* deploys a sophisticated range of narrative strategies which are integrated with systems more familiar to the visual arts, marking the novel out as a technical achievement beyond anything he had previously managed. In particular, its original engagement with, and absorption of, the paintings of Pierre Bonnard render the novel a unique artistic expression in literary fictional form and illustrates how the imaginative power of images drawn from the past can infuse existence with significance. In Banville's literary retelling and narrative assimilation of Bonnard's paintings, the fiction is also constructed in sympathy with the artistic principles that governed the French artist's paintings. For example, as with Max's poignant recollection of the final months and beyond of his dying wife, Anna, Bonnard too continued to paint his wife, Marthe, long after she died, but always at the age at which they met; in both cases the actuality of their subjects is imaginatively transfigured and preserved but—crucially—in apparent fluid, life-giving, movement rather than fixed stasis.

The Sea is the novel in which Banville's artistic imagination achieves its most refined expression because it is where his embedded philosophical discourse on art, in all its complexity, is ultimately most coherently reflected in its own status as a work of art; self-reflexive discourse assumes full authority as artistic expression in its own right. The coherent and subtle narrative texture is evident in multiple ways throughout. For example, *The Sea* exemplifies Banville's habit of constructing a secondary allusive ontology, beneath, or beside, the primary surface reality of plot, via a complex interconnected patterning of literary, artistic, and mythical resonances. The character Carlo Grace is, for instance, both man and God, "the one who appeared to be in command over us all, a laughing deity, the Poseidon of our Summer" (123), but in further shape-shifts, he is a "grinning goat god" (125) and a satyr (233) with "furred hind legs" (79). His family members, the Graces, are simultaneously flesh-and-blood children *and* the Graces of Greek myth, while Myles, Carlo's son, is both a boy and a "godling" (61), as well as a "malignant sprite" with webbed toes (226). His sister Chloe, at one point, blows "an archaic pipe-note on a blade of grass," echoing Pan, while the almost casual manner of the twins' apparent suicide by drowning reinforces the notion of them as gods simply retreating from material existence. Furthermore, Rose, who heavily dominates Gabriel Godkin's imagination in *Birchwood* (1973), drifts in and out of view in *The Sea*, at one point a figure in one of Max's imagined tableaus, "all rush and color," while at another she is "poor demented Ariadne on the Naxos Shore" (245–46) and, finally, he confirms her otherworldly aura and acknowledges that unlike Chloe and her mother, Rose was created by "another unknown, hand" (224), suggesting that she too has a multitextured ontological presence. Similarly, our narrator goes by two different names (Max and Morden) and is a "lyreless Orpheus" (24) lost and broken after the death of his wife, which infuses much of the texture of the novel with an elegiac quality. Banville is not simply borrowing the allusive significance of these mythic figures; in fact, the secondary intertextual frame is so pervasive that the primary ontological frame is frequently punctured by it, as when Constance Grace at one point practically transforms, in Max's adolescent, sexualized, delirium from woman to demon and back to woman, in "an instant of divinity" (118). One moment she is "Connie Grace, her husband's wife, her children's mother, the next she is an object of helpless veneration, a faceless idol, ancient and elemental" (118)—and immediately thereafter she returns to being a mortal woman and is never again the same in his imaginative consciousness, as though the glimpse his brief vision afforded him is powerful enough to transform existence.

CHAPTER 3

The impact of such persistent allusive doublings, or what Imhof calls "an echo chamber of literary quotations and allusions,"[6] on the narrative texture of Banville's fictional ontology is that the characters and their environment are perpetually both themselves (fictional humans holidaying in a seaside town, loving, living, dying) and other. This also extends, at times, to Max's engagement with material reality when he feels that everything "seemed to be something else" (65)—further extending a sense of the multiplicity of things. Characters and events continually shimmer in and out of view, slipping out of a fixed sense of identity or sharp focus, and reasserting themselves in new unexpected ways, while the very fabric of the novel is frequently suffused with subtle echoes, colors and sounds because of references to various branches of the arts. For example, late in the novel, Max observes that Rose is playing Schumann's *Kinderszenen* (or, *Scenes of Childhood*) on the piano, and self-consciously nudges us with the statement, "As if to prompt me" (220). The prompt is intended for the reader as much as it is for Max, and leads one to consider the possible parallels between *The Sea* and *Kinderszenen*. There are thirteen movements in *Kinderszenen*, many of which feature titles that might be seen to nominally correspond to specific moments in the novel, like the opening "Of Foreign Lands and Peoples" which resonates with the arrival of the Graces, the gods, in the humble seaside town, with their allure of unique otherness. Similarly, "Child Falling Asleep," the twelfth movement, may be interpreted as corresponding to the scene where Chloe and Myles calmly and silently vanish into the ocean, into death, and the final movement, "The Poet Speaks," is potentially identifiable with the presence of the self-conscious narrative voice which perpetually meditates on the nature of memory, time, and the transformation of the world of remembered experience into image and narrative shape in the novel. Perhaps even more emphatic is the way in which this final movement resonates with the closing lines of the novel in which Max is awoken from his reverie about Anna's death and informs us that he feels as though he is walking into the sea, the point at which, in the novel, the multiple ontological levels (the text itself, Max's present, his various memories, the rhythm of the novel, and life itself) merge into a single word—sea (263). While it may be unwise to extend this interpretive logic to a full mapping of all of Schumann's individual movements, the presence of echoes and partial allusions seems clear, and akin to the fragmentary but potent, gathering of shards of memory that Max himself summons in his efforts to invent a feasible transfiguration of his own mixed memories. The presence of Schumann thus adds another textured layer to the imagined landscape of *The Sea*.

The sense of multiplicity of being is also enhanced throughout by the use of the visual arts. So when Max offers up one of his many electrifying glimpses of the world, he imbues it with an artistic zeal that far outstrips descriptive reportage: "It was a sumptuous, oh, truly a sumptuous day, all Byzantine coppers and golds under a Tiepolo sky of enameled blue, the countryside all fixed and glassy, seeming not so much itself as its own reflection in the still surface of a lake" (45). Framed against an intertextual reference to Tiepolo's richly textured frescoes, Max's scene-setting contains an acknowledgment of its own invented, or reflective, mirroring. The world, he admits, is both itself and imagined other—as such the declared version carries with it the ghost of the world before it was remade in the imagination. Multiple other references to the visual arts shape the layered way that we imaginatively inhabit the storyworld of the novel and one is repeatedly confronted with compelling variations of the world rather than with a fixed image. Reflective of Max's desperate efforts to forge a sense of himself, there's a reference to one of Van Gogh's self-portraits, "not the famous one with bandage and tobacco pipe and bad hat, but that one from an earlier series, done in Paris in 1887, in which he is bare-headed in a high collar and Provence-blue necktie with all ears intact" (130–31), while Claire's "spindly legs and big bum, that hair, the long neck especially," makes Max think of "Tenniel's drawing of Alice" (44). Likewise, Miss Vavasour, we are informed at one point, is in the pose of "Whistler's mother" (256). All such painterly allusions do more than just declare a visual allusive frame, or likeness, as is frequently the case in Banville's previous work; in *The Sea*, characters, events, and places become othered by this frequent practice, overtly reminding us that all forms of representation generate parallel ghostly presences in the forms of art.

Similarly, while the mythic references generate a doubling of the characters, especially the Grace family, they also intertextually amplify the texture of the fictional ontology to such a degree that it shimmers in its own duality. During the frolicsome game on the beach, "a series of vivid tableaux, glimpsed instants of movement all rush and color" (125), when Rose is being pursued by Constance Grace, Max sees them as "two barefoot maenads" framed in a scene reminiscent of several European paintings of Greek and Roman myth, "by the bole and branches of the pine, beyond them the dull-silver glint of the bay and the sky a deep unvarying may blue all the way down to the horizon" (126). The description of the postpicnic games, as Pan Huiting argues, "might easily have sprung right out of the paintings of the bacchanalia, of nymphs and satyrs by painters such as Titian (*Jupiter and Antiope, Bacchanal*

CHAPTER 3

of the Andrians).... Poussin (*Nymph Syrinx Pursued by Pan, Nymph and Satyr, Bacchanalia*) and Peter Paul Reubens (*Nymphs and Satyrs, Pan and Syrinx*)."[7] Furthermore, the manner in which Constance Grace, woman and demon, lazily lies upon the ground, "supine on the bank with her head leaning back on the grass and flexed one leg," while her emptied glass "swoons" as it falls over (116), strongly echoes, in Pan's view, "the numerous fleshy, voluptuous and sleeping maenads that litter the ground in the history of art (two of which can be found in Titian's *Bacchanal of the Andrians* and *Jupiter and Antiope*)."[8] The substitution of temporal sequence with stilled, stylized tableaux—Max sees Rose, "from the waist up racing through the ferns," with "her black hair streaming behind her"—momentarily permits the characters to slip from one mode of textual existence to another, radically slowing the movement to stillness while retaining the illusion of movement.

On several other occasions in the novel, most pointedly perhaps when Max encounters Constance Grace washing Rose's hair in the garden, narrative tableaux are powerfully used as substitutes for temporal narration. Making overt reference to Vermeer's *The Milkmaid* (1657–1658), as she washes Rose's hair, Constance is described as being in the "pose of Vermeer's maid with the milk jug, her head and her left shoulder inclined, one hand cupped under the heavy fall of Rose's hair and the other pouring a dense silvery sluice of water from a chipped enamel jug" (222). The narrative resemblance to Vermeer's still life permits a suspension of the temporal narrative flow by framing the scene with ekphrastic stillness; this offers a clear indication of the extent to which Banville has integrated the spatial and temporal arts in *The Sea*. With reference to this particular scene, Joakim Wrethed observes that this is "obviously a still life, in which the descriptive narration slows down and becomes one with a possible contemplative moment in front of a painting,"[9] in effect mirroring the way in which we read paintings. Susanne Peters claims that Banville's use of ekphrasis "reaches its apotheosis in *The Sea*"[10] but it seems clear that the novel extends far beyond even comprehensive deployment of ekphrasis, particularly in the way that he splices paintings together, shifting, for example, from Vermeer to Watteau in the space of a few lines (222), and the manner in which the paintings are partially integrated into the narrative of the novel. Furthermore, Monica Facchinello usefully differentiates between Banville's previous use of paintings and *The Sea* as follows:

> Morden's predecessors refer to or re-create specific paintings mostly in the attempt to increase vividness by generating realistic visual accounts of this character or that landscape. Morden instead uses

> Bonnard's pictorial human figures and settings as models for his settings, human figures and even for himself.[11]

While one could argue that something similar occurs, especially with the landscape, in *Ghosts* (1993), the saturated degree to which paintings act as reflective models in *The Sea* distinguishes the novel. The instances of ekphrasis, the still lifes, and the tableaux derived from various literary, mythic, and artistic sources blend into the fabric of the greater imagined universe, until it is fashioned out of various glittering moments from the arts. Such instances act as sites of illumination for Max's ontological questions, in particular those related to the past, or more precisely, how one accommodates the past in the present.

Funneled through Max's memory, the "Milkmaid" scene is presented in the present tense, offering a careful detailing of the clothing the women wear, the way that they each wear their hair, and the manner in which the light intervenes to visually sculpt the figures in the morning air. "Memory dislikes motion," Max assures us, "prefers to hold things still," suggesting a reason for the tableau that he fixes in our line of vision. The momentum of the narrative sequence is temporally halted—although, as with Vermeer's still lifes, the illusion of movement is retained—and the fictional storyworld is once again modulated to accommodate the waves of memory that repeatedly peak and trough from the opening to the closing pages. This modulation is directly connected to the technical act of blending the attributes of literary narrative and the visual image. Wrethed's observations on this are astute:

> In for instance *The Sea*, the narrator often imitates the stillness and silence of a painted scene so that the manner of narration comes close to appearing as a series of word paintings or still lifes, carefully linked together in the softly flowing rhythm of the prose. This technique challenges the prevalent idea of the distinction between the temporal and spatial arts.[12]

In fact, the novel itself may be viewed as an extended technical demonstration of the merits of a fusion between the temporal sequence and key spatial moments. Furthermore, Banville's novelistic still life extends beyond Vermeer's extraordinary feats of three-dimensional illusion and perspective. Despite the observations of many critics that Banville somehow retains a complex relationship with realism—and he arguably does[13]—caution is required when considering *what* he does with it. This scene, for example, is not simply an ekphrastic rendering of Vermeer. Instead, it alludes to the way one of the character figures, Constance, positions herself, and seeks to extend beyond the

CHAPTER 3

limits of both Vermeer and the moment itself, by merging the still life, via the focal point of the jug, with another of Banville's familiar artistic presences. As the water falls from Constance's jug it touches "the crown of Rose's head" and "makes a bare patch that shakes and slithers, like the spot of moonlight on Pierrot's sleeve" (222). The Pierrot is Watteau's *Gilles*, returning again to register his presence in the fabric of Banville's world. The scene then, fittingly for a work of art, draws us into an extended discussion on Rose's visual features, in which her profile, we are initially told, generates an illusion like one of those "fiddly Picasso portraits" (223) that prevents one from ever truly seeing her head-on. She would also sometimes "seem a Duccio Madonna, melancholy, remote, self-forgetting, lost in the somber dream of all that was to come" (223) or, he might have said, hardly there at all, at least in a specific materialist sense.

Throughout the novel, Banville offers scene after scene that seek to transfer some of the attributes of painting to his prose narrative. In another hushed moment in Max's memory of Constance Grace, the arrangement of the scene is telling:

> There is a multi-coloured patch in my memory of the moment, a shimmer of variegated brightness where her hands hover. Let me linger here with her a little while, before Rose appears, and Myles and Chloe return from wherever they are, and her goatish husband comes clattering on to the scene; she will be displaced soon enough from the throbbing centre of my attentions. How intensely that sunbeam glows. Where is it coming from? It has an almost churchly cast, as if, impossibly, it were slanting down from a rose window high above us. Beyond the smouldering sunlight there is the placid gloom of indoors on a summer afternoon, where my memory gropes in search of details, solid objects, the components of the past. (86–87)

The point at which the sunbeam meets Constance's hovering hands, and offers a promise of some unseen realm beyond the immediate scene, is akin to the vanishing point of a painting, or the point at which all the converging lines, or visual emphases appear to meet, while retaining the alluring promise of the unseen. More explicit are Max's observations when describing a remembered moment in which he stands outside a scene in which Chloe acts out a kind of dumb-show:

> Chloe was still standing in the shadow of the pine tree, holding something in her hand, her face lifted, looking up intently, at a bird, perhaps, or just at the latticework of branches against the sky,

and those white puffs of cloud that had begun to inch their way in from the sea. How pensive she was yet how vividly defined, with that pine cone—was it?—in her hands, her rapt gaze fixed amongst the sunshot boughs. Suddenly she was the centre of the scene, the vanishing-point upon which everything converged, suddenly it was she for whom these patterns and these shades had been arranged with such meticulous artlessness: that white cloth on the polished grass, the leaning, blue-green tree, the frilled ferns, even those little clouds, trying to seem not to move, high up in the limitless, marine sky. (123–24)

Here Max explicitly names Chloe as the "vanishing point," in effect momentarily transporting her to the stillness of a fixed visual narrative, giving her a kind of concentrated significance for a few moments. And yet, all such moments are, in some sense, attendant narrative innovations compared to the central significance of Pierre Bonnard in the novel.

In *The Sea*, Max (Morden) is writing a book on Bonnard (1867–1947), offering explicit reason for the multiple references to his paintings and life. Beyond such plotted material, however, the presence of Bonnard in Banville's novel is of immense significance; while direct references do not in any sense dominate the surface narrative, and the degree to which his paintings are ekphrastically explored is not extensive—unlike the overt treatment of several paintings, real and imaginary, in the art trilogy. Nonetheless *The Sea* is literally saturated with Bonnard, from casual references to familiar items in his paintings, to direct allusions to his work and life, to the infusion of his theories and practices of art into the self-conscious Banvillean narrative universe, and to an almost total absorption of some of these ideas in the literary fictional rendering of several major events in the novel. The sequential textual proximity of both of Max's dead females—his wife, Anna and his first love, Chloe—to Bonnard's paintings in the novel also offers an indication of the centrality of each of these figures in the interwoven visual pattern that emerges.

Overt allusions to Bonnard are strewn throughout the novel, to which Max himself frequently draws our attention, as when he describes the weathered wood of the shed, and observes that Bonnard "would have caught that texture exactly, the quiet sheen and shimmer of it" (43). More important, perhaps, is the way in which he embeds subtle allusions into the fiction; Max recalls the specifics of his first visit to "The Cedars" as follows: "So there I am, in that Edenic moment at what was suddenly the centre of the world, with that shaft of sunlight and those vestigial flowers—sweet pea? All at once I seem to see sweet pea" (89). As Facchinello has observed, "*Sweetpeas* is the title of one

CHAPTER 3

of Bonnard's 1912 paintings featuring a vase of sweet pea on a table";[14] this illustrates one of the ways that Bonnard's world seeps into that of Banville. To self-reflexively emphasize the painterly connection, Max's description of the scene, "the centre of the world," with its "shaft of sunlight," is also suggestive of the vanishing point in *his* textual painting of the scene. So too with the small black woolly dog that Max remembers and relates, in the present tense, only to then puzzle over whose dog it may have been, a dog he never sees again in his memories (92). Black dogs are a recurring, significant presence in several of Bonnard's paintings, including, *Two Poodles* (1891), *Marthe Bonnard and her Dog* (1906), *The Red Checkered Tablecloth or The Dog's Lunch* (1910), *Woman with a Dog* (1922), and in the painting that is central to *The Sea*, *Nude in the bath, with Dog* (1941–1946) (Figure 3).

While the significance of such allusive, playful, gestures should not be overstated, they certainly reveal a certain artistic seepage between Bonnard's and Banville's works and demonstrate one of the ways in which *The Sea* reaches beyond a simple, linear form in an effort to integrate other ontological modes. Such integrative gestures proliferate in the novel, as does the frequency of reference to windows, doorways, and frames of various kinds— elements which dominate many of Bonnard's late interiors. In addition, Banville's familiar habit of musing on the architectural features of the house, rooms, and corridors extends to *The Sea*, as a metaphorical code that speaks to the progressive condition of Max's understanding of his context. For example, midway through the novel, his confusion with the disjunction between memory and materiality is apparent and the house, once again, forms the focus of his thinking:

> I found that the model of the house in my head, try as it would to accommodate itself to the original, kept coming up against a stubborn resistance. Everything was slightly out of scale, all angles slightly out of true [. . .] I experienced a sense almost of panic as the real, the crassly complacent real, took hold of the things I thought I remembered and shook them into its own shape. (*TS*, 156)

Near the close of the novel, the house instead becomes a locus of harmonization in which Max's accommodation with the complex mutability of living has been reached: "In the house all was tranquil and still. I moved among the rooms as if I were myself a thing of air, a drifting spirit, Ariel set free and at a loss" (247). Similarly, the domestic settings of many of Bonnard's late interiors mirror the potent brooding presence of Banville's houses. For Bonnard, in his late interiors, Nicholas Watkins tells us that rooms were "analogues of human experience" and his aim:

> was to draw the spectator into a painting on a contemplative journey, in which familiar objects are encountered as though for the first time, forming unexpected relationships and assuming new meanings, and generating in the process a consciousness of the complexity of the experience that constitutes awareness on entering a room.[15]

In a more overt intensification of the seepage between the works of Banville and Bonnard, in *The Sea* Max notices a shimmering outline of color in another of Bonnard's paintings that bears resemblance to Chloe's forehead: "her handsome, high-domed, oddly convex forehead—like, it suddenly strikes me, remarkably like the forehead of that ghostly figure seen in profile hovering at the edge of Bonnard's *Table in Front of the Window*" (137)—an, importantly, barely discernible human figure. Similarly, one also can discern a vague outline of barely distinguishable color in *White Interior* (1932) bending beside the table, and again in *Corner of the Dining Room at Le Cannet* (1932) a female presence stands, back to the viewer with part of her head cropped. The figures, crucially, bear resemblance to life, but they are also something other, something more; they are autonomous presences in art. In *The Sea* Banville seeks to permit something of those presences, via Bonnard, to take up residence in his words, as when Max experiences a moment in which he momentarily witnesses himself as an image, from outside himself: "I had a sudden image of myself as a sort of large dark simian something slumped there at the table, or not a something but a nothing, rather, a hole in the room, a palpable absence, a darkness visible" (193). This shape, like that which "no-one at the séance sees until the daguerreotype is developed" (194), echoes Dita Amory's evaluation of the substance of Bonnard's late interiors in which people are absorbed into the extravaganzas of color: "In the end, the dialogue in Bonnard's paintings is not a dialogue between people. It is a conversation between objects, colors, and the geometry of interiors, between bursts of light and their attendant hues, between those who are present and those who are absent."[16] And in Banville's variation, Max thinks that he is "becoming my own ghost," reminding us of the frequency of such imagery in the novel from the outset when he thinks that someone has walked over his grave (4), to the luminous presence of the word revenant—"a thing known returning in a different form" (10)—in the novel, which is what we aesthetically experience in *The Sea*. The Banvillean

CHAPTER 3

world repeatedly returns, in new forms, new extravaganzas of color, bearing with it numerous echoes from his storehouse of fictions.

Like Banville, Bonnard too insisted that "art" was not "nature" and foregrounded the primacy of the act of composition.[17] In fact, Bonnard felt that close proximity to the object, the real, was destabilizing for the work of art. His composition process involved only minimal interaction with the object and he preferred to paint from ideas, rough sketches. "'I am very weak,' he explained, 'it is difficult for me to keep myself under control in the presence of the object.'"[18] Similarly, as with Banville, the self-conscious mode evolved to be a central part of his work, particularly with the series of paintings among which *Table in Front of the Window* (1934–1935) (Figure 4) belongs, with its doubling of picture- and window-frame, complete with the illusion of an easel vertically slicing the image in two. Similarly, the earlier *Dining Room Overlooking the Garden* (1930–1931), and the later *In the Bathroom* (1940), among others, utilize a pictorial variation of the self-reflexive mode, drawing attention to their own status as framed works of art, alerting one always to the centrality of the notion of composition for Bonnard. As Julian Bell observes, the "self-conscious mode persisted during the following years, through mirrors, windowframes, scenes within scenes" while the enormity of the historical events unfolding about him apparently "bypassed him."[19] The self-conscious mode is, of course, the visual equivalent of the self-reflexive tradition in literary texts, from Cervantes and Sterne onward, but that which acquired particular emphasis in late modernism and postmodernism.

While Banville's persistent deployment of the self-reflexive mode, to varying degrees, throughout his work might even be considered an identifiable narrative marker in his work, the pictorial doubling that one encounters in Bonnard also literally corresponds to the use of windows and reflections of various kinds in *The Sea*. For example, when Max and Anna visit Mr. Todd to receive her cancer diagnosis, a subtle but quite extraordinary inversion of the apparent surface reality occurs. Unsettled by the prospect of simply sitting while awaiting the diagnosis, Max prefers to instead gaze out the window, "the glass wall," as he calls it, with his back to the room. However, he then sees Anna "palely reflected in the glass," like one of Bonnard's ghostly presences, portrait-like, "very straight on the metal chair in three-quarters profile," with "one knee crossed on the other and her joined hands resting on her thigh" (15). Anna, framed as she is by the window, simultaneously occupies two ontological layers in the scene. A little while later, and again involving Anna and Max, a framing window is used to generate a sense of visual doubling: "Light from the window behind me shone on the lenses of her spectacles where they hung at her collar bone, giving the eerie effect of another, miniature she standing close in front of her under her chin with eyes cast down" (21). The sense of proportion, and pictorial illusion, via the doubly reflected light and glass (window and spectacles), both emphasizes the essential ontological instability of the subject, Anna, while deriving benefit from the spatial stillness of the visual image.

Bonnard was a nonrealist, and is most frequently considered a Postimpressionist painter, although some critics consider this classification inaccurate and misrepresentative of his radical technical achievements with color.[20] Particularly in his later years, he refused to consider himself part of any specific school. His work repeatedly champions the composition above the subject and in his later most important work, as Wilkins notes, he didn't directly paint real life at all, preferring instead to preserve ideas in notes, or charcoal sketches, which were later transformed into basic color outlines and, eventually, to oils on canvas (43). And, even then, he would sometimes return to revise paintings years later—he is reputed, for example, to have changed paintings in museums and galleries while a friend distracted the attendant-in-charge.[21] As a result, Picasso famously referred to Bonnard's work as "a pot pourri of indecision."[22] Picasso, in turn, receives an intertextual rebuke from Max, a Bonnard scholar after all, in *The Sea*, when he dismissively refers to "fiddly Picasso portraits" (223).

In his midtwenties Bonnard met his lifetime companion, and future wife, who claimed her name was Marthe de Meligny and that she was aged sixteen; both details were inventions that Bonnard only apparently discovered thirty years later—her real name was Maria Boursin and she too had been in her midtwenties when they first met. In Banville's novel Max notes Bonnard's habit of repeatedly painting Marthe in her bath, continuing the series long after his model had passed away (152). The figures in his late paintings, Marthe included, are more phantoms than people, haunting the canvases, like Banville's revenant characters haunt the novel. One of Bonnard's most famous paintings of his wife, *Nude in the Bath, with Dog*, occupies a position of central significance in *The Sea*, and Max's ekphrasis reveals much about both the painting and his narrative response to his own subject, Anna:

> In the *Nude in the Bath, with Dog*, begun in 1941, a year before Marthe's death and not completed until 1946, she lies there, pink and mauve and gold, a goddess of the floating world, attenuated, ageless, as much dead as alive, beside her on the tiles her little brown

CHAPTER 3

> dog, her familiar, a dachshund, I think, curled, watchful on its mat or what may be a square of flaking sunlight falling from an unseen window. The narrow room that is her refuge vibrates around her, throbbing in its colors. Her feet, the left one tensed at the end of its impossibly long leg, seem to have pushed the bath out of shape and made it bulge at the left end, and beneath the bath on that side, in the same force-field, the floor is pulled out of alignment too, and seems on the point of pouring away into the corner, not like a floor at all but a moving pool of dappled water. All moves here, moves in stillness, in aqueous silence. (152)

The immediate connections between Bonnard's and Max's subjects are clear from the basic details of Marthe's dying within a year of the painting being initiated and the subsequent gestation period of the painting thereafter. In fact, Imhof suggests that Bonnard's painting "provides an exact correlative to the narrative."[23] Max overtly states that he is reminded of Anna when he looks at the painting: "Her right hand rests on her thigh, stilled in the act of supination, and I think of Anna's hands on the table that first day when we came back from Mr. Todd, her helpless hands with palms upturned" (153). Anna's hands, of course, were also featured in the quasi-portrait that Max witnesses in the reflected glass of Mr. Todd's window, like Marthe's, "resting on her thigh" (15), completing a sequence of associative visual images. Anna too took to the bath when she was ill, like Marthe, seeking relief. She and Max, like Marthe and Bonnard, also closed themselves away from the world, in "a deep dreamy silence" (154), that echoes the very fabric of Bonnard's domestic interiors. In Bonnard's painting, reality is governed by what lies on the fabric of the canvas. The floor, we are assured in Banville's ekphrastic reading pours away into the corner and the bathtub is reshaped. The floor has become a pool of dappled water. "All moves here," Max notes, "moves in stillness, in aqueous silence." Movement, stillness, and silence come together and the transformation of the idea of the real is apparent in the visual-spatial moment that Banville replicates in his own text—primarily to permit some of that same quality to take up residence in his narrative. In fact, Anja Müller has made a similar observation in her analysis of the "extensive ekphrastic passages" in the art trilogy, suggesting that the effect is to "incorporate a notion of space into the temporal verbal medium, creating moments in which the flux of time seems to be momentarily suspended to experience an immediacy of presence."[24] While the ekphrastic passages are not quite as extensive in *The Sea*, those that feature are supplemented by a general transference and/or mirroring of pictorial methods, the use of tableau, and the frequent "framing" of events in mirror or window reflections, as well as the deep thread of connections between Bonnard's and Max's subjects, Marthe and Anna.

Both women exist and yet don't exist in the novel, as figures enshrined in the respective portraits of their effective creators. They primarily exist as paintings, transformed into the other world of art. Although Marthe was seventy-three when she died, Bonnard continued to paint her as a young woman, retaining her as a model of sorts but the woman that existed in material reality has but tangential significance for the figures in these paintings. Bonnard's Marthe, in the painting, is always more a shape, an impression of vibrant color, a fluid presence, than a "real" woman, and Anna too seems but half present in Max's late descriptions of her: "She said so many strange things nowadays, as if she were already somewhere else, beyond me, where even words had a different meaning. . . . Her face, worn almost to the bone, had taken on a frightful beauty" (155). Max even outlines her own self-conscious awareness of her insubstantial nature. At one point, earlier in his recollections, she looks at her hands in her lap, "frowning, as if she had not noticed them before" (16). We even "other" ourselves, it is implied, further emphasizing the spectral atmosphere in the novel.

With reference to Max's ekphrasis of *Nude in the Bath, with Dog*, Wrethed suggests that "the passage partly amalgamates the two (narration and image) into a serene lament over the insolidity of the seemingly solid world of exteriority."[25] While this is certainly an amalgamation of sorts, whether it is actually a lament or not is debatable, considering Bonnard's reputation for this very insolidity, a feature that Wilkins sees as a distinguishing feature of his aesthetic: "his love of the ephemeral and the evasive; they depend on his ability to conjure ambiguity and unexpectedness out of the familiar and the thoroughly understood."[26] This, of course, is also a feature of Banville's fictional landscape in *The Sea*, in which characters and events from the past shape-shift, lose focus, and reemerge as figures in a beautifully wrought poetic landscape, much like those of Bonnard. Bonnard's interiors frequently exhibited a replacement of material reality with floods of blended color, or as Wilkins points out: "Figures merge with furniture or walls, sliding towards the boundaries of the canvas, moving past the limits of peripheral vision to hint at expanses beyond the edges of the picture."[27] And there are times when one can observe Banville's descriptions approach a similar painterly (in Bonnard's sense) quality, as when Miss Vavasour enters a room, "a moving wraith in the shadows of the twilit room" (219). Interestingly Julian Bell's interpretation of an earlier Bonnard painting of Marthe, *Nude in the Bath* (1937) offers

CHAPTER 3

an indication of the possible merging of the subject with twilit shadows, or any other suffusion of colors that characterize his paintings:

> Yet his work at its most extended . . . with its imperious reconfiguration of nature, can seem less a shared meditation than a submersion of one woman's individuality in the interests of one man's singular vision. What had the frail, ageing, distracted Marthe to do with the fluctuating mirage devised by her harried husband? Bonnard's transmutations of the objects of his gaze—his admirers have often reached for the term "magician"—can seem willfully solipsistic. A true solipsist, however, would not make pictures for others to see; and Bonnard, always intent to learn, was under no illusion about the power of his art. "When one distorts nature, it still remains underneath, unlike purely imaginative works."[28]

Bell's curious commentary seems to not recognize that "transmutations" of the objects are inevitable, and that the artistic response, while ultimately connected to the original object, undergoes radical adjustment, simply because it must, as a work of art. As Bonnard himself insisted in 1939: "One always speaks of submitting to the demands of nature. . . . There is also submitting to the demands of the picture." The painter's "principal subject," he noted, "is the surface which has its color, its laws, over and above those of objects."[29]

The "demands of the picture" make similar claims on Banville and, in his highly nuanced self-conscious work, direct or indirect commentary on the nature of the works' own processes is always a constituent part of the novels. With *The Sea*, this habit is extended, although not with a direct metaphorical method, like science or history or via the overt discourse about the nature of art that one finds in the trilogy, particularly in those moments where Freddie Montgomery seeks to assess the role of imagination or to imaginatively reconstruct the girl who has been lost. *The Sea* instead offers a more integrated approach and blends a more subtle form of artistic discourse into its narrative fabric—and this is key to the novel's success; Banville weaves a series of artistic concepts into the narrative without destabilizing the fiction itself, which is what arguably progressively occurs in the Frames Trilogy, culminating in the presence of an obtrusive aesthetic discourse in *Athena*. In *The Sea*, alternatively, in addition to the multiple allusions to painters and the narrative adoption of the pictorial mode, the reader is continually reminded of the essential complacency or indifference of the world, often in quite a casual manner: "that is all I have ever truly wanted, to burrow down into a place of womby warmth and cower there, hidden from the sky's indifferent gaze and the harsh air's damagings" (60–61). More emphatically, Max informs us, "I marveled, not for the first time, at the cruel complacency of ordinary things. But no, not cruel, not complacent, only indifferent, as how could they be otherwise?" (20). Banville's work has always been concerned with the sense of otherness that an indifferent world generates, and this indifference or "disinterestedness" is also presented as reciprocal in that while the world stands aloof from us, the artist too must locate a corresponding sense of distance from his/her subject. Such a position is embedded in Anna's intensely objective approach to photography in the novel, to the point that she almost erases her personality.[30] She becomes "like a blind person" when she holds the camera, whose eyes "went dead, an essential light was extinguished." Max marvels at her transformation from human to artist, with "her raptor's head out sideways," as she took "shockingly raw, shockingly revealing" photographs of him (173).

The sense of distance between the imaginative mind and the world upon which it muses is, according to Denis Donoghue, a key quality that resides at the center of artistic activity: "Autonomy, disinterestedness, and impersonality are the values to be recognized."[31] For Donoghue, the autonomy of art corresponds with the disinterestedness of the artist (and even, perhaps, the reader) and argues that this sense of distance is frequently evident on a linguistic level, in instances of what he terms catachresis: "the wrenching of language from the propriety of its normal reference"[32] ceases to be merely referential and "there are entire works which are catachreses in principle, such as *Finnegans Wake* and the Alice books."[33] In this, Donoghue envisages fictional universes in which language is in extended play with its own possibilities. Literary art thus itself becomes a center of otherness, governed by its own rules; so, a condition of accomplished artistry is akin to self-containment, and separateness from material reality. Walter Pater similarly argued that art strove to be independent of the "mere intelligence . . . to get rid of its responsibilities to its subject or material,"[34] while Banville frequently assumes a similar position with respect to subject matter.

Banville has frequently voiced his conviction that the world's strangeness, and his characters' puzzlement in the face of it, best defines his work.[35] It is thus no surprise to be informed in the opening lines of *The Sea* that the gods departed "on the day of the strange tide" (3), or that Max openly puzzles over what he calls the uncanny: "How is it that in childhood everything new that caught my interest had an aura of the uncanny, since according to all the authorities the uncanny is not some new thing but a thing known returning in a different form, become a revenant? So many unanswer-ables, this the least

CHAPTER 3

of them" (10). *The Sea* effectively seeks to echo the world's strangeness rather than present an ordered, plausible version of reality. The novel's role is thus to engender a sense of the strangeness that characterizes the world for Banville while simultaneously expressing the corresponding strangeness of art via its special relationship with material reality. In this sense the very texture of the fictional context, almost as an unavoidable characteristic, lies in true relation to the world from which it was originally derived. In fact, Steven Connor has, with respect to the general tendencies of some postmodern fictions, suggested that, "fiction and the world seem absolutely to interpenetrate, seeming more and more to be woven from the same fabric," pointing, in particular, to the problem of the "world and the world-making act up against each other."[36] The connection between world and text is relational rather than representational and effectively represents a renegotiation of the connection between art and existence. Furthermore, it may also be the case, especially with an author like Banville or Beckett, that the fictional world doesn't need to have a natural counterpoint in social reality beyond limited surface signposting.

Linda Hutcheon raises this very point in an effort to acknowledge the possible autonomous nature of certain fictional worlds: "In literature words create worlds; they are not necessarily counters, however adequate, to any extraordinary reality. In that very fact lays their aesthetic validity and their ontological status."[37] This validity is often expressed—and intensified—via Shklovsky's process of *Ostranie*, or defamiliarization[38] ("Art is a way of experiencing the artfulness of an object; the object is not important.") and we see many instances of this throughout the novel. For example, at one point Max recalls an inexplicable, destabilizing, incident on the beach, while in the company of Myles and Chloe:

> Myles runs ahead. But who is it that lingers there on the strand in the half-light, by the darkening sea that seems to arch its back like a beast as the night fast advances from the fogged horizon? What phantom version of me is it that watches us—them—those three children—as they grow indistinct in that cinereal air and then are gone through the gap that will bring them out at the foot of Station Road? (*TS*, 136–37)

Max's sense of himself as a phantom, or as a returning "revenant" (98), is a constant in the novel, as is a persistent slippage between different temporal versions of himself, and a fluid movement between his roles as subject and object. In pivotal moments like the above example, he encounters his self as a separate entity and the shift between he and his friends, from "us" to "them," to "those three children," firmly renders all of them as figures in the imagined landscape. The establishment of this as a fixed sense of normalcy is profound, with the surface texture of the world repeatedly resisting ordered patterns, only to be replaced by a moving surface of persistent strangeness, which Banville has claimed is "the mark of art."[39] But rather than being simply suggestive of an incomprehensible world, the novel, as Imhof claims, "offers a meditation on the indifference of the world,"[40] and "underscores the contingent nature, the capriciousness, the arbitrariness of life" and associates it with the "strange swell" that encircles so much of the novel.[41] As such, strangeness, and mystery, are elevated to the status of integral components of existence. Rather than simply registering ignorance, or antiknowledge, they are presented as states of being in themselves.

The oddness of memory has always fascinated Banville and, as early as novels like *Birchwood* and *The Newton Letter*, it has frequently served as a complex mediating factor between the world and the ambivalent modeling of past events, and as a constituent part of the imaginative process of seeking to recover those events. In interviews Banville has also frequently alluded to the intimate connection between memory and the strangeness of remembered things:

> Well, yes—I've become more and more convinced that we don't actually remember things as they actually happened. We make models of things which we carry into the future and which account for the fact that, when we return to a place or meet a person we once knew, the place or the person is different—not entirely different, of course, but in strange ways. Rooms have moved around, the color of their eyes has changed. It's because we don't actually remember these things. The brain is constantly modeling what it scans. That's what memory is—a series of models.[42]

These views correspond with many instances in *The Sea* where one's attention is explicitly drawn to confusion between what is remembered and what could have feasibly occurred, as with the uncertainty surrounding Max's first kiss with Chloe (162) which, initially, yields a remarkable clarity ("when I concentrate, I can see us there" [160]) but swiftly unravels as a true account. Despite the frequency of moments in which temporality is frozen "within the relentless flow of time," as Peters has it,[43] the recovery of past moments is an intensely aestheticized process, rather than an untroubled act of recollection. This, of course, is part of the significant pathway to understanding what accompanies Max's late period: "Yet how easily, in the end, I let it go. The past, I

CHAPTER 3

mean the real past, matters less than we pretend" (157). Such a perspective also explains the function of the pictorial-inspired tableaux or, as Wrethed argues, with respect to the Vermeer ekphrasis: "The narrator imitates the painting of a recollection, in which the memory image is given a stability that memory in general does not have."[44]

Wrethed's explanation of the function of memory images in the novel is accurate, and it is also important to conceive of the "stability" as an important anchoring point in a novel that so heavily embraces the sea as a central metaphor. As Imhof rightly observes, the sea also "stands for memory itself, more than anything else."[45] Max's observations about Bonnard's pictorial freezing of his dead wife in time, his own parallel attempts to transfigure Anna into a linguistic art figure, and the multiple instances of temporal suspension that proliferate the novel, all serve a similar aesthetic purpose. In a fictional storyworld that is so heavily invested in conveying an almost overwhelming sense of living (and remembering) as a strange, surging, multitextured process, it simultaneously registers moments of illumination that somehow signify human agency in an indifferent world. The achieved elegance of the novel owes much to the way that these competing energies coalesce, right up to its final lines. When Max follows the nurse inside to encounter his dead wife's body, he feels as though he were "walking into the sea" (263), offering a final self-conscious reminder of the seamless fusion of actual sea, the sea as metaphor for time, and the title of the novel itself—in this final moment the distinction between the sea of memory and the multitemporal space of the novel is complete but the wavelike ebb and flow of the novel's structural patterning is evident throughout. As Hedda Friberg convincingly points out, the "connection between Anna's death and the bay at Ballyless" is apparent when one considers the figurative framing of her final days. Max "feels the room sinking below the surface of the sea," and Anna is described as being "in the underwater glimmer of nightlight," which stresses both the significance of the sea as metaphor for memory while simultaneously ascribing yet another otherworldly quality to the texture of the novel, echoing, again, the aqueous imagery of Bonnard's paintings of Marthe.[46]

The sense of remembered time as elusive, ghostly, and capable of moments of illumination, ultimately conditions the surface texture of the narrative. Max is aware of the fluid sea of memories swirling around his consciousness from relatively early in the novel and, as always with Banville's narrators, offers us astute self-conscious observations on the nature of his own narration: "The truth is, it has all begun to run together, past and possible future and impossible present" (96). The implications for Max's own ontological status are, in turn, conditioned by the sense of mutable composition that accompanies his sense of self, and the deep sense of gratuitous pain that hangs over the lives of most of the main characters. In this, the form of the novel, replete with its attempts to assimilate the forms of the visual arts into its own frame and the mirroring of the strange indifference of life, ultimately stand in close relation to the haunted sense of loss and dying that define the novel from beginning to end. Similarly, Max's ghostly status as a phantom, or a revenant, conditions both his account of the world and his conception of his self but this quality is simply presented as a condition of existence rather than a lack of achievable solidity, and is frequently articulated in moments of illumination:

> On occasion in the past . . . I had felt myself break through the membrane of mere consciousness into another state, one which had no name, where ordinary laws did not operate, where time moved differently if it moved at all, where I was neither alive nor the other thing and yet more vividly present than ever I could be in what we call, because we must, the real world. And even years before that again, standing for instance with Mrs. Grace in that sunlit living room, or sitting with Chloe in the dark of the picture-house, I was there and not there, myself and revenant, immured in the moment and yet hovering somehow on the point of departure. Perhaps all of life is no more than a long preparation for the leaving of it. (*TS*, 97–98)

The formal fluidity of *The Sea* echoes through Max's tenuous grasp of his own being; his identity, like the novel, is a shimmering construction, layered with memories and invention, moments of beauty, and the inevitable pain and loss. In many respects, it is precisely the progressive unveiling of this construction that lies at the center of the novel.

The tension between Max and his split or othered self pervades his conception of himself in numerous ways. For example, he alerts readers to his many difficulties with mirrors, but stresses that "mostly they are metaphysical problems" (128). So, when he offers an extended commentary on his fright at viewing himself in the bathroom mirror it is clear that his discomfort is ontological rather than material. The subsequent comparison of his reflected image with Bonnard's and Van Gogh's self-portraits further imbues his face with the otherness of artistic image. Particularly with the latter painter, he allows the lines between mirror image and painting to bleed into one another, as when he moves from the "pink-tinged pallor" of his sunken cheeks to the

CHAPTER 3

radiance of Van Gogh's "stark and sickly" cheeks (131), which then glint "on the glass before me and sank into the distemper of the walls, giving them the parched, brittle texture of cuttlefish bone" (131–32). Van Gogh's radiance shines through his own bathroom mirror and Max is "transported for a moment to some far shore, real or imagined, I do not know which, although the details had a remarkable dreamlike definition, where I sat in the sun on a hard ridge of shaly sand holding in my hands a big flat smooth stone" (132). In moments like this the profound enormity of Max's ontological complexity is evident rather than indicative of any epistemological limitation, while the reach of his intertextual consciousness is emphatically rendered on a page that begins with a blending of Max and Van Gogh, traverses the sack of Troy and the sinking of Atlantis, and ends with a striking allusion to Stephen Dedalus's late diary section in *A Portrait of the Artist as a Young Man*: "All brims brackish and shining. Water-beads break and fall in a silver string from the tip of an oar. I see the black ship in the distance, looming imperceptibly nearer at every instant. I am there. I hear your siren's song. I am there, almost there" (132).[47] The appropriateness of the narrative artistic transfiguration in the fusion of painting and mirror image is, of course, linked to the fact that Bonnard's and Van Gogh's paintings, as Mark O'Connell reminds us, are also "remorseless in their depictions of their creators' frailties" in old age;[48] again the textual layers align while circling around the fundamental question of being that ultimately hums most loudly and persistently in Max's consciousness.

All of Max's musings ultimately lead to the following Kleistean[49] questions: "Who, if not ourselves, were we? All right, leave Anna out of it. Who, if not myself, was I?"(*TS*, 217), or more specifically, "Anyway, where are the paragons of authenticity against whom my concocted self might be measured?" (218). This is what Banville's protagonists have always asked in various ways, without ever being able to provide an answer. In Kleist's *Amphitryon*, Amphitryon's identity-confusion is derived from his puzzlement in the face of the deceptive antics of the Gods, which is more comprehensively exploited as a motif in Banville's subsequent novel, *The Infinities* (2009). In *The Sea*, the question of his own ontology, or authenticity, echoes forth from Max's tapestry of intertwined temporal zones, shifting senses of self—from child to old man, from Morden to Max—and overlapping intertextual and interpictorial frames. The rhetorical question about the paragons of authenticity against whom his concocted self might be measured requires no answer that the novel has not already provided. There is no knowing, no fixity, no finality to the question of self, as has always been the case for Banville's heroes. Speaking to Laura Izarra while writing *The Sea*, Banville suggested as much: "So there will be no masks, no actors, no business of theatre, and I realize that's absolute nonsense. Of course, there will be masks, of course there'll be actors, it will be the same book again in a different form."[50] And it is the same book as always, itself a kind of revenant, or something returned but in different form—and it is the ambitious shift in formal arrangement, in the aestheticizing positioning of the self in the maelstrom of time, what Max calls "the historic present" (248), that ensures *The Sea* attains a level of accomplishment beyond any of the previous works.

Notes

1. John Kenny, *John Banville* (Dublin: Irish Academic Press, 2009), 177.

2. Mark O'Connell, *John Banville's Narcissistic Fictions* (London: Palgrave Macmillan, 2013), 215.

3. For example, see the following interviews: Mark Sarvas, "The Long-Awaited, Long-Promised, Just Plain Long John Banville Interview—Part Two," *The Elegant Variation Blog* (September 19, 2005); "Fully Booked: Q & A with John Banville," interview by Travis Elborough, *Picador*, June 29, 2012, http://www.picador.com/blog/june-2012/fully-booked-q-a-with-john-banville (accessed August 31, 2016).

4. Ibid.

5. Kenny, *John Banville*, 178.

6. Rüdiger Imhof, "*The Sea*: 'Was't Well Done?'" *Irish University Review* 36, no. 1, Special Issue: John Banville (Spring-Summer 2006): 167.

7. Pan Huiting, *Aesthetic Configuration* (M.A. Thesis, Nanyang Technological University, Singapore, 2013), 15.

8. Ibid., 15–16.

9. Joakim Wrethed, "'A Momentous Nothing': The Phenomenology of Life, Ekphrasis and Temporality in John Banville's *The Sea*," in *The Crossings of Art in Ireland*, eds. Ruben Moi, Brynhildur Boyce, and Charles I. Armstrong (Bern: Peter Lang Publishing, 2014), 199.

10. Susanne Peters, "John Banville, *The Sea*." in Susanne Peters, Klaus Stierstorfer and Laurenz Volkmann, ed. *Teaching Contemporary Literature and Culture*, 6 vols. (Trier: Wissenschaftlicher, 2006–2008), 50.

11. Monica Facchinello, "'The Old Illusion of Belonging': Distinctive Style, Bad Faith and John Banville's *The Sea*," *Estudios Irlandeses*, no. 5 (2010): 43.

12. Wrethed, "A Momentous Nothing," 192–93.

13. Derek Hand, *John Banville: Exploring Fictions* (Dublin: The Liffey Press, 2002), 19–20; Kenny, *John Banville*, 118.

14. Facchinello, "The Old Illusion of Belonging," 39.

15. Nicholas Watkins, *Bonnard* (London: Phaidon Press, 2004), 52.

CHAPTER 3

16. Dita Amory, "Pierre Bonnard (1867–1947): The Late Interiors," in *Heilbrunn Timeline of Art History*. New York: The Metropolitan Museum of Art, November, 2010, http://www.metmuseum.org/toah/hd/bonn/hd_bonn.htm.
17. Julian Bell, *Bonnard* (London: Phaidon Press Ltd., 2003), 17.
18. Ibid., 22.
19. Ibid., 18.
20. Karen Wilkin, "Pierre Bonnard's Late Interiors," *The New Criterion* (March 2009). For example, Wilkin firmly argues that the term Postimpressionist is too conservative a nomenclature, and points to his experiments in colour, and "radical structure" (40) in which the works "threaten to dissolve into pure painting incident" (43).
21. Bell, *Bonnard*, 21.
22. Bell, *Bonnard*, 17.
23. Imhof, "*The Sea*," 176.
24. Anja Müller, "'You Have Been Framed': The Function of Ekphrasis for the Representation of Women in John Banville's Trilogy (*The Book of Evidence, Ghosts, Athena*)," *Studies in the Novel* 36, no. 2 (Summer, 2004): 187.
25. Wrethed, "A Momentous Nothing," 195.
26. Wilkin, "Pierre Bonnard's late interiors," 40.
27. Ibid., 41.
28. Bell, *Bonnard*, 23.
29. Wilkin, "Pierre Bonnard's late interiors," 43.
30. This again recalls various Modernist writers' aesthetic attitudes toward impersonality, as alluded to in the introduction, with respect to T. S. Eliot and James Joyce.
31. Denis Donoghue, *Speaking of Beauty* (New Haven: Yale University Press, 2003), 81.
32. Denis Donoghue, *On Eloquence* (New Haven: Yale University Press, 2008), 135.
33. Ibid., 137.
34. Walter Pater, *The Renaissance: Studies in Art and Poetry: The 1893 Text*, ed. Donald L. Hill (Berkeley: University of California Press, 1980), 106.
35. Hedda Friberg, "John Banville and Derek Hand in Conversation," *Irish University Review* 36, no. 1 (2006): 206.
36. Steven Connor, ed. *The Cambridge Companion to Postmodernism* (Cambridge: Cambridge University Press, 2004), 79.
37. Linda Hutcheon, *Narcissistic Narrative: The Metafictional Paradox* (Waterloo: Wilfrid Laurier University Press, 1980), 102–3.
38. Victor Shklovsky: "The purpose of art is to impart the sensation of things as they are perceived and not as they are known. The technique of art is to make objects 'unfamiliar,' to make forms difficult, to increase the difficulty and length of perception because the process of perception is an aesthetic end in itself and must be prolonged. Art is a way of experiencing the artfulness of an object; the object is not important." Victor Shklovsky, "Art as Technique," in *Modern Criticism and Theory: A Reader*, ed. David Lodge (London: Longmans, 1988), 20.
39. Friberg, "John Banville and Derek Hand in Conversation," 200.
40. Imhof, "*The Sea*," 165.

41. Ibid., 177–78.

42. Kevin Breathnach, "John Banville Interviewed," in *Totally Dublin*, June 28, 2012, http://totallydublin.ie/arts-culture/arts-culture-features/john-banville-interviewed/ (accessed September 31, 2016).

43. Susanne Peters, "John Banville, *The Sea*," in Susanne Peters, Klaus Stierstorfer and Laurenz Volkmann, ed. *Teaching Contemporary Literature and Culture, 6 vols.* (Trier: Wissenschaftlicher, 2006–2008), 49.

44. Wrethed, "A Momentous Nothing," 200.

45. Imhof, "*The Sea*," 166.

46. Hedda Friberg, "Waters and Memories Always Divide: Sites of Memory in John Banville's *The Sea*," in *Recovering Memory: Irish Representations of Past and Present*, ed. Hedda Friberg, Irene Gilsenan Nordin, and Lene Yding Pedersen (Newcastle: Cambridge Scholars Publishing, 2007), 255.

47. James Joyce, *A Portrait of the Artist as a Young Man* (Harmondsworth: Penguin, 1992). In the diary entry of 16 April, Stephen's aesthetic reverie anticipates his departure from Ireland, itself a self-reflexive act of becoming and artist in the novel, as follows: "The spell of arms and voices: The white arms of roads, their promise of close embraces and the black arms of tall ships that stand against the moon, their tale of distant nations. They are held out to say: We are alone. Come. And the voices say with them: We are your kinsmen. And the air is thick with their company as they call to me. Their kinsman, making reading to go, shaking the wings of their exultant and terrible youth" (275).

48. O'Connell, *John Banville's Narcissistic Fictions*, 135.

49. The original quote from Kleist's *Amphitryon* reads as follows: "And who, except me is Amphitryon?" from, *Amphitryon* in *Selected Writings*, ed. and trans. David Constantine (Indianapolis: Hackett Publishing Ltd.: 2004), 116.

50. Laura P. Z. Izarra, "Interviewing John Banville," in *Kaleidoscopic Views of Ireland*, ed. Murina H. Mutran and Laura P. Z. Izarra (Sao Paulo: Humanitas, 2003), 235.

Figure 1. Jean-Antoine Watteau, *L'Embarquement pour Cythère* (1717)

Figure 2. Willem Drost, *Portrait of a Woman* (1653-5)

Figure 3. Pierre Bonnard, *Nude in the Bath, and Small Dog* (1941-6)

Figure 4. Pierre Bonnard, *Table in Front of the Window* (1934-5)

Figure 5. Pablo Picasso, *The Old Guitarist* (1903-4)

Figure 6. Édouard Manet, *Déjeuner sur l'herbe* (1863)

4

The Art of Self-Reflexivity

The Cleave Novels

*T*HE *SEA* INTERRUPTS THE SEQUENCE of novels that directly and indirectly feature Alex Cleave, Cass Cleave, and Axel Vander—*Eclipse* (2000), *Shroud* (2002), and *Ancient Light* (2012). While Banville has de-emphasized the idea of the trio of novels as a series,[1] they clearly enact, via the interlinked mirroring of Alex, Axel, and Cass, an extended sequence. They each speak to the doubled nature of reality within fictional ontologies that are even more self-consciously composed than previous Banville works, with the possible exception of *The Sea*. Extending beyond the use of counterfeit and fake paintings in the Frames Trilogy, the "Cleave" novels deploy specific, resonant, metaphors associated with acting, actors, and puppetry (Alex Cleave is an actor, as is Dawn Davenport from *Ancient Light*, and Axel Vander is an impersonator), and the narrative voices are repeatedly given to observations about their own perpetually dislocated personas. In *Eclipse*, for example, Alex complains that he has "lived amid surfaces too long" (23), while in *Ancient Light*, he speculates about the essential intangibility of one's own personality when he acknowledges that he is getting lost in the persona of the character he is to play, Axel Vander:

> I seemed to see the shadowy first and valid Axel Vander faltering and falling without a sound and his usurper stepping seamlessly into his place and walking on, into the future, and overtaking me, who will presently in turn become a sort of him, another insubstantial link in the chain of impersonation and deceit. (*AL*, 82)

Axel Vander, who had originally assumed the real Axel's identity, now seeps into Alex Cleave, who is to play him in a film, becoming a version of the impersonator, rather than the original. All this occurs in a convoluted game of identity-usurpation and fictional doubling. The fake Axel ends up, in a sense, replacing the actor Alex; their personas, like their names, echo each other, seep into one another. They are all puppets after all, eking out insubstantial existences, learning to mimic each other's thoughts and habits, in a sophisticated tissue of self-consciously aestheticized existence.

CHAPTER 4

Alex textually echoes Axel, in a perfect anagrammatic relationship, and their relationships with Cass, as father and lover respectively, are repeatedly blurred, stretched beyond the limits of literal characterization. For instance, in *Shroud*, while Vander is "goughing and grunting at her," the second time, Cass (impossibly) imagines her father entering the room, walking around, speaking, and smiling (129). She had long been prey to hallucinations of this kind but the imaginary presence of her father while she is midcoitus with Vander has led Patricia Coughlan to suggest the presence of "incestuous feelings,"[2] while also suggesting that Lily, in *Eclipse*, becomes a kind of substitute daughter to Alex.[3] While there is certainly validity in Coughlan's identification of such a thread it is also perhaps to assign too firm a material substance to characters that more closely resemble variations of each other than specific pretend humans. Cass, for example, is variously described as a "close relative, her own twin, perhaps . . . somehow hollow-seeming" (*S*, 74), as an actor, like Alex, in *Eclipse* (71), and she also resembles one of the parade of red-haired interlopers in Banville's extended fictional universe. She too has red hair (*S*, 93) and occasionally echoes their sly manipulative presences, as when Alex describes her in *Eclipse* in the following manner: "At times she has a look, a fleeting, sidelong, faintly smiling look, in which I seem to glimpse a wholly other she, cold and sly and secretly laughing" (71). She is, at very least, a variant of these near-perpetual presences in Banville's work. Readers are also repeatedly reminded by Alex of Cass's multidimensional nature:

> I had not been prepared for so many resemblances. She was my mother and father, and Lydia's father and dead mother, and Lydia herself, and a host of shadowy ancestors, all of them jostling together, as in the porthole of a departing emigrant ship, in that miniature face contorted upon the struggle for breath. (*E*, 41)

While such observations can be read literally, as physical family resemblances, Alex also observes, with reference to the dead Cass in *Ancient Light*, that "all my dead are alive to me" (242). The figuration of Cass, as literary presence, here takes more explicit shape; she is daughter, lover, ghost, perpetually alone, a stranger to herself, and resonant both with the presences of all her family members, and with all of Alex's dead who live on in his words. Her imaginatively textured existence far exceeds the limits of normal characterization.

Similarly, Hedda Friberg has argued that Cass exists on the "borderline of psychic illness."[4] While this perspective certainly has merit, the narrative complexity of her persona also, at very least, seriously complicates psychoanalytical analysis, given her role in the Cleave novels as multitextured aesthetic presence. As Alex observes of her: "She puts on a character with an ease and persuasiveness that I could never match. Yet perhaps she is not feigning, perhaps that is her secret, that she does not act, but variously is" (71–72). Cass's ontological status is more akin to a ghost in the novels, being both herself and others, powerfully echoing, as she does, Lily (*Eclipse*) and Dawn Devonport (*Ancient Light*). In fact she even haunts Alex in *advance* of her "actual" death in *Eclipse*, transcending the limits of her temporal and spatial zones. Furthermore, in *Shroud*, she is described as the "one true subject" and, as a result, she has no "detachment, could not divide herself from her subject" (320). Banville has even suggested that he may be Cass.[5] And yet he is also Alex, Axel, Freddie, et al., in an aesthetically doubled sense, just as all the major characters in the Cleave novels, within their fictional frames, occupy multiple modes of being. As Eoghan Smith argues: "The characters in these novels [*Eclipse*, *Shroud*] are identified as poseurs and actors, mask-wearers and frauds, whose lives are played out as a matter of style, and who are all suffering from an extreme crisis of authenticity caused by a life of deceit and role-playing."[6]

All of the main characters in the Cleave novels appear aware of their insubstantial natures, and their fictive status is relentlessly emphasized, as in *Eclipse*, when Alex's wife, Lydia (or Leah) suggests that he has become his own ghost, and he readily agrees (43). Similarly, there are, once again, numerous references to puppets and marionettes. Cass Cleave—in *Shroud*—claims that she "saw herself as a puppet, with lacquered cheeks and fixed mad grin, popping up in front of him, look at me, look at me!" (313). Specific figures from Banville's familiar intertextual repository also make allusive appearances, frequently being closely aligned with the characters themselves. For example, in *Eclipse*, Quirke is momentarily glimpsed "in the doorway in the pose of Vaublin's Pierrot, trying to find something to do with his hanging hands" (200), registering both a doubled presence and a powerful reminder of his prior existence in a "Vaublin" painting (effectively a Banville painting).

Similarly, in *Shroud*, Cass identifies with "the one-eyed glare and comically spavined gait" (4), of the grotesque figure of the Harlequin, who had previously been associated with Felix in *Ghosts* as the "smirking Harlequin astride his anthromorphic donkey" (96) in an ekphrastic moment. In *Shroud*, Cass is fascinated by the figure of the Harlequin but ultimately advises, that we should not "*suppose a relation with other human beings*" because he has none (Italics at source: 381). He is, after all, a perfect example of the artificial, where the visual arts meet the marionette figures that seek to live in Banville's "golden world,"

CHAPTER 4

his *monde d'or* (*G,* 128). The Harlequin is also afforded an ekphrasis-style self-reflexive interlude in *Shroud*, in which the *"inexplicable being"* is associated with Mercury and Proteus and is attributed with the creation of *"a new form of poetry, accented by gestures, punctuated by somersaults, enriched with philosophic reflections and incongruous noises"* (Italics at source: 380). The allusion here is to Watteau's painting, *Gilles* (Cover Image). This function is further evident in the way that the lines between Harlequins, puppets, and other artificial figures in the novels, are continuously blended or doubled with "real" characters. Vander insists, for instance, on his own puppet-like state, claiming that he is "all frontage; stroll around to the back and all you will find is some sawdust and a few shaky struts and a mess of wiring" (*S,* 329), and Alex Cleave tells us that he has "stepped through the looking-glass into another world where everything is exactly as it was and at the same time entirely transformed" (*E,* 121). The world to which he refers, is the world of pure artifice that both he and Banville's other characters inhabit. The self-referentiality is, however, unlike that of Banville's earlier works, which largely sought to draw our attention to the limits of language, and offered a self-conscious commentary on their own making. The Cleave trilogy extends the self-referential range because the novels appear to have a consciousness of themselves as multilayered fictional discourses. The characters are aware of their own status as characters, they each possess an intertextual consciousness that continually recalls other Banvillean fictional universes and a vast array of literary, philosophical and visual arts references; it is to the fabric of this world that the characters refer when they speak of their ontological conditions.

In Banville's most overt author-intrusive gesture, he inserts an author, "JB," into *Ancient Light*, as author of the text and film script for *The Invention of the Past*, the biography of Axel, in which Alex is set to play the lead. Mark O'Connell asserts that JB's work is in fact a movie version of *Shroud*,[7] which is only partly accurate, although the general point—that JB has written a version of a John Banville work is significant. In fact, JB, in a faintly comical self-portrait, appears as a kind of parody of Banville. In *Eclipse*, Banville similarly toys with his own authorial role when a line that Alex had delivered on stage that includes the place-name Ballybog, is mentioned; Ballybog is the town in which Banville's adaptation of Kleist's *The Broken Jug* (1994) is set. So Alex, a character in a Banville novel, has also acted in a play written by Banville, further thickening the intertextual soup. However, O'Connell suggests, with good reason, that *Ancient Light* is "his most openly self-referential"[8] novel, given the presence of JB himself as a character, and the high degree of commentary on counterfeits, and the mirroring of Axel and Alex on several potent levels (the film script, Cass's notes). Joan Acocella too has argued that *Ancient Light* is "the most reflexive novel that Banville has ever written"[9] because of the dual emphasis on acting and impersonation that brings Alex and Axel together. Furthermore, the familiar trope of the house, as metaphor for the house of fiction, is again reasserted, as is evident in Lydia's grief-stricken obsession that Cass is actually still alive but lost somewhere in the house: "It is a kind of sleepwalking, or sleeprunning, in which she is convinced our Catherine, our Cass, is still alive and a child again and lost somewhere in the house" (*AL, 18*).

In fact, all three Cleave novels are intensely self-reflexive artifacts, stemming perhaps from Banville's own observation that *Eclipse* was "as near as I've got to writing a book that has no real center,"[10] which he contrasts with the plot-driven *The Untouchable*. The absence of a real center, as he has it, effectively means that the novel is concerned primarily with its own being, rather than with a declared subject matter. This is a pattern that one can discern in all three Cleave novels. *Shroud* and *Ancient Light* are also acutely self-absorbed works, despite their respective semblances of dramatic suspense and sexual plots. *Eclipse* openly displays its constructed nature by inserting standard metafictional morphological features, like stage directions, into its narration: "Swish, and the curtain goes up on the last act. Place: the same. Time: some weeks later. I am at my table as before" (191). In addition, the novel, both literally and aesthetically, features an overt return to the trope of the house—as a plot-driven locus of convalescence for Alex and, structurally, as a reconceptualization of the aesthetic process for Banville. The house is as central here, as literary-creative metaphor, as it was in *Birchwood* forty years earlier, although its rendering is now far more sophisticated and deeply engendered as parallel process-commentary. From the outset, Alex fuses the literal and the metaphorical in a manner that has grown increasingly seamless in the years since *Birchwood*: "The house itself it was that drew me back, sent out its secret summoners to bid me come . . . *home*, I was going to say" (*E, 4*), to his "house of the dead" (*E, 49*), in which Quirke warns us, there are "always queer goings-on" (*E, 129*). Alex, in a more pointed manner, outlines his rationale for returning to the house, and simultaneously alerts us to one of the central aesthetic fascinations of the novel: "To be watchful and attentive of everything, to be vigilant against complacency, to resist habituation, these were my aims in coming here [to the house]" (*E, 45–46*). This echoes Viktor's Shklovsky's defamiliarization, a process "through which one might impart the sensation of things as they are perceived and not as they are known."[11]

CHAPTER 4

For Shklovsky, "The technique of art is to make objects 'unfamiliar,' to make forms difficult, to increase the difficulty and length of perception because the process of perception is an aesthetic end in itself and must be prolonged."[12] In this context, Alex proceeds to articulate his primary aesthetic challenge as he settles in to the house:

> *Making strange*, people hereabouts say when a child wails at the sudden appearance of a visitor; how was I to make strange now, and not stop making strange? How was I to fight the deadening force of custom? In a month, in a week, I told myself, the old delusion of belonging would have re-established itself irremediably. (Italics at source: *E*, 46)

The metaphor of the house serves as the initiation point for a self-conscious engagement with the process of conceiving of a sense of the fabric of reality. The objects and inhabitants of the house serve as both literal and metaphorical presences, a simultaneity to which he also speaks:

> I am amongst them, I am of them, and they are of me, my familiars. . . . When I speak of them being at the table, or the range, or standing on the stairs, it is not the actual stairs or range or table that I mean. They have their own furniture, in their own world. It looks like solid stuff among which I move, but it is not the same, or is the same at another stage of existence. Both sets of things, the phantom and the real, strike up a resonance together, a chiming. If the ghostly scene has a chair in it, say, that the woman is sitting on, and that occupies the same space as a real chair in the real kitchen, and is superimposed on it, however ill the fit, the result will be that when the scene vanishes the real chair will retain a sort of aura, will blush, almost, in the surprise of being singled out and fixed upon, of being lighted upon, in this fashion. (*E*, 48)

In the transformed universe, in which the strangeness of the reflected images illuminates objects, the "most humdrum phenomena" (*E*, 49) fill Alex with astonishment. The house thus becomes a center of introspective observation about the nature and texture of reality, and an extended demonstration of the strange relation between material reality and the ghostly presences that we fashion in its place. In the above extract, Alex points to the illuminating impact of the invented image on the materiality of the object being represented, imbuing it with an afterglow of imaginative concentration, echoing Gordon Graham's suggestion that literary devices can "illuminate."[13] In such moments, Banville seeks to articulate the nature of the way art illuminates the real and in some respects *Eclipse* is itself a prolonged meditation on precisely this aspect. The novel seeks to illuminate that which cannot be represented—a quality which Banville has alluded to in the figures of Watteau's paintings in an effort to explain their potency as works of art: "These glowing figures are very very moving; this is poetry."[14]

Throughout *Eclipse*, differences between images and material reality are blurred, and in characteristic self-reflexive fashioning, Alex claims that, "things are running together now, collapsing into one another, the present into the past, the past into the future. My head feels full of something" (*E*, 187). And even more overtly, he too closes his account with a declaration that echoes Gabriel's closing promise in *Birchwood* ("to live a life different from any the house has ever known") when he decides to give the house to Lily, who has hovered between ontological levels throughout the novel:

> Yes, I shall give her the house. I hope that she will live here. I hope she will let me visit her, la jeune châtelaine. I have all kinds of wild ideas, mad projects. We might fix up the place between us, she and I. . . . I shall ask her if I may keep my little room. I might write something about the town, a history, a topography, learn the place names at last. (*E*, 213)

Eclipse exemplifies the aesthetic development that characterizes all of the Cleave novels because it fully integrates a self-reflexive articulation of the complex problem of aesthetic response to reality within its fictional storyworld. *Shroud* enacts a similar aesthetic process albeit by different means: the metaphorical system of the house is replaced with an intensely focused treatment on the two central figures who dominate the fiction, Cass and Axel. Several critics have pointed to the correlation between Axel Vander and the lives and works of European intellectuals like George Steiner, Adorno, Thomas Mann[15] and Althusser and Paul de Man,[16] some of whom (Althusser and de Man) Banville affirms in the Acknowledgments at the rear of the novel. Imhof has argued, however, that the novel primarily makes use of the lives of some of these figures rather than representing a genuine engagement with post-structuralist thought.[17] Nevertheless, Kenny registers a more specific intellectual connection between Steiner's *Real Presences* and a chapter title of one of Vander's book titles, "Effacement and Real Presences." However, his attempt to implicitly connect Vander with the "alignments of high culture and high crimes against humanity in the Holocaust," and his suggestion that Vander addresses, "from the vantage point of the USA the combined philosophical and political

CHAPTER 4

crucifixion of language in old, war-torn Europe,"[18] extends the significance of the intertextual relationship into a crusading ethical enterprise that is generally anathema to Banville's aesthetics.

Furthermore, Axel Vander's presence has multiple competing, and more compelling, layers of significance. He is, for example, also associated with the Harlequin throughout *Shroud*, at one point referring to his "daily harlequinade" (405) which, as Imhof points out, refers to "a play in which a harlequin or buffoon stars."[19] Furthermore, he is also variously associated with the Shroud of Turin, with Nietzsche, and with Christ, or a "negative, diabolical Christ figure."[20] He is also a mirror image of Alexander Cleave, a feature that is registered via his relationship with Cass, and in his own acknowledgment of their echoing acting roles:

> I fear that between us we destroyed her, old Thespis and I. . . . An actor he is, or was, so she told me. I am sure we would have many things in common, he and I. After all, I am an actor too, though only an inspired amateur. The difference is that the part I play is mine alone, and may not be taken by anyone else, on or off the stage. (*S*, 395–96)

He is partly wrong, textually at least, because in *Ancient Light*, Alex prepares to play Axel in the work written by JB, but the self-reflexive condition that enfolds all the major characters is emphatically registered. Furthermore, the title of the novel itself also emphasizes the significance of the self-reflexive, referencing as it does the "Shroud of Turin," "the first self-portrait," according to Kristina. She conflates this with the Vander chapter title "Effacement and Real Presences," although she foregrounds the effacement aspect (*S*, 156).

The effacement of self is again emphasized later in the novel in an explicitly self-referential manner, when Axel ruminates on the way his work has been received by critics during his lifetime:

> I spent the best part of what I suppose I must call my career trying to drum into those who would listen among the general mob of resistant sentimentalists surrounding me the simple lesson that there is no self: no ego, no precious individual spark breathed into each one of us by a bearded patriarch in the sky, who does not exist either. (*AL*, 27)

Similarly, Banville has frequently alluded to aesthetic effacement, or authorial impersonality, in interviews, arguing, for example, that his work has nothing to do with his own life and that "true art is always impersonal."[21] This self-parodic gesture allows some of Banville's own views to permeate those of Vander. It is tempting to extend this connection further when Vander immediately admits that, in fact, he "cannot entirely rid myself of the conviction of an enduring core of selfhood amid the welter of the world" (*S*, 27). In turn, the "real presence" component of the Vander chapter title echoes through the image of the Shroud of Turin, and the novel entitled *Shroud*. Perhaps, after all, there is a ghost in the machine, something that Banville hints at via his use of the name Max Schaudeine, a red-haired "Felix"-style character whom the impersonator Axel encounters in his parents apartment, and whom Cass also meets. As Imhof correctly observes, Max Schaudeine is an anagram of *deus ex machina*,[22] alerting us to barely visible presences that might be governing the hidden motivations. In this, *Shroud* is perhaps more deeply engaged with the mystery of its own ontological possibilities than any previous Banville novel.

The potential alignment of Vander and Banville is furthermore expressed via the former's disgruntled thoughts about the reception of his work by critics who spoke of his "assertive elusiveness," his "mastery of the language" (61) and the "desolate lyricism" of his style, while also noting his early work on Rilke, Kleist, and Kafka (62). We might as well be referring to Banville—and perhaps we are, in a manner of speaking—Banville himself doubled via the illuminating presences of his own characters. If Banville is Vander then he is also his mirror reflection, Axel. In another turn of the fictive layering of personas, the fake Vander himself summarizes the original Vander's work as follows: "The poise and studied distance of Axel's style, with its high patrician burnish and flashes of covert wit," and "his call for the aestheticisation of national life" (214), and as a "dabbler, an opportunist of ideas" (208). The original Vander is then also an incarnation of Banville. The key here is that the central figures, in all their layerings, echo each other, and exist in a curious artistically sublimated relationship with Banville, while representing different variations of the kind of artistic process in which Banville is engaged. In fact, the author has suggested in several interviews that he thinks that Cass is Banville,[23] and has acknowledged a close relationship with Phoebe from the Benjamin Black novels, while he has also indicated that all his major characters are the same voice.[24] This does not simply suggest an autobiographical connection, but acknowledges that all these characters, and Banville-as-author, converge in the creative consciousness that perpetually investigates the relationship between material reality and the objects that one constructs in its place.

Throughout *Shroud*, an overwhelming sense that the novel itself is conscious of its own fictionalized status is evident. In response to Vander's

CHAPTER 4

collapse, for instance, Kristina and Franco "sprang up at once and began to bustle about like mechanical figures, as if his fall had somehow switched on a motor and set their parts moving" (*S*, 175). Similarly, akin to the use of stage directions in *Eclipse*, Axel here also interjects another medium into the narrated account: "I propose a series of scenes, as in a frieze, depicting a pale girl capered about by an old man, against the background of a marble cityscape. . . . In each of the panels he is striking an elaborate attitude for the girl's benefit" (*S*, 329). Furthermore, Axel makes repeated reference to his textualised context, particularly with respect to other characters, in a manner that mirrors Banville's fictional storyworld: "Perhaps it is not for him alone that I am grieving, but for all my dead, congregated in a twittering underworld within me, clamouring weakly for the warm blood of life" (241). The recurrence of this topos of the dead,[25] even at the close of the novel as Axel nears fictional annihilation, serves to emphasize the significant, doubled nature of the discourse that is deployed: "The dead, though, have their voice. The air through which I move is murmurous with absences. I shall soon be one of them" (405). He has, in fact, always been one of them, one of Banville's interconnected network of voices: "I am, as is surely apparent by now, a thing made up wholly of poses" (329).

In the Cleave novels, the temporal context too alerts one to the invented, self-sustaining universe. All three novels begin in April, and it almost always remains April in both the declared present contexts and in their memories of key events; the various voices repeatedly speak of the world in what appears to be a kind of temporal stasis. In *Shroud*, it is April when Axel meets Cass (276), it was April when he had his first sexual encounter as a boy (325), and it is to April his mind turns in certain nostalgic moments (91). In *Ancient Light* the temporal location itself becomes a subject of the text's own self-scrutiny. Initially, the young Alex alerts us to his time frame: "April, of course. Remember what April was like when we were young, that sense of liquid rushing and the wind taking blue scoops out of the air and the birds beside themselves in the budding trees?" (4). And yet, the emphasis on April is at odds with his (surely autumnal) recollections of the "hammered gold of fallen leaves" although he insists otherwise: "yet it was April, it had to have been April" (10). Such momentary imaginative dislocations persist throughout, a point which is openly addressed by Alex: "Whatever it was, we had it one watercolour April day of gusts and sudden rain and vast, rinsed skies. Yes, another April; in a way, in this story, it is always April" (26). Even when the temporal sequence leans toward alternative time zones, the imaginative insistence refuses to permit it: "The weather was strange—it was one of those hectic days that come sometimes in October, when it seems that out of sheer mischievousness the year has reversed itself temporarily and turned back to springtime" (89).

In a playful self-reflexive manner Alex continues to provoke the reader's temporal and spatial senses, drawing specific attention to his imaginative reordering of past events: "And look! In the square, when I come out, it is, impossibly, autumn again, not spring, and the sunlight has mellowed and the leaves of the cherry trees have rusted and Busher the rag-and-bone man is dead. Why are the seasons being so insistent, why do they resist me so?" (*AL*, 16). It appears that in Banville's artistic consciousness of the temporal and spatial storyworld a particular focus persists throughout, akin to a still canvas, which implicitly stalls the sequential movement, and offers a continuous, fixed present. The entirety of the fictional ontology is thus imbued with a quality akin to that of the visual arts, and the temporal patterning that one usually encounters in works of prose fiction is replaced with a perpetual present that seeks to speak of the illuminated qualities of aestheticized memory. While the curious temporality clearly speaks of a particularized aesthetic surface to the novel, it also again alerts one to the deep self-referential structure of the novel, a quality that is mirrored in the surface arrangement of plot and characterization.

From the outset, the names of the characters echo and mirror each other. In addition to the familiar Alex/Axel inversion, Celia (Mrs. Gray) is called Lily by her husband, echoing Lydia's "other" name Leah; they have doubled names and also echo each other. We also have a Billie Gray and a Billie Stryker and a Mr. Jaybee, who is actually JB. Eoghan Smith has also observed that several names have doubled initials—Dawn Devonport, Toby Taggart, Cass Cleave, and the anagrammatical Alex/Axel game extends to Fargo de Winter, who had discovered Axel Vander's identity.[26] His name is an anagram of Ortwin de Graef, the Belgian postgraduate student who uncovered several hundred articles written by Paul de Man during World War II, some of which had a distinct anti-Semitic focus. The novel initiates a process of doubling that is familiar to that of other Banville novels but in *Ancient Light* the composition of the narrative is almost exclusively framed against a poetics of self-reflexive doubling without the use of metaphorical parallels.

The two primary parallel plots—Alex's youthful affair with his best friend's mother when he was fifteen and she thirty-five, and his life fifty years later as he prepares to star in *The Invention of the Past*, a film version of Axel Vander's life—also effectively echo one another in how they each demonstrate

CHAPTER 4

that Alex's problems with comprehending life perpetuate throughout his life. As O'Connell points out, the adult Alex had been overtly unaware of his deceased daughter's role in Vander's life, just as the teenage Alex was oblivious to Mrs. Gray's terminal illness,[27] while in both temporal zones he is waylaid by the mysteries of his memories, "random; representative, perhaps, perhaps compellingly so, but random nonetheless" (*AL,* 3). With each plotline, of course, further ruptures to the notion of a single, linear reality proliferate. For example, Alex immediately acknowledges the manner in which he creates a multilayered image when he first meets Mrs. Gray: "I would have been hard put to give a fair description of her—if I had tried, what I would have described would probably have been a version of myself, for when I looked at her it was me that I saw first, reflected in the glorious mirror that I made of her" (*AL,* 12). The subjective consciousness generates dualities during the act of apprehending reality and Banville teasingly plays with this fact throughout, as when he further splinters reality in a mesmerizing transfiguration of Mrs. Gray into a dizzying sequence of images reflected in a set of mirrors:

> More confusingly still, there was another mirror, a full-length one, fixed to what would have to have been the outwards-facing side of the inwards-opening door, and it was in this mirror that I saw the room reflected, with at its center the dressing-table, or whatever it was, with its own mirror, or I should say mirrors. What I had, therefore, was not, strictly speaking, a view of the bathroom, or bedroom, but a reflection of it, and of Mrs. Gray not a reflection but a reflection of a reflection. (*AL,* 28–29)

A few pages earlier, Alex had requested that we bear with him, "through this crystalline maze" (28) warning us of the nonlinear model of the world that we inhabit as we read. Here, Mrs. Gray is a reflection of a reflection and, as he clarifies a little later, her body is as though dismembered, disassembled, in a "jumbled arrangement" because of the positioning of the mirror panels—almost a Picasso painting. She is doubled, and dismembered and the mirror reflections produce "in combination a magnifying effect" (30). Ultimately, he insists that what he has described "is what appears in my memory's eye, and I must say what I see" (*AL,* 30). The complex process of apprehension is again offered up as a parallel reality, contiguous with the thing-in-itself, about which Banville has mused from his earliest work. Here, however, the process of apprehension, doubling, magnifying, and disassembling is inherently declared in every gesture to such a saturated degree that it becomes its own subject matter. The only content, beyond a thin veneer of plot, is the process itself.

The emphasis on a disassembled multilayered ontology is evident in other ways, from the most basic level of characterization—when Billie Stryker is described as one who "might have been assembled from a collection of cardboard boxes of varying sizes that were first left out in the rain and then piled soggily any old way one on top of another" (74)—to the odd interpolation of Alex's otherworldly meeting with Fedrigo Sorrán. Fedrigo's vision of the mysterious universe alludes to a "vast invisible sea of weightless and transparent stuff, present everywhere, undetected, through which we move, unsuspecting swimmers, and which moves through us, a silent, secret essence" (172), and reveals an enormous, elegant, unknowable universe. Ultimately, his intuitive sense mirrors the novel's own sophisticated intuition of an endlessly mirrored universe:

> Now he was speaking of the ancient light of galaxies that travels for a million—a billion—a trillion!—miles to reach us. "Even here," he said, "at this table, the light that is the image of my eyes takes time, a tiny time, infinitesimal, yet time, to reach your eyes, and so it is that everywhere we look, everywhere, we are looking into the past." (*AL*, 172)

This is reminiscent of the use of reflected images utilized elsewhere in Banville, especially apparent in many of the post-2000 novels. In *Eclipse*, for example, precisely at the moment in which Alex's real and actor selves collide and he freezes on stage, it as though he is mocked by the doubled figuration of his reflected image:

> While I gagged and sweated, the young fellow playing Mercury, who in the guise of Amphitryon's servant Sosia was supposed to be cruelly taunting me on the loss of my identity, stood transfixed behind plywood crenellations, looking down at me with terrified eyes in which I am convinced I could see myself doubly reflected, two tiny, bulbous Amphitryons, both struck speechless. (*E*, 89)

Such mirroring metaphorically speaks of the duplicity inherent in one's sense of being, frequently generating a sense of oneself simultaneously as primary subject *and* as othered object. At certain key moments this extends further to a more essential form of dislocation, like when Alex literally steps outside himself and witnesses him and Mrs. Gray in midsexual embrace:

> She began to say something, and stopped, and then—it was the strangest thing—then I saw us there, actually saw us, as if I were standing in the doorway looking into the room, saw me hunched

CHAPTER 4

> against her, canted a little to the left with my right shoulder lifted, saw the shirt wet between my shoulder-blades and the seat of my wet trousers sagging, saw my hands on her, and one of her glossy knees flexed, and her face paling above my left shoulder and her eyes staring. (*AL*, 219–20)

Here, he becomes his own subject, and the moment transfigures into a scene from a painting, attaining a state of existence that is distinct from the material event unfolding. In the intense moment of self-apprehension, the illuminated image achieves a life of its own. Furthermore, the moment is eerily similar, albeit from a different perspective, to that moment in *Shroud* where Cass imagines Alex standing in the doorway to the bedroom looking at she and Axel in bed (129), effecting yet another textual proliferation of ontological echoes and levels.

The generation of multiple layers of textual reality operates on several additional levels, most obviously via the manner in which the film adaptation of the life of Alex Vander, *The Invention of the Past*, functions in the novel. Mark O'Connell views the Vander book to be a classic *mise en abyme*[28] and, although we only have limited access to the fullness of the book, it does appear to be an embedded version of at least the Vander strain of the plot that operates on a subservient diegetic level. Nonetheless, *The Invention of the Past* is also more complex than this partly because Banville's blurring of the diegetic levels problematizes such distinctions. The irony inherent in the mirrored and anagrammatical characterization of Axel and Alex also extends to Banville, considering the way that Vander is characterized in the book—the author of an "arcane and coded specialism," echoing the way Banville is frequently characterized in reviews (*AL*, 54). Similarly, if *The Invention of the Past* is a version of *Shroud*, or the Cleave Trilogy, it too is written by Banville, or JB as we have it here. This represents an extension of the self-reflexive range of the text beyond Banville's already self-conscious body of work and emphasizes that the primary subject of the work is its own process of construction. This extends to the additional presence of Cass's papers in *Ancient Light*, which may be read as a partial *mise en abyme*, in this case reflecting the Cass plotline. Reading his daughter's papers, we are again alerted to the doubled nature of all text, replete with hidden meanings and coded signals:

> I wanted to believe that what looked like the frantic scribblings of a mind at its last extremity were really an elaborately encoded message meant for me, and for me alone. And there were places indeed where she seemed to be addressing me directly. In the end, however,

> wish as I might, I had to accept that it was not me she was speaking to but someone other, my surrogate, perhaps, shadowy and elusive. For there was another presence detectable in those pages, or better say a palpable absence, the shade of a shade, whom she addressed only and always under the name of Svidrigailov. (*AL*, 144)

Svidrigailov is Vander and is also a kind of figuration of Banville in his "frantic scribblings." While such observations remind us of the essentially playful mode of discourse that Banville is using, it also mirrors—as befits its role as *mise en abyme*—the complications of reading *Ancient Light* which speaks in layered codes.

The incessant marveling at how the world surrenders to the redemptive capacity of art continually reflects back on the Cleave novels as creative acts and as such they are radically advanced variations of the self-reflexive novel. Everything is fictionally doubled, being both itself as apparent plot and, simultaneously, as component of the deep web of elaborate Banvillean artifice. At one moment in *Eclipse*, for example, the Banvillean surface of familiar gestures and characters gives way and Alex finds himself somewhere other than the concrete sense he had previously thought he inhabited: "I have stepped through the looking-glass into another world" (*E*, 121), and in *Ancient Light*, Cleave entertains the possibility of "a world next to this one, contiguous with it, where there might linger somehow the spirits of those no longer here and yet not entirely gone, either" (*AL*, 20), a concept also included in *The Infinities* in Old Adam's many worlds theory (*TI*, 202). This perpetual sense of doubling is Banville's way of asserting the contiguity of the content of reality—the material subject matter—and an illuminated aestheticized universe. The empirically tangible resides in close proximity to the imaginatively transformed. Sometimes the veil falls and the essential insubstantiality of the fixed material fictions that we erect to generate order is exposed. By the Cleave novels this is an established pattern in Banville's work; things are as they are, and yet simultaneously other.

In these novels, rather than availing of science, history, or the visual arts as metaphoric parallels to address the implications of the role of the creative imagination, Banville instead places the fictive zone itself at the center of his focus, albeit occasionally facilitated by the acting metaphor that resonates on many levels in all three novels. The fictional ontology is itself the direct subject of its own imagining. The primary characters, and the landscapes in which they play out their meandering plots, are all marked with a quality of having already been aestheticized and transformed. The Cleave novels also represent a

CHAPTER 4

formal evolution of the self-reflexive novel by retaining the deeply self-referential problematization of the artistic process that had characterized the metafictional novel form in works like *At Swim-Two-Birds* and, indeed, *Nightspawn* and *Birchwood,* while nonetheless seeking to illuminate the material world which the self-reflexive mode appears to disavow or evade. This is a crucial distinction between Banville's mature work and postmodernism. His work never fully abandons the self-reflexive mode but it does progress beyond a direct demonstration of the *limits* of knowing, saying, and representing that one finds in many metafictional texts. It instead progressively seeks an integrated method that both acknowledges the limits of representation and illustrates the power of an artistically charged illumination of what we name the real. The novels themselves effectively become demonstrations of this power by virtue of their verbal artistry, or what Denis Donoghue calls artistic eloquence—the "play of words or other expressive means" which he sees as central to art.[29] Similarly, like the postmodernism from which it emerged, Banville's work largely retains devices like parody, playfulness, irony, and auto-referentiality, all in an effort to draw one's attention to the complex relationship between what we call reality and fiction while simultaneously asserting the centrality of the transformative power of art.

Typically, Banville's novels demonstrate the complex problem of writing fiction though the act of writing fiction, like many postmodern novels, but his deployment of a pattern of ideas, in the Cleave novels, derived from Russian formalists like Viktor Shklovsky and Roman Jakobson, adds a particular dimension to postmodern poetics by re-empowering an aesthetic narrative focus that is neither ironically utilized nor subverted in any way. For Jakobson, art defamiliarizes the world by revealing the essential strangeness of things[30]—which is precisely the process that Alex is engaged with in *Eclipse* as he seeks to make things "strange" (46). This, in turn, reflects the sense of a doubled universe that is increasingly explicit in *Eclipse* and thereafter. Alex's dislocated sense in *Eclipse* offers a clear indication of the dual presence of the world rendered strange, via aesthetic apprehension, and the material world, which it shadows: "I was in the kitchen. I might never have been here before. Or I might have been, but in a different dimension. Talk about making strange! Everything was askew. It was like entering backstage and seeing the set in reverse, all parts of it known but not where they should be. Where were my chalk marks now, my blocked-out map of moves?" (114). Similarly, in *Shroud*, Axel frequently experiences a sense of the oddness of the world and in doing so illuminates it: "I watched the disheartened landscape with its raked shadows fleeting past and was struck yet again by the strangeness of being here, of being anywhere, in the company of all these deceptive singularities" (*S*, 26). Such moments of aesthetic apprehension are frequently transferable in Banville's work, as Cass, in *Shroud*, demonstrates: "Everything was so strange, all pulled out of shape and littered with torn-up things, like a stretch of shoreline after a storm. This old, old man. All at once, as she stood there gazing down at him, he was not he, or he was he and also not. She frowned, trying to unravel it" (*S*, 119). The world is again revealed by registering a sense of the mystery of things—Banville's declared primary reason for creating art, after all.[31] The doubled nature of the world reveals its essential strangeness when the mere materiality of things yields to the pressure of the imagining, subjective mind. Or, as Elke D'Hoker observes, citing the Russian formalists with respect to Banville's work: "'Making strange,' or defamiliarization is then an eminently artistic process in which ordinary reality is made into something unfamiliar, uncanny or strange or, put differently, in which habitual perception is disturbed and another unusual quality of reality is revealed."[32] Banville's weaving of the Russian formalist aesthetic position into his deployment of the self-reflexive mode demonstrates the innate aestheticization of reality that his characters engage with. So, the self-reflexive mode does as it has always done: it reflects on the process of its own construction.

The difference now is that Banville's creative energies do not end in the subversion of the fictional mode but instead seek to permit the highly aestheticized form of the work of art a privileged place in the seemingly paradoxical context of the self-subversive form. He does this, in part, by significantly de-emphasizing the role of content—or, as he claimed of *Eclipse*: "I'm encouraged, somehow, by *Eclipse*: I think that it's as near as I've got to writing a book that has no real center."[33] Artistically, this places Banville in the same company as the decidedly un-postmodern Flaubert who famously aspired to write

> a book about nothing, a book dependent on nothing external, which would be held together by the strength of its style, just as the earth, suspended in the void, depends on nothing external for its support; a book which would almost have no subject, or at least in which the subject would be almost invisible, if such a thing is possible.[34]

The aim, of course, is that the work of art is responded to primarily as a work of art, as opposed to a vehicle for "meaning" of some kind. The Cleave novels

CHAPTER 4

endorse an aesthetic mode that both refers to itself as an art form and also demonstrates a *particular* kind of art form, one that in a circularity of artistic momentum itself invites one to focus primarily on the artistry, the eloquence.

The plot lines in the Cleave novels are increasingly thin, the evocation of an aestheticized doubled sense of material reality is more emphatically apparent, and the primary focus on the ways in which experience might be illuminated by somehow revealing its strangeness is raised to the status of primary focus in the novels. Everything serves this aim, from Alex Cleave's return to the house of his youth, to the plot mystery at the heart of Axel Vander's bogus life, and the curious temporal zone in *Ancient Light*, which Alex declares to be no more than a "luminous and everlasting present; alive to me yet lost, except in the frail afterworld of these words" (242), an afterworld of words that has been openly and repeatedly declared on every page on the novel.

Notes

1. Banville: "It's not really a trilogy. I mean it could be considered that way, but I didn't intend it that way. In fact, it's funny because now that you've said it it's the first time I've thought of it as part of a trilogy I've built in the references to previous books as a kind of game with myself, but it's certainly not necessary to have read the previous two books." Kevin Breathnach, "John Banville Interviewed," in *Totally Dublin*, June 28, 2012, http://totallydublin.ie/arts-culture/arts-culture-features/john-banville-interviewed/ (accessed September 31, 2016).
2. Patricia Coughlan, "Banville, the Feminine, and the Scenes of Eros," *Irish University Review* 36, no. 1 (Spring-Summer 2006): 95.
3. Ibid.
4. Hedda Friberg, "'[P]assing through Ourselves and Finding Ourselves in the Beyond': The Rites of Passage of Cass Cleave in John Banville's *Eclipse* and *Shroud*," special issue: John Banville, *Irish University Review* 36, no. 1 (Spring-Summer 2006): 154.
5. Hugh Haughton and Bryan Radley, "An Interview with John Banville," *Modernism/Modernity* 18, no. 4 (November 2011): 857.
6. Eoghan Smith, *John Banville: Art and Authenticity* (Oxford: Peter Lang, 2014), 118.
7. Mark O'Connell, *John Banville's Narcissistic Fictions* (London: Palgrave Macmillan, 2013), 175.
8. Ibid., 174. Given that O'Connell's book was written before the publication of *The Blue Guitar*, his point holds good. However, I contend that *The Blue Guitar* effectively outstrips all of Banville's previous fictions in terms of its close figurative relationship with the author.
9. Joan Acocella, "Doubling Down: John Banville's Complicated Lives," in *The New Yorker*, October 8, 2012, http://www.newyorker.com/magazine/2012/10/08/doubling-down (accessed August 31, 2016).

10. Arminta Wallace, "'I'm at Last Beginning to Learn How to Write, and I Can Let the Writing Mind Dream,'" in *The Irish Times*, June 30, 2012, http://www.irishtimes.com/culture/books/i-m-at-last-beginning-to-learn-how-to-write-and-i-can-let-the-writing-mind-dream-1.1069902 (accessed August 31, 2016).

11. Viktor Shklovsky, "Art as Technique," in *Russian Formalist Criticism: Four Essays*, ed. and trans. Lee T. Lemon and Marion J. Reis (Lincoln: University of Nebraska Press, 1965), 12.

12. Ibid.

13. Gordon Graham, *Philosophy of the Arts: An Introduction to Aesthetics* (New York: Routledge, 2007), 145.

14. Hedwig Schwall, "An Interview with John Banville," *European English Messenger* 6, no. 1 (1997): 18.

15. John Kenny, *John Banville* (Dublin: Irish Academic Press, 2009), 33.

16. Lene Yding Pedersen, "Revealing/Re-veiling the Past: John Banville's *Shroud*," *Nordic Irish Studies* 4 (2005): 137–55.

17. Rüdiger Imhof, "'The Problematics of Authenticity': John Banville's *Shroud*," in *ABEI Journal–The Brazilian Journal of Irish Studies*, no. 6 (June 2004): 106–7.

18. Kenny, *John Banville*, 33.

19. Imhof, "Problematics," 115

20. Ibid., 105.

21. Travis Elborough, "Fully Booked: Q & A with John Banville," *Picador*, June 29, 2012, http://www.picador.com/blog/june-2012/fully-booked-q-a-with-john-banville (accessed August 31, 2016).

22. Imhof, "Problematics," 105.

23. Haughton and Radley, "Interview with John Banville," 857.

24. Wallace, "'I'm at Last Beginning.'"

25. Axel, in *Eclipse*, also informs us that he is "living in the house of the dead" (London: Picador, 2000), 49.

26. Smith, *Art*, 172.

27. O'Connell, *John Banville's Narcissistic Fictions*, 176.

28. Ibid., 177.

29. Denis Donoghue, *On Eloquence* (New Haven: Yale University Press, 2008), 3.

30. Roman Jakobson, "Art as Technique."

31. Schwall, "An Interview with John Banville," 15. Banville suggests that the "only reason for doing art" is to "show the absolute mystery of things."

32. Elke D'Hoker, *Visions of Alterity: Representation in the Works of John Banville*, (Amsterdam-New York: Rodopi, 2004), 223.

33. Wallace, "'I'm at Last Beginning.'"

34. Gustave Flaubert, *The Letters of Gustave Flaubert: 1830–1857*, ed. and trans. Francis Steegmuller (Cambridge, MA: Belknap Press of Harvard University Press, 1982), 154.

5

John Banville and Heinrich von Kleist—The Art of Confusion

The Broken Jug, God's Gift, Love in the Wars, and *The Infinities*

JOHN BANVILLE'S ADAPTATIONS of Heinrich von Kleist's plays, *Der zerbrochne Krug* (1811), *Amphitryon* (1807), and *Penthesilea* (1808), as *The Broken Jug* (1994), *God's Gift* (2000), and *Love in the Wars* (2005), respectively, are perhaps unsurprising given the recurring intertextual presence of the German playwright's work in his fiction.[1] In as early a work as *Mefisto*, Kleist's work features as a central part of the allusive framework and in *Eclipse*, *Shroud*, and *Ancient Light*, it registers a significant presence in both the plots and in the use of acting and impersonation metaphors that proliferate in these novels. Furthermore, Banville has frequently indicated his high regard for Kleist's work in reviews and interviews, considering him to be "one of the great artists of the modern era."[2] Similarly, he has praised what he sees as Kleist's "unwavering clarity that at the heart of things there is always ambiguity"[3] in a glowing review of Martin Greenberg's translations of Kleist in 1988. He has also suggested that *Amphitryon* is "one of the great works of European literature" and views it as Kleist's "superb, dark masterpiece."[4] Banville's full acknowledgment of the influence of Kleist is, of course, most emphatically registered in the adaptations of the three plays and in his rewriting of *Amphitryon* in prose fictional form as *The Infinities* (2009).

The earliest evidence of Banville's interest in Kleist appears in part I of *Mefisto*, "Marionettes," which alludes to Heinrich von Kleist's "The Puppet Theatre."[5] Kleist's essay offers a compelling aesthetic argument for the unnatural gracefulness of the marionette, in contrast to the stiff materiality of human dancers. The marionettes, or puppets, "have the advantage of being resistant to gravity. Of the heaviness of matter, the factor that most works against the dancer, they are entirely ignorant: because the force lifting them into the air is greater than the one attaching them to the earth."[6] For Erich

CHAPTER 5

Heller, the primary significance of Kleist's essay is derived from the fact that "the marionette displays in its motions a grace that is wholly unaffected—unaffected, that is, by even the slightest trace of self-consciousness, a grace that is not obtainable by any man or woman."[7] Kleist's unself-conscious puppet movement is purely artificial and quite distinct from the materiality of man; in keeping with Banville's familiar pattern of infusing his own texts with the philosophical and aesthetic fascinations of other writers, thinkers, and intellectual discoverers, *Mefisto*'s Gabriel Swan similarly acquires a puppet-like aura in the nonrealist fabric of the novel. John Kenny observes that the first part of *Mefisto* ("Marionettes") "includes scenes with broken puppets and theatrical costumes, and in his narrative Swan repeatedly refers to himself as a 'Pinocchio' who is trying to be real."[8] In this one can discern relatively early indications of the aesthetic influence of Kleist on a body of fiction that would repeatedly engage with oppositions such as illusion and truth, and reality and appearance and, ultimately, a belief in confusion as a prime marker of human experience. Kleist's essay is essentially a parable about the possibility of graceful movement and about the inhibitions generated by self-consciousness. Its importance to Banville cannot be overstated, particularly in the way its central opposition percolates throughout much of his writing. On many occasions hereafter when puppets are alluded to, Kleist's essay is the guiding spirit: Freddie in *The Book of Evidence* refers to his life as "all that puppet-show twitching which passes for consciousness" (38) and the representation of the character Victor Delahaye, in Benjamin Black's *Vengeance*,[9] is similarly offered in puppet-like terms: "He was looking all around, trying to see in all directions. He almost laughed to think of himself, like a wooden doll, his head spinning and his eyes starting in fright. Always, behind everything, there was a part of him that stood back skeptically" (150). Always, it might be added, Banville's characters slip in and out of such self-consciously invented moments and catch themselves gazing at their own images.

In similar terms, in *Eclipse*, Alex Cleave expresses *his* aesthetic fascination by spying on an unaware naked girl from his window: "The unadorned grave beauty of her movements was, it pained the performer in me to acknowledge, inimitable: even if I spent a lifetime in rehearsal I could not hope to aspire to the thoughtless elegance of this girl's most trivial gesture" (101). Banville's long-term fascination with Kleist's "The Puppet Theatre" is again clearly evident; the narrator is besotted by the absence of self-consciousness in the girl, by the objective grace that is unaffected by a consciousness of the external gaze. The fictive universe, it is implied, has its own world-rules and, in certain moments of unconscious abandon, the residue of human self-consciousness evaporates and one witnesses a purity of action usually denied to human beings—in this the marionette or puppet, for Kleist and Banville, was a perfect example of unconscious aesthetic expression.

A further demonstration of the aesthetic assimilation of Kleist in Banville's work is registered in the fact that Cleave had been an actor who froze on stage while playing the part of Amphitryon. It is a doubled moment of almost total loss of self, precisely at the point in Kleist's *Amphitryon* (or Banville's ironically titled *God's Gift*) when the main character, bewildered completely by the machinations of the Gods, has lost any precise definition of himself. Cleave dramatically offers an insight to his collapse as follows: "'Who if not I, then, is Amphitryon?' I cried—it is now for me the most poignant line in all drama—and suddenly everything shifted on to another plane and I was at once there and not there" (*E*, 89). Cleave's focus on this essentially ontological question in *Eclipse* becomes, as we shall see, a central facet of Banville's later adaptations of Kleist but it is also a line that frequently resonates throughout Banville's novels. In response to Kleist's line—"And who, except me is Amphitryon?"[10]—Cleave delivers his tortured version in *Eclipse* (89), and Max also offers his variations in *The Sea*: "Who, if not ourselves, were we? All right, leave Anna out of it. Who, if not myself, was I?" (217). In *The Infinities*, itself an adaptation of *Amphityron*, the line is toyed with in several ways, like when Helen wonders, "Who if not her husband was that monstrous man" (56) and later asks him "When you return, who will you be but you?" (60). In all cases the key issue is that of identity and, in turn, of phenomenological being, both in terms of their roles as characters within the fictional storyworld and as an expression of the limits of knowing oneself.

Other playful allusions to Kleist's work proliferate in many of Banville's novels. For example, the use of the letter "A." to designate Athena, or Art, in *Athena* (1995), echoes the comic and deceptive identity-play with the letters "A," for Amphitryon, and "J," for Jupiter, in Kleist's *Amphitryon* (97–98). There are numerous references to marionettes and puppets throughout Banville's work and his fascination with the Kleistean marionette also extends to the Benjamin Black novels; Inspector Hackett, of the Quirke novels, is repeatedly referred to in terms reminiscent of a marionette, while Phoebe, in *Christine Falls*,[11] stands with her "head bowed and her arms hanging at her side, herself a slack-stringed marionette" (189), and Leslie, from *The Silver Swan*,[12] is described as "long and gangly, with a stooping, sinuous, flat-footed gait, his long pale hands swinging at the ends of his arms as if they were connected to

CHAPTER 5

his wrists not by bone but skin alone" (91). Furthermore, several characters from the novels are explicitly involved in Kleist's work. Vander is said to have completed work on Kleist in his earlier career (*S*, 62) and Cass has also worked on Kleist. Alex isn't the only actor to play Kleist; Helen plays Alcmene (or "Alceme," as she declares it) but, in yet another intertextual pirouette, in Banville's translation of *Amphityron, God's Gift* which is set in Vinegar Hill. Less directly, as Hedda Friberg-Harnesk has observed:

> The masks and disguises of spy, actor, and impostor make opaque the worlds of John Banville's novels of roughly the past decade. In *The Untouchable* (1997), *Eclipse* (2000), *Shroud* (2002) and *The Infinities* (2009), issues of duplicity, the instability of identity, the trickery of memory, and the uncertain nature of reality, come to the fore.[13]

One could add *Ancient Light*, given Alex's musings on his old failure of self-expression as an actor of Kleist, and *The Blue Guitar* (2015), in which Oliver is both a thief and a deceiver. Given Banville's perpetual interests in split and mirrored selves, doubled realities, and epistemological confusion, Kleist's parallel fascinations offer a kindred philosophical frame, even if both writers are formally distinct.

Both *The Broken Jug* and *Love in the Wars* offer intriguing insights into how certain aspects of Banville's aesthetic, via Kleist, find expression on stage. While these two plays are less radically assimilated into Banville's novels than is *Amphityron*, there are clear resonances in both that speak to his broader aesthetic sense. Both plays, for example, reference other dramatic texts and frequently break the fourth wall, a dramatic variation on Banville's self-reflexive aesthetic. In *The Broken Jug*, Judge Adam responds to Lynch's sarcasm about suspending his disbelief by suggesting that there is "no better place to do that, friend, than here" (24), and several characters in *Love in the Wars* dismissively comment on the excessive performativity that they witness on stage (66, 70). Both plays also derive their dramatic energies from a fluidity of self, identity, impersonation, and pretense, all of which points to the creation of a doubled sense of being on the part of the major characters. In both plays there is a marked difference between the apparent and the real and much of the humor and pathos emerges from the tensions between these differences. In turn, this tension generates the unique form of strangeness that one finds throughout Kleist, in which the apparent world is forever presented as a mask to a simultaneously present oddness, a quality that Fattori equates with the Freudian *das Unheimliche* while explaining Banville's interest in Kleist.[14] Perhaps as a gentle parody of Friel's Ballybeg,[15] Banville situates his version of *The Broken Jug* in Ballybog, establishing a textualized context rather than a concretely real one. Again, the distinction between the real and the apparent is registered. While Fattori suggests that the play displays a "social concern" which is not found in the original Kleist, and thus sees evidence of "once again Banville's concern with Irish issues"[16]—primarily because of the attention the impoverished natives are given in the stage directions, and via oblique references in the dialogue—it is important to remember that stage directions don't appear on stage and, if anything, this amounts to a de-emphasis of the social setting. In fact, there is scant attention paid, beyond a few scattered references to any nuanced sense of a social reality, with much of the focus being directed at the identity confusion that envelops the major characters.

More persuasively, Fattori points to the Kantian distinction between "the *Phenomenon*, the world as it appears and as we experience it," and "the *Noumenon*, the world as it really is (the thing-in-itself, *das Ding an sich*)" a distinction that she suggests governs much of Kleist's work, including *The Broken Jug*.[17] Thus, while Kleist's and Banville's plays conclude in apparent resolution, this may be viewed as being indicative of the world-as-Phenomenon, or as Schein (appearance), while the truth of things remains concealed. In reality, as a result of the action of the play, certain wounds have been opened that cannot be closed—Eve no longer trusts Robert and makes it clear that whatever she did, it was for her own good, not his—and a barely visible uncertainty lingers beneath the surface. In fact, as Fattori points out, the closing to Banville's version is, if anything, even less reconciled than Kleist's, with the final stage directions even suggesting an odd complicity between Eve and the Judge. The closing stage directions read as follows: "Eve says nothing, slowly moves to the door, where she pauses and glances back at JUDGE ADAM, who lifts his head and returns her glance."[18] The barely contained social model momentarily displays a fissure in its veneer, only to again recede into silence, more Beckett than Kleist in its final ringing echo.

Banville's version of Kleist's *Penthesilea—Love in the Wars*—similarly pivots on the difficulty of knowing one's self or other, and the passionate furies that such a struggle provokes. Mohammad Kowsar usefully points to Kleist's radical rewriting of the legend in which he has the Amazon queen, Penthesilea, murder the love-struck Achilles, unlike all earlier versions, in which Penthesilea is brutally murdered,[19] and Banville fully adopts this female-focused emphasis. For Kowsar, this represents a de-emphasis of the contextualizing legend and an energized refocusing on what he terms a "remorseless eroticism."[20]

CHAPTER 5

Certainly, much of the action revolves around a highly charged sequence of battles between Achilles and Penthesilea in swift succession, accompanied by several shifts in attitude to each other, from hostility, to surrender, to devotion, followed ultimately by deception and death. The speed of the action, as well as the rapid shifts in emotional positioning generates a powerful uncontrolled quality to the play, in which the two primary characters appear to have little concrete sense of themselves and appear bathed in confusion from the moment they first meet. As Mahlendorf argues, both Penthesilea and Achilles struggle to maintain "a cohesive sense of self" throughout.[21] *Amphitryon*, and Banville's *God's Gift*, are also framed against a powerful poetics of confusion. Much of the action is based around the lack of fixed coherence that ultimately underpins our sense of ourselves.

Banville has specifically deployed Kleist's *Amphitryon* throughout his later work, particularly in the Cleave novels, but it is also the framing myth that underpins *The Infinities*. His reasons for doing so appear obvious, given the way in which Kleist's play is dominated by impersonation, dissolving identities or, as Hugh Haughton has described it, *Amphitryon* is a "grotesque hall of mirrors, it is a tragic-comic study of real people usurped by actors, actors who in this instance happen to be gods."[22] While *The Broken Jug* and *God's Gift* both clearly resonate with Banville's fiction and offer useful insights to his fascination and interconnectedness with Kleist, his adaptation, or version, of *Amphitryon*, and subsequent rewriting of both his own version, and Kleist's, in *The Infinities* serves as another marked developmental stage in Banville's evolving aesthetic. In both of these texts (*God's Gift* and *The Infinities*), Banville raises the acting and deception motifs to more profound levels of ontological confusion than previously, while simultaneously permitting the narrator Hermes a central artistic role as detached observer of human existence in the novel.

God's Gift and *The Infinities* are significantly different versions of Kleist's play, itself an adaptation of Molière's comic version of the Greek myth. Thus, several interpretative shifts, from Kleist to Banville, and from drama to fiction present themselves as questions of critical significance. Banville's double appropriation of the tale establishes a deeply resonant texture that exceeds any simple notions of adaptation and also offers an opportunity to evaluate the relative merits of Banville's prose and dramatic rendering of Kleist. Kleist's own reconstruction, or "reworking" of Molière too is significant; according to David Constantine, his version differs most clearly from that of his predecessor in its infusion of serious subject matter in what was essentially a ribald comedy, a seriousness that is primarily located in the "developed character of Alcmene and, as in *Jug*, it is incongruous in a context of coarse comedy."[23] In turn, it is also necessary to consider the implications involved in the multiadaptive move from Kleist's *Amphitryon* to Banville's *God's Gift*, and thereafter to *The Infinities*. Banville's adaptation of Kleist, or his "version," as the subtitle to *God's Gift* declares, offers insights to his tacit approval of Kleist's specific focus but also reveals some key ways in which he overwrites Kleist.

This has implications for what E. L. Doctorow means when he argues for the cultural and historical translatability of Kleist's drama: "A Kleist play may be set in ancient Greece, in Holland, or in seventeenth-century Prussia, but the fortress of consciousness is where the action occurs; inevitably, the walls are breached and the ramparts overrun."[24] The inherent significance of the dramatic enactment lies not in its representational value but in the deeper capacity to illuminate the more fundamental question of being—embodied in Amphitryon's (or Ashburningham's) ontological confusion. The primary significance of Kleist's *Amphitryon* and Banville's *God's Gift* lies precisely in the inherently unnerving tension of Doctorow's "fortress of consciousness." Despite several commentators noting the historical and cultural significance of Banville's *God's Gift* being set in Ireland in 1798,[25] and his *The Broken Jug* being set in the Irish Famine,[26] Kleist's work is primarily of interest to Banville not because it offers him a plot to imbue with social or ideological implications but because of a shared sense of the essential strangeness of human existence, or as Kleist claimed in a late letter: "The world is a strange set-up. And we are not at home in it. God, if he exists, is incomprehensible. . . . There seems to be some mismatch between the way we are and the way the universe is constituted."[27] He also claimed that "everything in me is confusion," while Constantine argues that this is also embodied in Kleist's characters: "Their confusion is legendary. Their patterns fail them; playing familiar roles they discover that the lines no longer make much sense. The usual categories collapse."[28] Constantine could have been writing of Banville's characters' similar confusion, or as Freddie Montgomery of *The Book of Evidence* puts it: "I have never really got used to being on this earth. Sometimes I think our presence here is due to a cosmic blunder, that we were meant for another planet altogether, with other arrangements, and other laws, and other, grimmer skies" (26–27). Banville insists that this is one of the few true statements he has made in a novel.[29] Similarly, with respect to *Amphitryon*, Goethe argued that "Kleist, in his delineation of the main character, aims for a confusion of emotions."[30] The philosophical and comic energy of both Kleist's and Banville's Amphitryon plays lies in the demonstration of, and exploitation of, a relentless ontological confusion and

CHAPTER 5

loss of a coherent sense of self. Granted, this is predicated on the primary narrative level of a comic gesture derived from a marauding Greek God but the metaphorical power of the myth, for both Banville and Kleist, lies in the world of the fraught mind, or Doctorow's "fortress of consciousness," rather than in the literal immediacy of the represented context on stage.

On its most obvious level, Banville's version simply registers another way to permit Kleist's resonance to be felt in his intertextual universes. In some respects, however, *God's Gift* both extends and reframes Kleist's *Amphitryon*. Firstly, as Friberg-Harnesk points out in some detail, the transference of the Theban wars to an Irish setting is a fundamental adjustment, as is the renaming of some of the central characters: "Amphitryon and his wife Alcmene, of Kleist's play, become the English General Ashburningham and Lady Minna; the servant Sosias and his wife Charis become Souse and Kitty."[31] However, the reconstitution of Thebes to Wexford and the Theban wars to the 1798 rebellion is perhaps not necessarily as significant as first appears to be the case. The retention of Mercury and Jupiter inevitably universalizes the context and Banville's version, while historically specific, is far less detailed than Kleist's and rarely extends beyond a backdrop. In fact, some of the Ireland-specific references are indicative of typically Banvillean anachronistic play, as is the case with the reference to the song "The Auld Triangle," from Brendan Behan's play *The Quare Fellow* (1954), which is mentioned by Mercury: "Let's go and see the rebels being flogged/And hear the old triangle jingle-jangle" (23). The historically specific 1798 setting could not have featured a Behan song but the cross-temporality of Mercury transcends all limits, as is often the case in Banville's intertextual universes.

Secondly, Banville also makes far more extensive use of stage directions in a few key areas as a narrative device than does Kleist. Rarely extending beyond very basic scene-setting in Kleist, the stage directions in Banville, perhaps typically for a novelist (Beckett's precise and elaborate use of stage directions looms large), occasionally offer more detail, some of which allude to Banville's prose fictions. For example, the directions at the beginning of scene 2 make reference to "golden light" (18) as a quite dramatic depiction of events is provided. A few lines later, Jupiter himself tells Minna that "this day that's starting now will be/A day out of your days, a golden day,/The light of which will burn throughout your days" (21), and Minna herself refers to having been upon "some golden mountaintop" (*GG*, 35). The golden world, or *Le monde d'or*, is also the painting that radiates at the center of Banville's *Ghosts*, and is ascribed to the fake painter, Vaublin. The descriptions of *Le monde d'or* in *Ghosts* speak of an otherworldly existence, of an artistically framed world, pastoral in imagery, godly in appearance, that Freddie aspires to. As Joseph McMinn claims, "*Le monde d'or* serves as a kind of visual parable of Freddie's world, a landscape, even an escape, he yearns for, but one which he will never enjoy."[32] So in *God's Gift*, Banville finds a way to infuse his narrative with allusions to his extended house of prose fiction, and simultaneously manages to generate a similar sense of nonrealist fictive otherness that one finds so often in the novels. To extend the thought one step further, we realize that if the golden world in the play is intertextually invented by the fake painter Vaublin (Banville), then the depiction of the landscape is effectively a self-reflexive acknowledgment of the novelist's own artistry. Kleist's *Amphitryon* is not framed against such intertextual echoes.

There are other differences between the two plays: Banville's *God's Gift* is a significantly truncated version of Kleist's play, offering two acts rather than three; in particular there is a diminishing of emphasis on the heavy comic play between Sosias and Mercury in the opening scenes and a stripping away of detail pertaining to the war and the role of the citizens and officers in the final scene. Furthermore, while Banville's Minna remains relatively prominent, she is certainly less so than Kleist's Alcmene, particularly in the closing scenes. Crucial too are the respective differences between the endings; in Banville, there is far greater emphasis on the differences between the worlds of Gods and men, with Mercury sneeringly referring to the human world as the "(With a contemptuous wave) bright world of beauty, hope and joy," only for Jupiter to reply that the human world is "warmer, though, than our cold lifeless Heaven" (*GG*, 72). The distinction between worlds extends beyond the literal heaven/earth opposition in Banville's version, with numerous references to a distinction between the real and the artistically constructed, with Souse, from the outset, remarking that "The sun appeared, and then went down again,/ As if some hand had pulled it by a string" (11). Similarly, there are several instances of direct address to, or gazing at, the audience (16, 65) as Banville self-reflexively breaks the fourth wall, in keeping with his novelistic narrative habits, while characters are frequently described as artistically conceived entities like statues (46) and paintings:

> He seemed a living portrait of himself,
> A Painting by a master, showing him
> Exactly as he is and yet transformed!
> Standing there, he was—I don't know what:
> A dream; a fantasy; and yet a man. (51)

CHAPTER 5

God's Gift extends the Kleist version with the familiar Banvillean usage of metaphorical structures (science in the tetralogy, art in the Frames Trilogy, acting in the three Cleave novels, and painting in *The Sea*) and the play thus becomes a commentary on the difference between the theatrical and the real. A play in which many of the main characters are either acting, or being acted to, or are unsure of their own selves, is perfect subject matter for a novelist whose work has always been populated by figures who pursue self-reflexive theatrical existences in worlds that are self-evidently staged. The fact that Banville eventually chose to rewrite his own adaptation of Kleist's *Amphitryon*, as *The Infinities*, testifies to his residing interest in the imaginative possibilities of the mythic frame and also suggests that there were other, unfulfilled, possibilities that might be explored in prose fiction.

The direct implications of working in the dramatic form are, in Banville's case, more pronounced in *God's Gift* than in his other Kleist dramatic renderings. This is so because the compelling concerns in the play more comprehensively resemble the central fascinations of much of Banville's prose fiction. The fundamentally different narrative properties of drama and fiction, ensure that the embodiment of the Amphitryon story in *The Infinities* and *God's Gift* necessarily takes quite different shape in each form. Daniel K. Jernigan, with respect to Stoppard's plays (as opposed to his only novel *Lord Malquist and Mr. Moon*) for example points to the "decidedly complex tightness and completeness" of the plays (146).[33] Alternatively, Rabinowitz suggests that "In terms of audience dynamics, narrative is more complex than drama."[34] In a sense, both of them are accurate, particularly in terms of itemizing genre-specific narrative attributes. More specifically, H. Porter Abbott points out that the move from fiction to stage (and film) involves, in one sense, a reduction in narrative content: "Adaptation to the shorter, continuous forms of stage and screen is, then, a surgical act," although this may enhance the clarity of the key issues because the "finished form" may depict what "readers of the novel often find themselves struggling to understand: the story's constituent events. We see much more clearly than in the novel how one event leads to the next. . . ."[35] This struggle to understand is, somewhat paradoxically, key to Banville's aesthetic in *The Infinities*. While he has suggested that *Amphitryon* is really just retained in skeletal form in *The Infinities*,[36] it is nevertheless clear that the "constituent events" in Kleist's and Banville's dramas, and in *The Infinities*, are directly intertwined with the ontological confusion at the heart of the lead characters; the narrative method may differ but the central issues remain consistent. However, given the distinctly different narrative focuses of drama and fiction, there are significant adjustments made to the artistic framing of the subject matter. *God's Gift* explicitly foregrounds acting, or pretending, and the doubled-impact of being presented on stage amplifies the effect by generating an implied self-consciousness rather than the direct diegetic intrusion more familiar to Banville's novels. In addition, the rapid temporal momentum in a play that already features ample amounts of confusion and misapprehension significantly adds to the audience impact, precisely because it is focused in a containable theatrical space that largely confirms to the Aristotelian unities. Thickets of ontological shifts, varied narrative points of view, and plot convolutions, on the other hand, characterize its prose fictional counterpart, *The Infinities*. The impact of each form is decidedly different with the tightly focused mayhem of the theatrical mode capable of a more immediate, disorientating effect. Still, the narrative dynamics of each form are simply different. In both forms we find that what W. Michelle Wang terms "a synthesis of its thematic and stylistic qualities (or the medium's particularities),"[37] is generated, and each set of particularities impact on the reader or audience is different ways.

Abbott's distinction between film and prose fiction is instructive in this context, with the attributes of film resembling those of drama for him: he argues that film (and drama) in adaptation acts as an interpretive gesture of a novel by emphasizing "the story's *constituent events*"[38] and argues that "the story line move[s] with greater clarity and simplicity in a film." Abbott's different generic properties are useful to consider how Banville's reexploration of *Amphitryon* (and *God's Gift*) in *The Infinities* differ: "One way to describe the difference [between novels and films] is the quality and degree of retardation, or the slowing down of the narrative discourse that the media can tolerate." He adds that film's "tolerance is much more restricted than that of novels" and the audience cannot tolerate the expansiveness of the novel form on stage, although he does concede that much "figurative flexibility" is also lost in drama.[39] Porter Abbott's observation holds good for prose fictions that are heavily dependent on the allegorical or metaphorical implications of complex plots, and the sophisticated narrative form and less condensed treatment of temporal sequence of *The Infinites* largely correspond to Abbot's observations about prose fiction. However, the distinctions between drama and prose are not necessarily always so starkly delineated. While Keir Elam, for example, has argued that drama is "mimetic rather than strictly diegetic"[40] in its narrative logic, Bartosz Lutostański, with reference to Beckett's *Molloy*, has challenged the notion that the diegetic and the mimetic are binary opposites. He instead

CHAPTER 5

argues that novels like *Molloy* should be considered "excessively mimetic" rather than diegetic because "mimetic principles penetrate and permeate each and every aspect of the novel leading to the generation of a 'theatrical' semantic, which, to some degree, approximates theatre."[41] The declarative narrative presences of Banville's narrator-voices are similar to those that we find in Beckett's novels, although without the same degree of progressive syntactic and sequential disruption. His narrators have always been less characterized by a diegetic desire to name and explain than to performatively demonstrate their progressive failings in monological terms. Thus, in some senses, the shift to the dramatic form may be viewed as retaining what was already a performative impulse. *God's Gift* too retains many of the essential core fascinations than one finds in the novels: reality and fiction; impersonations or fakes; confusion at the world's strangeness; ontological uncertainty; and the breakdown of knowledge systems. The direct audience impact of *God's Gift*'s treatment of such matters is, given the immediacy and condensed form of drama, more direct, but the novel form is not entirely bereft of the theatrical deployment of ostension (or showing forth). Because the voice in Banville's prose monologues (notice how little dialogue there is in most of his novels) has always been essentially performative rather than diegetic, the novels have always felt closer to drama. In fact, the plot elements of his versions of Kleist have rather less of the monologue properties of the plays, which carry over much of Kleist's intricate plotting.

It is clear why Banville has always found in Kleist a kindred artistic and philosophical voice, a fellow champion of the idea that existence is defined, in its truest form, by the way we negotiate our ways through labyrinths of confusion, and not by seeking merely to resolve confusion into order. That ontological confusion is contextualized quite differently in Banville's use of drama and prose fiction: the performative impact of ontological confusion and identity erasure works particularly well on stage, especially because of the latent self-consciousness than is generated. While *The Infinities* is not an adaptation, it certainly engages with the same core elements and arguably manages to convey a more profound sense of the complexity of ontological confusion by virtue of its multiple narrative levels. One of the achievements of Banville's multitextured prose fictional world is the sense that existence itself is inherently mysterious in ways that extend far beyond the overt actions of characters. Nonetheless, Brian Richardson, arguing for a distinct narrative poetics of drama, insightfully suggests that the performative nature of drama radically impacts on the notion of representation in the work:

> [H]earing words being uttered in an auditorium defamiliarizes the more usual (and usually mimetic) conventions of representation. Likewise, deep traditions of stylization (verse drama, and so on), nonillusionistic theater (for example, asides), and the material conditions of the playing space (lighting effects, coughing) all work against the illusion of representation.[42]

The otherness that is created via Richardson's defamiliarized dramatic representation is a special attribute of theater that distances one from realism no matter how authentic the representative zeal aspires to be. But Banville's fiction also offers an array of defamiliarizing and self-reflexive techniques, including a perpetual sense of the theatrical, that serve to deflate any sense of realist representation. The distinctions, while certain, may not be as oppositional and distinct as is sometimes suggested.

Banville's *The Infinities* doesn't simply reinterpret and transplant the same story; it enlarges the metaphorical possibilities offered by Kleist's dramatic model by adjusting the emphasis of the role of Mercury (here named Hermes). By adding several alternative narrative layers, permitting both young Adam, via free indirect discourse, and old Adam, via first person narration, to offer their perspectives, it also expands the cast of central characters and, crucially, it more fully situates the events of the basic plot in Banville's complex, allusive fictive universe. In *The Infinities* the motif of the house is again used in a self-reflexive manner:

> They round a bend and the house comes into view. Really it is, Adam sees, not for the first time, an impossible sort of folly, square and mad-looking, with its yellow-painted walls and pale-blue shutters and that winged tin figure—ahem!—atop the single turret. Viewed from this perspective the entire structure seems to lean slightly to one side, drunkenly. (*TI*, 105)

Populating the "mad-looking" house are cast members who are familiar from other Banville novels; the vaguely demonic Benny Grace, with "goatish hoofs" (177) is a reincarnation of Carlo Grace, "a grinning goat god" (125) in *The Sea* who was, in turn, a revised version of Felix, and several others. There are numerous references to clowns, a familiar presence in Banville; even young Adam and Petra, are dressed in "clownishly ill-fitting pairs of pyjamas" from their childhood (*TI*, 11), and Old Adam is both a character in the novel and is yet simultaneously resonant of other figures from Banville's work, and from art more generally: "In an armchair facing this irate godhead Adam sits, hapless and distracted, his hands resting limply in his lap with palms upturned,

CHAPTER 5

like one of the *commedia dell'arte*'s mournful clowns" (*TI*, 124). Availing of a familiar set of artistic allusions, the narrator Hermes also asks, "Is it not a quaint scene?—a moment out of Watteau, it might be, these figures about their ambiguous business, in uncertain light, as the day wanes" (264). And, like *God's Gift*'s allusion to Banville's *Ghosts*, via *Le monde d'or*, *The Infinities* frequently makes direct references to Banville's fictional universe. Cheekily alluding to *Birchwood*, for instance, we are told that the peculiarly childlike Petra is "nineteen and so much younger than her years, and yet possessed too of an awful ancientness—'That one,' Granny Godly used to say of her darkly, 'that one has been here before'" (9). Granny Godly is also clearly a reincarnation of Granny Godkin from the early novel. She is correct about Petra who is certainly "possessed of an awful ancientness"; she has been in Banville's world before, as Flora, as Cass Cleave, and many other female figures whose recurring expressions of otherness are as constant as any other feature in his work. Furthermore, we are informed that Ivy Blount had originally sold the house to Adam Godley: "She clings on in a two-storey cottage at the corner of a crooked field where the gates to the property once stood" (39). The house, with its gate lodge, is yet another reconstituted version of the houses in *Birchwood* and *The Newton Letter*.

All of this intertextual play serves primarily to remind one of the essentially invented landscapes that one inhabits and, as always in Banville, the world appears to coalesce into an invented visual universe of paintings. Hermes even guides us to see the world in such a fashion at one point:

> What a striking tableau we must have made, a genre scene by one of the minor Dutch masters, me in the bright doorway and she in the smouldering dimness of the room and the still-life chicken on the table; look at the cat, the crockery on the dresser, delph, they call it—from Delft!—the red and black floor-tiles, and that glimpse of the sunlit day behind me in the door, mute and calm as money. Poor Ivy braced a hand on the table to support herself and looked at me with a look so needy and defenseless even I experienced a qualm. Something to say? I had nothing to say. I was just amusing myself, toying with one of my creatures, as so often is the way.
>
> Turning to go, I nodded in the direction of the jug. "That milk," I said, "is gone sour." (*TI*, 87–88)

Apart from the familiar (for Banville) allusion to Dutch still-life portraits, the final remark is a playful reference to Vermeer's *The Milkmaid* (1657–1658)—the milk is sour because it has been still for so long in that other universe of art that we frequent so often in Banville's work, in that "for ever now" perpetual present, as Cheeke has it.[43]

All such devices and games demonstrate the manner in which many diverse interrelated elements are woven into the texture of Banville's temporally and spatially fictional multilayered worlds. His godlike figures, Hermes, Benny Grace, Zeus himself, all contribute an obvious extra-real dimension but it is in the multitextured world of art that Banville's universes acquire their true complex identities. Hermes may be a god but figures like old Adam, himself a revenant from numerous Banvillean parables about the creative imagination, exhibit the ghostly behavior of the reborn (from other texts)—they are themselves *and* other, simultaneously:

> A plain steel desk and a bentwood chair, a block of graph paper in loose sheets and a plentiful supply of pencils, of course, his famous Ticonderogas No. 4, extra hard, yellow with a green band and pink eraser, specially imported by the boxful; these are, were, the tools of his trade, the implements of the Arcanum. When he was famous first, caricaturists pictured him as a monk in a windowless bare cell, wild-eyed and hydrocephalic, hunched with his pencil over a gridded page of parchment; also as a spaceman in a globular helmet popping out of a hole in the sky. (43)

He could be any number of Banville heroes, or Banville himself perhaps, in a novel that is saturated with various self-referential comments and casual asides.

The manner in which Kleist's *Amphitryon* is folded into the narrative of the novel is exploited in several distinct ways. Helen is playing "Alceme" in a version of Kleist which, she says "could have been set here" (192) in the house—which, in a sense it is, although her self-reflexive consciousness doesn't extend to this level of awareness. The version that she is playing is John Banville *God's Gift*, set in Vinegar Hill during the 1798 rebellion, but she also references Kleist's version. Roddy, however, cautions her that Old Adam, the creator wouldn't have approved of tampering with the classics (192), a wry moment of self-conscious humor on Banville's part. In addition, the scientific model of old resurfaces to strike a self-reflexive note when Benny Grace dismissively summarizes Old Adam's aspiration "that it should be possible to write equations across the many worlds, incorporating their infinities, see, and therefore all those other dimensions" (*TI*, 202), suggestive of Banville's metaphorical transference across doubled fictional spaces. Hermes too extends a sense of the world as multifarious, doubled, and the trickster role of the gods which is, for Banville, synonymous with the strange unpredictability of art:

CHAPTER 5

> To us your world is what the world in mirrors is to you. A burnished, crystalline place, sparkling and clear, with everything just as it is on this side, only reversed, and infinitely unreachable. A looking-glass world, indeed, and only that. Hence our melancholy, our mischievousness, too—oh, to put a fist to that blank pane and burst through to the other side! But all we would meet is mercury. Mercury! My other name, one of my other names. (*TI*, 260–1)

The manner in which certain elements bleed across the generic differences between *God's Gift* and *The Infinities* also augments a sense of the deliberately fictional. The theatricality of Banville's prose fictional world is immediately obvious, from clownish dressing to puppet-like movements—Ivy Blount and Duffy the cowman, for example, are "a faded Columbine and her rustic Harlequin" (298)—to numerous references to performances and imitations. At one point Hermes suggests that,

> Adam feels light-headed, weightless, seeming to float an inch above the floor. He supposes it is to do with the supply of oxygen to the brain, or lack of it. His sister is right, he is not used to being up at this hour—*everything is different*—when the world looks like an imitation of itself, cunningly crafted yet discrepant in small but essential details. (*TI*, 13)

The fact that many of the characters are acting, or pretending, also resonates with the theatrical inheritance, as does the general sense of contrivance that Hermes generates, even before the "happy faun" (177), Benny Grace, arrives to add further layers of illusion and disruption. Zeus too perpetrates his godly deception in disguised relations with Helen, as in Kleist's original, although its significance is somewhat diminished in the novel, becoming simply another facet of a complex web of disguise and performativity.

Banville's fiction, including *The Infinities*, is always comprised of a multiplicity of narrative threads that defy any simple notion of extracting key constituent elements. It is clear why Banville has found in Kleist a kindred artistic and philosophical voice. The way that ontological confusion is contextualized in prose fiction here seems more potent in its execution, primarily because the form of Banville's novel is more complex. One of the achievements of Banville's multitextured fictional world is the sense that existence itself is inherently mysterious in ways that extend far beyond the overt actions of characters. For example, near the close of *The Infinities*, Hermes, Banville's expression of the creative imagination in the novel, offers a final statement about the world that we have just encountered:

This is the mortal world. It is a world where nothing is lost, where all is accounted for while yet the mystery of things is preserved; a world where they may live, however briefly, however tenuously, in the failing evening of the self, solitary and at the same time together somehow here in this place, dying as they may be and yet fixed forever in a luminous, unending instant. (300)[44]

In the dense verbal tapestries of Banville's nonrealist, richly complex worlds, the aesthetically reconceived surface reality is sought and articulated. The dramatic texts of both Banville and Kleist depict a confusion of self, and the overt strangeness of the human capacity to grasp the complexity of being. The dramatic form well illustrates the comedy and tragedy of our tentative grasp on the existences that we laud so highly. But *The Infinities* takes us beyond the confusion of self, it guides us through the maddening labyrinths of existence that offer context to our confusion. The essentially insubstantial nature of being begins to lose focus in Banville's poetical fictions and for all the world-depiction that is possible, for all the immediacy and the here-and-now qualities of drama, it may well be that, in certain instances, the novel form, as conceived by Banville at least, may offer a more comprehensively imagined metaphor for a world that has no boundaries, and that has confusion at the very core of its ontology.

Notes

1. Banville, *God's Gift: A Version of Amphitryon by Heinrich von Kleist* (Oldcastle: Gallery, 2000); *Love in the Wars: After Kleist's Penthesilea* (Oldcastle: Gallery, 2005).
2. Hedwig Schwall, "An Interview with John Banville," *European English Messenger* 6, no. 1 (1997): 14.
3. John Banville, "The Helpless Laughter of a Tragedian," *Irish Times*, December 3, 1988. W.9.
4. Anne K. Yoder, "The Millions Interview: John Banville," *The Millions*, February 24, 2010, http://www.themillions.com/2010/02/the-millions-interview-john-banville.html.
5. Kleist's "Über das Marionettentheater" has been variously translated as "The Puppet Theatre" and "The Marionette Theatre."
6. Heinrich von Kleist, "On the Puppet Theatre," in *Heinrich von Kleist: Selected Writings*, ed. and trans. David Constantine (Cambridge: Hackett Publishing Company, 2004), 414.
7. Erich Heller, *The Poet's Self and the Poem: Essays on Goethe, Nietzsche, Rilke and Thomas Mann* (London: Athlone Press, University of London, 1976), 47–48.
8. John Kenny, *John Banville* (Dublin: Irish Academic Press, 2009), 170.

CHAPTER 5

9. Benjamin Black, *Vengeance* (London: Mantle, 2012).
10. Heinrich von Kleist, *Amphitryon* in *Selected Writings*, ed. and trans. David Constantine (Indianapolis: Hackett Publishing Ltd., 2004), 116.
11. Benjamin Black, *Christine Falls* (London: Picador, 2006).
12. Benjamin Black, *The Silver Swan* (London: Picador, 2007).
13. Hedda Friberg-Harnesk, "In the Sign of the Counterfeit: John Banville's *God's Gift*," *Nordic Irish Studies* 9 (2010): 71.
14. Anna Fattori, "'A Genuinely Funny German Farce' Turns into a Very Irish Play: *The Broken Jug* (1994): John Banville's Adaptation of Heinrich von Kleist's Der zerbrochne Krug (1807)," in *Angermion: Yearbook for Anglo-German Literary Criticism, Intellectual History and Cultural Transfers/Jahrbuch für Britisch-Deutsche Kulturbeziehungen* 4 (November, 2011): 77.
15. Brian Friel set several of his major works in the fictional Donegal town of Ballybeg, which was closely based on Glenties.
16. Fattori, "'A Genuinely Funny German Farce,'" 82.
17. Ibid., 87.
18. Ibid., 84.
19. Mohammed Kowsar, "Fugitive Desire: The Figural Component in Heinrich von Kleist's 'Penthesilea,'" *Theatre Journal* 40, no. 1 (March 1988): 62.
20. Ibid., 63.
21. Ursula R. Mahlendorf, "The Wounded Self: Kleist's Penthesilea," *The German Quarterly* 52, no. 2 (March 1979): 253.
22. Hugh Haughton, "The Ruinous House of Identity: The fictions of John Banville," in *The Dublin Review*, no. 1 (Winter 2000–2001): 109.
23. David Constantine, "Notes to *Amphitryon*," in *Heinrich von Kleist: Selected Writings*, ed. and trans. David Constantine (Cambridge: Hackett Publishing Company, 2004), 431.
24. E. L. Doctorow, "Foreword," to *Heinrich von Kleist: Plays*, ed. Walter Hinderer (New York: Continuum, 1995), vii.
25. Friberg-Harnesk, "In the Sign," 73.
26. Fattori, "'A Genuinely Funny German Farce,'" 80.
27. Constantine, "*Notes to Amphitryon*," xviii–xiv.
28. Ibid., xxi.
29. "John Banville: A Life in Writing." With Stuart Jeffries, June 29, 2012, https://www.theguardian.com/culture/2012/jun/29/john-banvill-life-in-writing (accessed August 31, 2016).
30. Walter Hinderer, "Introduction," to *Heinrich von Kleist: Plays*, ed. Walter Hinderer (New York: Continuum, 1995), xi.
31. Friberg-Harnesk, "In the Sign," 73.
32. Joseph McMinn, *The Supreme Fictions of John Banville* (Manchester–New York: Manchester University Press, 1999), 124.
33. Daniel K. Jernigan, "Tom Stoppard's Fiction: Finding His Form," *The Review of Contemporary Fiction* XXXIV, no. 1 (2014): 146.

34. Peter Rabinowitz, "Narrative Difficulties in Lord Malquist and Mr. Moon." *The Cambridge Companion to Tom Stoppard*, ed. Katherine E. Kelly (Cambridge: Cambridge University Press, 2001), 55–67.

35. H. Porter Abbott, *The Cambridge Introduction to Narrative* (Cambridge: Cambridge University Press, 2002), 115.

36. Yoder, "The Millions Interview."

37. W. Michelle Wang, "Writing for the Ear: Alasdair Gray the Playwright," *The Review of Contemporary Fiction* XXXIV, no. 1 (2014): 104.

38. Abbott, *The Cambridge Introduction*, 115.

39. Ibid., 116.

40. Keir Elam, *The Semiotics of Theatre and Drama* (London and New York: Routledge, 1980), 224.

41. Bartosz Lutostański, "Theatrical Narrative—Samuel Beckett's *Molloy*," *The Review of Contemporary Fiction* XXXIV, no. 1 (2014): 225.

42. Brian Richardson, "Voice and Narration in Postmodern Drama," *New Literary History* 32, no. 3, Voice and Human Experience (Summer 2001): 685.

43. Stephen Cheeke, *Writing for Art: The Aesthetics of Ekphrasis* (Manchester: Manchester University Press, 2008), 51.

44. Indicative of the major significance of the intense self-containedness that these lines articulate, a near exact replica previously appeared in *Ghosts*:

> This is the golden world. The painter has gathered his little group and set them down in this wind-tossed glade, in this delicate, artificial light, and painted them as angels and as clowns. It is a world where nothing is lost, where all is accounted for while yet the mystery of things is preserved; a world where they may live, however briefly, however tenuously, in the failing evening of the self, solitary and at the same time together somehow here in this place, dying as they may be and yet fixed forever in a luminous, unending instant. (*G*, 225–31)

6

Art and Crime

Benjamin Black's Quirke Novels

For an author whose fiction has always been densely populated by fakes, stereotypes, and self-consciously invented characters, John Banville's adoption of a pseudonym, Benjamin Black, as the pen name for his crime novels, should be treated with caution.[1] His writing has always included elaborate games, counterfeits, characters reincarnated from earlier novels, sinister (or absent) twins, and mirror universes, and it has repeatedly offered up fictional scenarios in which the surface plot barely conceals complex networks of ideas. All are indicators that the Benjamin Black novels may amount to more than they initially seem. Banville's work has also been repeatedly infused with criminality, as observed by Seamus Deane almost thirty years ago,[2] while Carol Dell'Amico has suggested that Banville has had a career-long interest in evil.[3] In addition, Joseph McMinn has written of what he sees as a "psychology of fear"[4] in the early *Long Lankin*. Similarly, sinister characters, like Felix and close variants of him, proliferate in Banville's extended fictional universe, while *The Book of Evidence* has a gratuitous murder at its center, and the threat of violence, crime, suicide, and general intrigue extends throughout novels like *The Untouchable*, *Athena*, *Shroud*, *The Sea*, *The Infinities*, and *Ancient Light*.

Banville's and Black's novels are, however, far more deeply interconnected than the presence of criminal acts alone suggests. The former's novels are all constructed around a variant of the detective genre—the philosophical detection quest. His heroes are typically engaged in journeys toward a realization that the landscapes they inhabit fail to yield their philosophical secrets. Typically, as in the case of Freddie Montgomery in *The Book of Evidence*, these journeys are frequently interwoven with aspects of the creative process. Framed within a recurring narrative form of disappointed quest, the fictional mode deployed by Banville is not dissimilar to the detective genre employed in the Quirke novels with their intellectual mystery games, stock criminals, seemingly

CHAPTER 6

irresolvable crimes (at least in a larger sense), all revolving around an unconventional protagonist-detective figure (in Quirke's case, a pathologist-detective). Furthermore, as with much of detective fiction, the Quirke novels— where my primary emphasis lies in this chapter—tend to reveal the nature of the crime from the outset after which the reader is drip-fed information that leads to the denouement. In Banville's *The Book of Evidence* a similar pattern is evident: Freddie Montgomery reveals from the outset that he is in jail charged with murder, after which readers embark on a complex philosophical journey rather than a convoluted plot. Modernist fiction, as observed by Brian McHale, frequently employs this narrative strategy: "The detective genre is affiliated with the poetics of modernism, since both detective fiction and modernist fiction are animated by epistemological quests."[5] Black's detective novels also retain this inheritance in their narrative structure primarily because the compulsive quest motif and the perpetual puzzlement of the protagonists are also important features of the Quirke novels. The narrative structures of Black's Quirke novels also pivot on the consciousness of their central character as part of the central motivation of the novels, as do the Banville novels. In this sense Black's immediate literary context mirrors that of Banville, although the significance of the detective novel genre is also central to an understanding of Banville's aesthetic aims in writing the Quirke novels.

Several reviewers, in part fueled by Banville's suggestion that the Black novels are craft works,[6] have implied that they have less literary significance than Banville's novels. At the heart of this critical condescension is the suggestion that detective fiction is a lesser, formulaic form of the novel that is too heavily invested in plot. The detective novel was praised by P. D. James for its "highly organised structure and recognised conventions"[7] but these are precisely the qualities that also appear to limit the form. In fact, the condescending attitude to crime fiction that often rests on a belief in the apparent primacy of plot (at the cost of artistry) also appears to be weakly conceived especially when one considers Raymond Chandler's particular fascination with style,[8] and the manner in which writers like Hammett and Simenon are frequently celebrated for their unique linguistic methods. John Scaggs too argues that, for Chandler, "plots are often nothing more than frameworks upon which to hang Marlowe's values and through which to emphasize his view point,"[9] diluting the significance of the overt "whodunnit" logic of such novels. Furthermore, as Jon Thompson suggests, in the context of his defense of the genre, a common accusation is that "crime fiction suffers from formulaic restrictions that true fiction or literature transcends."[10] Of course, such an accusation, on the basis of generic conventions, is extremely limiting in terms of our understanding of how literature functions. Banville has frequently insisted on the importance of crime novels, even arguing that Georges Simenon's work "is better than Camus or Sartre"[11] and he has repeatedly cited the influence of Simenon's *romans durs*[12] on the Quirke novels. While he seems less impressed by Simenon's Maigret novels,[13] clear generic parallels and character types exist between them and the Black novels. Banville has himself indicated that he dislikes the way that genre is deployed as a mode of hierarchal classification and insists that work by James M. Cain, Raymond Chandler, Richard Stark, and Georges Simenon represents some of the best writing of the twentieth century, work that "shouldn't be put off into a ghetto."[14] Thompson similarly argues against the application of rigid generic categories "as a basis for determining literary merit," which both tends to "obscure the hybrid nature of genres" and is indicative of an interpretative process that reads a text "exclusively in terms of the genre to which it has already been assigned."[15] In fact, the Black novels resonate with some of the stylistic, thematic, and structural elements of the Banville novels to such a degree that they are themselves indicative of the essentially hybrid narrative structure of the detective novel form, and assertions about literary merit thus appear to be made on the basis of habitual bias rather than genuine critical insight.

Similarly, the distinction between high forms of literature and detective fiction has its roots in the critical inheritance of high modernism which is characterized, in Thompson's view, by a "dense, complex, allusive, and self-referential style" unlike that of detective fiction that, alternatively, "lacked a sense of verbal texture."[16] It is doubtless true that much that is significant in modernist literature is encoded in innovative, aesthetically self-conscious linguistic structures. Apart from the ostensible distinction in terms of linguistic artistry, Thompson's observation also points to the detective genre's reliance on "realist modes of representation" which better lend themselves to less figurative, more direct forms of discourse. In fact, David Platten argues that "the enduring appeal of crime literature may be attributed wholly or in part to the ways in which it has mined, and continues to mine, a realist aesthetic."[17] It is clear that the linkage between detective fiction and realism is derived from the persistence of direct stylised urban representation in writers like Hammett, Chandler, Stark, and Benjamin Black himself (in both the Quirke series and in his own "Chandler" novel, *The Black-Eyed Blonde*[18]) but Thompson also points to ways in which urban modernity is inextricably linked to crime fiction and thus, arguably, at a certain point transcends the nineteenth-century

CHAPTER 6

realism that appears to govern its narrative structure. For Thompson, the crime genre offers,

> myths of the experience of modernity, of what it is like to live in a world dominated by the contradictory forces of renewal and disintegration, progress and destruction, possibility and impossibility. The capacity of crime fiction to evaluate different historical moments in the experience of modernity is not an accidental feature; rather, it is a dominant convention of the genre.[19]

While Benjamin Black's novels offer a unique test case for Thompson's observations, particularly in the context of Banville/Black's ambivalent attitude to his treatment of Irish social and political history in the novels, it is clear that modernism is inextricably connected, in particular, to the hard-boiled forms of the urban detective form.

The immediate cultural context for Benjamin Black's emergence, during something of a flowering of detective fiction in Ireland, also holds implications for his particular deployment of this most urban of forms. Colin Bateman, Ken Bruen, Ingrid Black (pseudonym of Eilis O'Hanlon and Ian McConnel), Declan Burke, Tana French, Declan Hughes, Adrian McKinty, Stuart Neville, Éilís Ní Dhuibhne, Peter Tremayne, John Connolly, and Brian McGilloway—among others—have all authored crime fiction series that are still being written, while hybrid forms of literary and detective fiction like Eoin McNamee's masterful *Blue* trilogy, have been Man-Booker listed. The fact that much of this work has been written during the Celtic Tiger years, or in the crash and recovery years since—like Banville's Quirke novels (2005 to the present)—and is based in Irish cities like Dublin, Galway, and Belfast or regional towns like Sligo and Dingle means that specific urban and social issues are to the fore. Despite Banville's claims to have little political interest in the 1950s social milieu—of which more presently—it is not difficult to see in Quirke's engagement with corruption in the Catholic Church, illegal adoptions, political intrigue, a harsh economic climate and a spate of murders connected to all these issues, a historicised mirror-image of contemporary Ireland. It seems likely, for example, that the placing of church corruption at the center of many of Black's plots reveals something of a contemporary consciousness at work. Written after 2005, or after church corruption had become a commonplace trope in the Irish narrative, Black reflects back much of Banville's own contextual awareness.

Furthermore, much of the Irish crime fiction written during these years has openly engaged with the Celtic Tiger and its aftermath by engaging with what Andrew Kincaid describes as "the violence, ugliness, the distrust, the moral conflicts, and tempo that are inherent" in the social fabric of these years.[20] Kincaid argues that the classic characteristics of hard-boiled detective fiction,

> are particularly well-suited to exposing basic modern contradictions between democracy and capitalism, crime and justice, glamor and poverty, city and suburb, gender and conformism, art and dross. And no society in Europe over the last twenty years has been so exposed to the rise and fall, the wonders and disillusionment, of fast-track capitalism as Ireland.[21]

Many of Kincaid's contrasts certainly resonate with the Quirke novels, or with what Elizabeth Mannion has termed, with respect to the interest of the majority of Irish crime series, the "historical scars or legacies of nation."[22] Audrey McNamara, in particular, has itemized the close correlations between the Quirke novels and a litany of social ills in Irish society, including the general social stagnancy, the collusion between church and state, illegal adoptions, the abuses in the industrial schools, the shame of suicide, and the multifaceted mistreatment of women.[23] The urban context that is effectively a defining characteristic of the genre lends itself particularly well to such matters. The mix of economic well-being, social and ethical shallowness, and economic hardship that defines Chandler's or Hammett's Los Angeles has much in common with the alienating streets of contemporary Irish urban centers, which Kincaid calls "transient, oppressive, and cold."[24]

The modern urban city is a fundamental part of the aesthetic veneer and thematic focus of the hard-boiled detective novel. As Scaggs observes, citing Willet, the "modern city of hard-boiled fiction is 'a wasteland devastated by drugs, violence, pollution, garbage and a decaying physical infrastructure,' and it is down the mean streets of this urban wasteland that the private eye must go."[25] For Scaggs, the detective figure, in turn, is "a quick-fisted urban cowboy"[26] on an idealistic quest for truth and justice, and a "reincarnation in the indigenous American tradition in the Western."[27] The quest that the hero embarks on is also a fixed trope in high modernist literary texts like *Ulysses*, *The Wasteland*, *Heart of Darkness*, and *Mrs. Dalloway*, as is the alienation that was a distinguishing characteristic of these texts. Furthermore, a shared desire to articulate an unintelligible landscape of confused signals, seemingly unreachable truths, and epistemological challenges is equally evident in writers like Joyce and Chandler. Thompson concludes that "crime fiction dramatizes the

CHAPTER 6

contradictory experience of modernity" rather than simply offering "reassuring myths of modernity."[28] In the process of such dramatization, the detective novel seeks to do what its central narrative logic demands: it outlines a process of detection, analysis, and harmonization. The degree to which this is achieved depends, of course, on the individualized deployment of the form but writers like Chandler and Benjamin Black operate in fictional landscapes in which a brooding sense that justice is never absolutely achieved permeates the experiences of the hero-detectives. Irrespective of the resolutions of individual crimes, the larger conundrum of human existence is usually rendered even more puzzling at the close of the plots than at the beginnings. In this context, Scaggs's summary of the unintelligible world of the hard-boiled detective novel emphasizes even further the resonance that the form has for modernist writing, in general:

> The fakery and artifice that characterise the modern city of hard-boiled fiction drive a wedge between what is seen and what is known, and in this way the private eye's quest to restore order becomes a quest to make sense of a fragmented, disjointed, and largely unintelligible world by understanding its connections, or, more often, its lack of connections.[29]

Again, Thompson's argument in favor of the critical usefulness of a hybrid genre is clear, especially when one considers the way that some of these works function, although the narrative cross-currents with high modernist writing are not the only compelling generic fingerprints that one can trace. Thompson himself suggests that the investigative impulse of crime fiction can be traced back to Oedipus,[30] while Irwin points out that "for Chandler, the private investigator represents a plausible form of modern knight-errant"[31]—a term that Rose sarcastically associates with Quirke (203) in *Even the Dead* (2015).[32] This motif also extends to many other hard-boiled heroes, with their emphasis on adventure and the pursuit of justice, even if their quests are often only partially completed.

There is something of the self-consciousness of Don Quixote in many hard-boiled detective stories, with varying degrees of irony and self-mockery built into their personas. The self-consciousness of Quixote, of course, has also been influential on postmodern fiction; it is precisely in this intersection that the well-established interrelationship between postmodern fiction and crime fiction is evident, to the degree that the genre—postmodern crime fiction—is itself an established subgenre. There are several reasons for this connection.

Knight argues that "Postmodern crime fiction has a special importance because major early postmodernists employed the genre to establish their positions against rationality and humanism."[33] He proceeds to suggest that writers like Borges, Butor, and Eco, in particular, showed "how crime fiction can, by being less determinate and simplistic than usual in its processes and outcomes, be a means of questioning certainties about the self, the mind and indeed the ambient world."[34] Arguably, hard-boiled detective fiction had already become progressively "less determinate and simplistic" than earlier forms of analytic detective fiction, like the novels of Agatha Christie, which Banville calls "crossword" novels.[35] There is little doubt, however, that writers like Pynchon, Auster, and Eco, as Knight sees it, lead to more dissolute representations, as with *The Crying of Lot 49*—"an irrational and unresolved detective quest."[36] This description also applies to Banville's *Nightspawn*, a parody of the detective form in which the narrator-hero has no real understanding of the plot. John T. Irwin also identifies the postmodern narrative "commitment to an increasingly self-conscious analytic posture" as being strongly evident in postmodern crime fiction.[37] While there is clearly a significant difference between Chandler and Pynchon, or Black and Auster, the contrast between Banville's unresolved tales of self-conscious aestheticism and Black's plotted confusion may not be absolute. The distinction, as with modernism and postmodernism, is one of degrees rather than essential difference, and it may even be the case that such categories disguise more fundamental shared-values and aesthetic aims that at first seem obvious.

While the structures of the Black novels are intimately connected to Hammett, Chandler, Stark, and Simenon, Banville's densely intertextual storyworlds are also everywhere evident in the Quirke novels. To mention a few instances: Professor Silas Kreutznaer from *Ghosts* reappears as Dr. Kreutz, still dealing with visual images, albeit of a more sleazy kind, in *The Silver Swan*. There is a Morton in *A Death in Summer*,[38] corresponding to Morden in *Athena* and *The Sea*, while Wilson Cleaver in *The Lemur*[39] is a near-relative, no doubt, of Alexander and Cass Cleave from *Eclipse* and *Shroud*. A variant of Inspector Hackett, a constant fixture of the "Quirke" novels, also appeared in *The Book of Evidence* as Inspector Haslet, and as Inspector Hackett in *Athena*, while Quirke, the central figure in all seven of Black's "Quirke" novels is himself resurrected from his role as caretaker and father to Lily in *Eclipse*. Quirke too has a daughter, Phoebe, in the Benjamin Black novels, echoing not only Quirke and Lily but also Cleave and Cass, and Max and Claire from *The Sea*. Fathers and daughters continually return, slightly modified, in Banville, and it

CHAPTER 6

is clear that Quirke and Phoebe correspond to their Banvillean counterparts.[40] Lily, the strange daughter of Quirke in *Eclipse*, also makes a reappearance in *Holy Orders*[41] as the simple daughter of a traveler woman with whom Black's Quirke has a brief liaison. Finally, with something of the shape-shifter about her, there is Rose who reappears in *Christine Falls* as Quirke's stepmother (twice removed if we remember that Quirke was adopted by Judge Griffin) but later marries Mal, becoming Quirke's sister-in-law. She and Quirke also had a brief liaison in the past. In Banville, Rose is the name given to Gabriel's lost sister (who never appears) in *Birchwood*.[42] She also features as both the governess Rose, and Rose Vavasour, caretaker of "The Cedars" boarding house in *The Sea*. Banville's characters have always moved through his varied storyworlds, mutating, adopting new disguises and names, half-remembering each other and compulsively repeating the same obsessive ghost-like adventures; they have now transgressed the boundaries between Banville's and Black's fictional ontologies. Black's novels may initially appear distinctly different from Banville's because they offer an alternative generic approach, largely avoiding the highly self-conscious voice of Banville's first-person narrative focus, but the surface seepage of characters between the respective worlds offers early indications that Black's world resonates with much of the significance of Banville's.

The name Benjamin Black itself has a curious fictional lineage: Benjamin White is the main character in Banville's early "The Possessed," while in his first novel, *Nightspawn* (1971), he appears as the detective figure, Benjamin S. White and there is also a murder victim named Black, who never appears. The Black/White game is reinforced by the existence of another character named Erik Weiss (or white), and the entire novel is loosely built around a series of black/white chess images. The name of the author Benjamin Black emerges from this lineage more than thirty-five years after the original publication of *Nightspawn*. In fact, Banville claims that he originally intended for his crime novelist's pseudonym to be Benjamin White, only to be dissuaded by his publisher and agent.[43] That Benjamin White, in *Nightspawn*, is also a self-conscious writer who becomes enmeshed in a murder story and sinister political plot adds to the density of resonances between the early work and the Black novels.

Benjamin Black has also written two novels for commission that don't feature Quirke: *The Lemur* (2008) and the Raymond Chandler title *The Black-Eyed Blonde* (2014). *The Lemur*, written for serial publication in *The New York Times Magazine*, is set in New York and features the formerly celebrated journalist, John Glass, who finds himself in the midst of a murder plot linked to his father-in-law, William Mulholland. As with many of the Black novels, there are multiple allusions to literature, film and the visual arts, including *Alice in Wonderland*, *Ulysses*, Emerson, Dickens, *Some Like It Hot*, Gene Hackman in *The Conversation*, Man Ray, and two of Banville's oft-cited painters, Modigliani and El Greco. Similarly, the landscape of the novel is repeatedly registered as something fake, or invented; John Glass is described as someone "living in a play," "spouting clichés," and "like a clown who has got something stuck to the sole of his big, floppy show and cannot shake it off" (*L*, 104–5). This is extremely reminiscent of the surface texture of both Banville's work and Black's Quirke novels.

More recently, Banville has written a Raymond Chandler Marlowe novel using one of his predecessors's planned titles. Unlike the Quirke novels, in true Chandler style, *The Black-Eyed Blonde* is written in the first person, and is thus closer, technically, to Banville's usual narrative style. Similar too is the Chandler sense of irresolution that one repeatedly encounters in Banville's literary fiction. According to Banville, Chandler wasn't particularly concerned with endings and cites him as such in several interviews: "I don't happen to care who killed Professor Plum in the library with the lead pipe."[44] Several other Banvillean elements seep into Black's Chandler novel, including a hint of the literary sensibilities that one encounters in Banville and Black. Apart from the Irish thread that runs through the plot (via Dorothea Langrishe), he also alludes to *Doctor Faustus*, Herman Melville, Scott Fitzgerald, S. T. Coleridge, John Keats, P. B. Shelley, and Lewis Carroll, among others, while the Langrishe family name is likely borrowed from Aidan Higgins's novel *Langrishe, Go Down*, playfully reminding us of the immobility at the heart of Higgins's masterpiece when Mrs. Langrishe is inaccurately recorded as "Mrs. Languish" in a message. Similarly, the word-play that is so frequently a feature of Banville's novel occasionally emerges in his Chandler novel:

> I came across a nice word recently: palimpsest. The dictionary said it was a manuscript with the original text partly erased and a new one written over it. What I was dealing with here was something like that. I was convinced that behind everything that had happened there was another version of things that I couldn't read. (*BEB*, 225)

While few of Banville's heroes would be unaware of the word palimpsest, the overt self-conscious reminder of his ventriloquist's dummy version of Marlowe is classic Banville, as are the frequent quasi-postmodern observations about

CHAPTER 6

the unknowability of one's existence: "Now I know that decisions we think we make are in fact made only in hindsight, and that at the time things are actually happening, all we do is drift. It doesn't trouble me much, this awareness of how little control I have over my affairs" (*BEB*, 175*)*. Such statements wouldn't be out of place in any Raymond Chandler novel in which Marlowe is frequently detached and disenchanted. Moments like this serve to remind one again of the implicit connections between the crime fiction genre and the modernist philosophical detection mode.

The Black novels which are of primary relevance in this chapter are those that feature Quirke, the chief pathologist at the Holy Family hospital in 1950s Dublin. Beset by alcohol dependency and a complex family life (as a child he was adopted by Judge Garrett Griffin and grew up as a member of a privileged household, with one brother, Mal), Quirke repeatedly gets drawn into convoluted criminal plots with Inspector Hackett that derive from his profession but which also frequently implicate his family. His adoptive father (in reality, his true father as revealed in *Even the Dead*), is connected to a series of crimes linked to the Catholic Church. The unfamiliar (for Banville) sociopolitical subject matter is closely linked to many of the crimes that are unearthed from the first Quirke novel (*Christine Falls*) to the most recent (*Even the Dead*) ensuring that in one crucial sense Black's novels differ from those of Banville—an important distinction which will be considered hereafter.

Ultimately, despite differences in the overt plotted surfaces, I contend that far from being distinctly different writerly universes, Benjamin Black's storyworlds are intertwined with Banville's fiction. If one considers Black's novels, in totality, to be an extended, elaborately plotted retelling of Banville's extended fictional universe in the guise of crime fiction, much of the logic for creating an overtly acknowledged pen name becomes clear.[45] The Benjamin Black novels themselves represent an intertextual mystery with a slew of clues everywhere to be seen but so seamlessly absorbed into the texture of Quirke's fictional universe that it does not initially seem apparent. With Banville's own name so self-consciously positioned at the center of Black's work, as well as the presence of so many Banvillean figures and tropes, Quirke's world approaches a metaleptic storyworld, even if it is one that still ostensibly retains its own self-contained, primary narrative frame. In a sense, then, this chapter is also a sleuth work of sorts, in which the complex narrative relationship between Banville's and Black's worlds is investigated, a relationship that is itself an overt self-conscious game.

In addition to the parallels between modernist epistemological quests and detective fiction, the Black novels also represent an artistic alternative to the overtly philosophically motivated Banville novels. Rather than view the Black novels as Banville-lite, I suggest that the fictional universe is reconstituted in a different genre, retaining several of the characters and tropes while also engendering an alternative landscape that is hauntingly similar to the worlds in which the Banville characters exist. Black's detective novels contain a double-crime frame. On an overt level, the Quirke novels are conventional crime-detection novels but a philosophical detective plot also exists on a more self-reflexive, novelistic level. Quirke's puzzlement in the face of the world's significance is typically expressed in tandem with the unfolding of the crime plot and, in this way, the philosophical imperatives that impose themselves so profoundly in Banville's work also assert themselves in Black's work, albeit in modified form.

A characteristic feature of Banville's fictions has always been the complex intertextual web that underpins much of their surface texture. The dominant artistic presence, for example, in *The Sea*, is Pierre Bonnard; the explicit positioning of the French artist's paintings of his beloved Marthe, even after her death, parallels Max's desire to imaginatively recover his dead wife's existence in his mind. Bonnard's paintings thus mirror Banville's textual images and vice-versa. All art, it is implied, reconfigures its material in new forms. Bonnard is again summoned in Benjamin Black's *A Death in Summer* (*DS*, 289–90), while his sweetpeas are again prominent in *Even the Dead* (*ED*, 60, 125). In *A Death in Summer*, Matisse, Jacques Louis David, Douanier Rousseau, Atget, and Paul Henry are all also mentioned, while in *Vengeance* (2012), a Mainie Jellett abstract hangs in the Delahaye house (*V*, 50, 184, 257), which later, oddly, reappears in Mal's house in *Even the Dead* (*ED*, 10). Its deployment in *Vengeance* mirrors the way that Banville integrates paintings in *The Sea*, in conjunction with the almost mischievous interference of the reflected sun in the window: "The window and the sunlit garden beyond were reflected in the glass, so that he had to move his head this way and that to see the picture properly. He did not think much about it but supposed he must be missing something" (*V*, 184). Similarly, Phoebe's sense of herself, in *Holy Orders*, as akin to a figure in a painting (most likely by Berthe Morisot), is strongly reminiscent of several of the female figures in Banville's art novels: "She was conscious of herself as a figure there, as if she were posing for her portrait. *Young Woman by a Window*" (*V*, 257).

CHAPTER 6

The habit of offering casual allusions to art, literature, and myth in Banville is also prevalent, if not quite as relentless, in all the Black Quirke novels. In the first Quirke novel, *Christine Falls*, there are numerous references to Pierrot, the hunchback of Notre Dame, Punch and Judy, Shakespeare, and, more generally, to theatre, myth, painting, and film, while more recent novels similarly refer to Greek myth (*HO*, 238), Pound's Cantos (*ED*, 117), Fragonard, El Greco, and Watteau's *Gilles* (*V*, 111, 266, 200), Sherlock Holmes, and Cary Grant, and numerous others. Similarly, in a playful, surreal sequence in Black's *Holy Orders*, Quirke meets his intertextual namesake, Thady, an old man who has apparently lived in Trinity Manor for more than sixty years, and with whom he imagines having an extended conversation—it transpires, in fact, that no such Thady lives there; Quirke has imagined him.

In addition, many of the Black novels echo key moments in Banville's work, like when *The Silver Swan* concludes with an overt declaration of bewilderment that might be from any number of Banville novels, especially with reference to the desire to bring his living daughter "back to life," a desire that dominates Banville's *The Book of Evidence*, *Ghosts*, and *Athena*:

> She was his daughter. He must find a way to bring her back to life. That was how he thought of it, those were the words that formed themselves in his head: I must bring her back, bring her back, to life.... He tried to make himself move, to walk, to get away, but in vain: his body would not obey him. He stood there, paralyzed. He did not know where to go. He did not know what to do. (*TSS*, 344–45)

In fact, some of the central motifs of the art trilogy repeatedly assert themselves throughout Black's work, particularly in terms of Freddie's "failure of imagination" (*BoE*, 215), or as we have it in Black, "a failure of attention" (*HO*, 155). Similarly, the impact of imaginative scrutiny, as expressed via the imagined painting of the girl in *The Book of Evidence*, when the unnerved girl reveals after seeing her completed painting that she "had expected it would be like looking in a mirror, but this is someone she does not recognize, and yet knows" (108). On meeting Dr. Evelyn Blake for the first time Quirke similarly "felt he had never been looked at in this way before; indeed, it was as if he were being looked at for the first time in his life, and he was unnerved" (*ED*, 109). Furthermore, the painter of the girl in *The Book of Evidence* is described as looking at her "with impersonal intensity," in a way that no one "has ever looked at her like ... before" (*BoE*, 106–7), just as Quirke notices that Dr.

Blake had a way "of concentrating her gaze, on an object or a person, so that it seemed as if everything else around had fallen away, into a fog of insignificance . . . he was not accustomed to being looked at like that, with such calm intensity" (*ED*, 153). This in turn echoes Stephen's student explanations of Aquinas' aesthetics in *A Portrait*, demonstrating Banville's continued conscious engagement with aesthetics.[46]

Also in keeping with Banville's self-conscious reminders of his characters' invented statuses, Black repeatedly asserts the constructed, even grotesque nature of his character-creations. Many are referred to as marionettes or puppets, again emphasizing the reliance on stock literary and artistic figures in his work but also implicitly acknowledging the pure artistic presence of literary characters. This pattern continues throughout all the novels with Hackett and Quirke described as "a pair of mannikins," in *A Death in Summer* (115), Mal, Quirke, and Rose as "life-sized waxworks" (*ED*, 60), and Quirke himself as a "kind of clown, in outsize trousers and long bulbous shoes," a la *Gilles* (*V*, 200). All echo Banville's fascination with clowns, puppets and mannikins. Furthermore, the major characters in both Banville's and Black's worlds frequently experience a sense of dislocation, a sense of their own ontological intangibility, compounded by an awareness of their roles as caricatures or marionettes.

Throughout the Black novels, Inspector Hackett is repeatedly referred to in terms reminiscent of a marionette or manikin: "Hackett's flat, square face had the look, in its wooden imperturbability, of a primitive mask" (*TSS*, 49); "he had a large rectangular head and a slash for a mouth and a nose like a pitted and mildewed potato" (*CF*, 119); and "the light shining upwards from the desk lamp made his face a mask, with jutting chin and flared nostrils and pools of empty darkness in the eye sockets" (*CF*, 120). But the construction of character as manikin is the norm in the Black novels. Phoebe stands with her "head bowed and her arms hanging at her side, herself a slack-stringed marionette" (*CF*, 189) and Leslie, from *The Silver Swan*, is described as "long and gangly, with a stooping, sinuous, flat-footed gait, his long pale hands swinging at the ends of his arms as if they were connected to his wrists not by bone but skin alone" (*TSS*, 91). The point here has less to do with simply tracing intertextual echoes but with the aesthetic motivation that lies behind Banville's and Black's characters, and the narrative framing of the fictive world. By overtly transplanting much of the aesthetic rationale that governs Banville's worlds, the author is self-consciously alerting us to the logic of Black's world, both beyond, and in tandem with, the *topos* and character types of the crime novels.

CHAPTER 6

One of the advantages of adopting the detective genre for the Quirke novels is precisely that the persistent use of marionettes, stock criminals, and grotesques, facilitates the creation of a disorientating landscape in which the sense of alienation is enhanced. The characters live a purely textual existence, appearing and reappearing, reborn from other fictional universes, as ghost-like posthumous creatures. Quirke's world is also populated with unnerving grotesques who generate a sense of unease and otherworldliness throughout. The Delahaye twins have "long, straw-pale heads," (*V*, 165), while the policeman, Jenkins, has a "pin-head on a stalk of a neck" (*V*, 218–19), and Philbin, a brain specialist has "a long, narrow head the top of which was a slightly flattened, shiny curve, like the crust of a loaf" (*ED*, 3). Dolores Moran, of *Christine Falls*, exemplifies a more layered usage of the grotesque and is described almost in the same terms as the fox-fur stole that hangs around her neck: "she appeared again . . . with a fox-fur stole around her neck that had the fox's sharp little head and little black paws still attached. . . . A lipstick mouth . . . was painted over her real one. Her eyes and the fox's were uncannily alike, small and black and shining" (*CF*, 33). The significance of such compositional features lies in the fact that the novels at times seem to operate on two or more levels. Everything is simultaneously itself and yet other or, as Max tells us in *The Sea*, "everything seemed to be something else" (65). This sense of doubling too is apparent in numerous ways in the Black novels. One is repeatedly reminded, for example, of the coexistence of different layers of reality such as when Quirke visits Bewley's café in *A Death in Summer* only to discover the extraordinary foreignness of literal reality: "It seemed so long ago, that time, a kind of sun-dappled antiquity, as if it were an Attic glade he was remembering and not a shabby and overcrowded café in a faded little city with a past that felt more immediate than its present" (*DS*, 216). Similarly, the very fabric of material reality is subverted on many occasions by the characters' puzzlement at the generic props that materialize in their midst, as seen during an intimate moment between Quirke and Sarah: "He sat forward so abruptly her gloves on the table seemed to shrink back from him, clasping each other. How lifelike they looked, Sarah thought, a pair of black leather gloves. As if some otherwise invisible third person at the table were wringing their hands" *(CF*, 162). Many characters also have a sense of themselves as doubled with the Black novels offering perpetual reminders of the distinction between self and other, between representation of self (even to oneself) and a deeper, unnamable other, as in the case of Mona Delahaye: "Sometimes she thought of herself as a separate object, a figure outside herself that she could regard from a distance, appraising, approving, admiring" (*V*, 144).

The impact of such doubled moments on the texture of fictional reality in the Black novels is compounded by the fact that many of the characters also exhibit a powerful, recurring sense of the strangeness of existence. John Banville has frequently alluded to the "puzzlement" of his narrators: "So, the world is puzzling. . . . All the narrators of my books talk about how baffled they are. Puzzlement, bafflement, this is my strongest sensation, my strongest artistic sensation."[47] He was speaking of the novels written in his own name but the same sense of oddness at *being* exists throughout the Black novels. For example, Inspector Hackett, in *Elegy for April* (2011),[48] in a rare introspective moment, reminds himself that to take "reality as it presented itself was to miss an entirely other reality hidden behind" (112), and concludes that a kind of strangeness lies at the center of his sense of reality:

> But it was the strangeness that stayed with him, the out of the ordinariness of the spectacle of a grown man sitting there at the too-small desk, crying his heart out, in the middle of an otherwise ordinary morning. . . . All around lay the surface of the ocean, seeming all that there was to see and know, in calm or tempest, while, underneath, lay a wholly other world of things, hidden, with other kinds of creatures, flashing darkly in the deeps. (*EA*, 114)

The strangeness of being is coupled with Hackett's sense of the world as forever doubled, with the world of hidden things sending flickering signals without ever fully materializing. Many characters in the Black novels have a similar sense of their environments as other and strange. As Jack Clancy of *Vengeance* muses: "This street was strange, always had been, so hushed and secretive, with a silence all of its own, flat yet echoing" (*V*, 103) or, as Quirke himself observes, with respect to the strange familiarity of certain momentous events: "How strange it was, Quirke thought, the way certain things, the most momentous, seemed to come not as something new and unexpected but as mere confirmations of things already known" (*ED*, 122). The characters seem to shimmer in their strange unfixed appearances, stubbornly refusing to move into sharp focus: "There was something about Maggie, something faintly but definitely strange. . . . You felt when she looked at you that she was not seeing you straight" (*V*, 102). In many respects this recurring feature of the Black novels is ultimately an aspect of being, as the narrator of *Holy Orders* observes: "Quirke caught himself thinking how strange it was to be here; how strange to

CHAPTER 6

be anywhere" (*HO*, 167). For Banville, strangeness is intimately connected to one of the primary constituent qualities of art and, echoing Shklovsky's process of *ostranenie*, or defamiliarization,[49] he has asserted that strangeness is "the mark of art."[50] The residue of Banville's persistent use of the word strange, and its variants, is not just alluded to in the Black novels. At times, in fact, there is a sense that the characters reveal an awareness of the deeper significance of the term, as when a dying Mal complains that he has lost "the knack of being normal" and is unnerved by the oddness of his new state of being, his new perspective, but comforts himself by claiming that "nothing stays strange for very long" (*ED*, 132).

A constituent part of Banville's aesthetic, particularly from *Eclipse* onward, has been an engagement with the sense of strangeness that characterizes the experiences of the major characters. His heroes have always been occupied with considerations of the Kantian "thing-in-itself,"[51] or fascinated by the problem of the transformative nature of art and—a variation of this—the unyielding and disinterested nature of the real. This generates a continual sense of the world as odd and knowable only in glimpses. While the self-conscious anxiety that marks Banville's novels is largely absent from the worlds of Benjamin Black, the essential sense of separateness from the tangibility of material reality continues to assert itself. For example, returning to his flat in *Elegy for April* after spending time in St. John's drying-out center for recovering alcoholics, Quirke marvels at the "suddenly estranged and sullen surroundings" (*EA*, 34), and is disturbed that all "should have remained intact and unaffected while he was away suffering such trials" (*EA*, 33). More recently, in *Holy Orders*, it is clear that Phoebe believes that she has inherited her father's "gift" of impersonality, her sense of dispassionate remove (*HO*, 119), a point that we are again reminded of in the recent *Even the Dead* during her meditation on the essential difference between objects and humans:

> It occurred to her how dissimilar things were from people [. . .] but objects were always obstinately themselves. Or, no, not "obstinately," that was the wrong word. "Indifferently," that was what she meant. She recalled what her father had said to her once, long ago, in the days before she knew he was her father. "The thing to remember, Phoebe," he had said, "is that the world is indifferent to us and what we do." . . . she had never forgotten him saying it. (*ED*, 179)

The world will always remain other and, while Banville's first person protagonists generally reflect more self-consciously than Black's characters, their intuitive awareness of the unyielding reality is the same. Indeed, one could argue that, as the Black novels proceed, a developing feature of Quirke's character is precisely a growth in his overt sense of self-awareness that increasingly resembles that of Cleave, or Max, or Oliver Orme from *The Blue Guitar*. In *Even the Dead*, for instance, his adventure concludes with a reflective consideration of his own indifference: "Quirke felt nothing, nothing at all. He wondered if his indifference, like his acknowledgement at last of who his parents had been, was perhaps a sign that 'something momentous' had indeed occurred" (*ED*, 260). The association of the quality of indifference with the possibility of a momentary flash of awareness is perhaps more Banville than Black, although the distinction grows increasingly less with each novel.

The central significance of such moments in Black's work lies in the fact that they resonate so deeply with corresponding moments in Banville's work. For example, Max (Morden) from *The Sea* also offers insight into Quirke's sense of the uncanny when he considers the world of his childhood:

> How is it that in childhood everything new that caught my interest had an aura of the uncanny, since according to all the authorities the uncanny is not some new thing but a thing known returning in a different form, becoming a revenant? So many unanswerables, this the least of them. (*TS*, 10)

The uncanny notion that Quirke senses is, for Max, a thing known returning in a different form. Max has a more acute awareness of his own role as a perpetual inhabitant of Banville's worlds, while Quirke's self-consciousness does not extend beyond his own introspective intensity. Banville's characters, as noted earlier, appear and reappear in modified guises throughout his work and often display a self-reflexive awareness of their prior incarnations. Banville, for instance, litters *Ghosts* with his characters' awareness of their previous existences: "*I have an habitual feeling of my real life having passed, and that I am leading a posthumous existence*" (Italics at source: 25). And as the ever-recurring Mephisophelean figure, Felix, reminds the puzzled day-trippers: "'Yes, yes,' he said impatiently. 'Everyone feels they have been here before'" (*G*, 48). But Quirke too has a similar sense of having lived before and of now living a posthumous existence. In *Christine Falls*, he observes, "*All this happened before somewhere*" (297) and he also has an intense sense of the repetition of things in *Vengeance* when he observes, "So many things that were happening had happened before, in identical circumstances" (200). In addition, Quirke's dubious proximity to the dead frequently hints at some in-between ontological

CHAPTER 6

existence, akin to literary characters themselves: "It sometimes seemed to him that he favoured dead bodies over living ones. . . . He suspected, too that he was becoming more like them, that he was even in some way becoming one of them" (*CF*, 63). Phoebe, increasingly more significant as the Quirke novels develop, also muses that she "never got used to being alive" (*EA*, 59), further emphasizing the unstable ontological status of the primary characters in the Black novels, especially in terms of how they relate to the Banvillean world in their fictional posthumous existence. The difference, however, rests on the degrees of self-consciousness that the characters possess, with Black's characters less overtly conscious of their fictional status.

The familiarity of the detective novel form also lends itself to a very particular staged sense, a quality that Kevin Boyle has recognized as "slightly cartoonish"[52] in Black's work. But rather than being indicative of a parodic relationship with the source-genre this is simply a surface indication of a far more complex sense of artistry at work in the Black novels. The surface texture of the fictional worlds is a *bric-a-brac* reconstruction drawn from a tissue of quotations, which hovers continually on the edge of instability; the characters are largely puppets, grotesques or stock figures borrowed from other crime fiction novels and films, or are reborn from Banville's novels, suffering a sense of estrangement, disorientation, and puzzlement in the face of the mess of existence, similar to that experienced by so many Banville heroes who have long quested for order and harmony.

Despite the rarefied veneer that can ultimately be discerned in both the Banville and Black novels the primary narrative mode, as with most hard-boiled detective novels, is derived from a relatively stripped down, direct mode of description. In fact, Fintan O'Toole has argued that Irish crime fiction, in general, in recent years "has become arguably the nearest thing we have to a realist literature adequate to capturing the nature of contemporary society."[53] Similarly, Elizabeth Mannion points to the tendency among Irish crime fiction writers to explore their historical moment as a defining feature. She argues that the "leading detective writers are producing novels that feature cultural allusion, and this is likely part of their international appeal"[54]—a point that may, in fact, be a defining difference between Banville and Black. The implication is that crime-fiction tends toward an accessible form of realist writing which in turn has been part of the reason for the recent popularity of Irish crime fiction. David Platten argues that the success of the form itself also "derives from an aesthetic commitment to the creation of whole worlds, to the depiction of the individual and society as 'complete entities' which Georg Lukács saw as the hallmark of 'true, great realism.'"[55] Whether Black's variation on the form meets either O'Toole's realist model or Lukács's essentially politicised aspiration is worth considering, given the highly intertextual aestheticized surfaces that repeatedly confront one in his storyworlds. Still, Andrew Kincaid argues that "Even the most self-conscious of Ireland's current crop of noir is ideological, and they can be interpreted as harnessing, however residually, the original energy of noir to the very different context and problems of modern Ireland."[56] In contrast to Banville's less culturally identifiable fictional worlds, Benjamin Black's historically specific 1950s landscapes appear to lend themselves to a more politically energized focus. However, Banville's observations in interviews, reviews and essays, generate a certain degree of confusion in this respect. For example, when Hugh Haughton asks, in an interview with the author, is he is correct in detecting "a more politically conscious writer about the historical Ireland" in the Benjamin Black novels, Banville strongly disagrees:

> Well, I wish that I could agree with you, but I don't feel that. I really believe that any writer who imagines he has a social voice is in trouble. If you mix politics and art, you get bad politics and bad art. I can imagine, of course, if, for instance, it seemed to me tomorrow that the civil war in the North would make a subject for a novel for me, that I could write it as a novel rather than a commentary on war, then I would do it, but that would be incidental. I think this is always true. For art, subject is always incidental, or at least secondary, to the work itself.[57]

These observations extend the kinds of comments that Banville has made about the social novel throughout his career, insisting that subject matter is secondary to formal significance. In the Banville novels, in general, this position can be validated—despite several notable attempts to emphasize Banville's Irishness.[58] But Haughton's observations with respect to the Quirke novels do have some merit. Throughout the Quirke novels the crimes, and general air of corruption, repeatedly circle around the Catholic Church and the quasi-political organization with which it was so closely aligned, as well as around a compromised judiciary—via Quirke's deeply implicated father. In addition the typically Banvillean motifs of lost brothers or sisters are reconfigured in the Black novels as abused orphans, including Quirke's own orphan-past in Carricklea or children torn from their mothers in mother and baby homes and sold in illegal adoptions to rich Americans. The cruelty heaped upon those mothers is a constant sore in the novels. Many of the crimes with which Quirke becomes embroiled are connected in some circuitous way to the central dark presence of

CHAPTER 6

the church, suggestive, on the surface, of a clearer political significance to the novels than one can find in his more "literary" offerings.

The Black novels were originally conceived of as a commissioned TV miniseries for RTÉ and ABC television (Australia) that was intended as a "dark story of political and religious chicanery in the 1950s," which was never brought to completion.[59] Banville has also revealed that it was only much later in his life that he saw "the potential of 1950s Dublin as a setting for his [Black's] *noir* novels,"[60] although he has frequently emphasized the generic rather than the historical when explaining his choice of setting. Speaking of his reasons for selecting the 1950s he reveals: "It was a strange, dark time, full of secrets, with lots of cigarette smoke and fog, and clandestine sex; a perfect time to set a noir novel in."[61] However, he does concede that the period was historically interesting in itself: "The '50s are a fascinating decade. People of my generation tried to forget about the '50s. In Ireland especially, the things we're discovering now about things that went on in the '50s makes it fascinating."[62] Furthermore, Quirke's era coincides with Banville's youth and he admits that the palpable controlling presence of the Catholic Church was "impossible to ignore" when writing the Black novels.[63] A clear sense of moral objection is evident in some of Banville's interviews, in which he frequently likens the enslavement of the Irish Catholic Church in the 1950s and beyond to the fate of countries behind the Iron Curtain:

> Of course, we were under the yoke of an iron ideology. We were told in those days that the Soviet satellite countries, behind the Iron Curtain, they are not free there. We are free. It was only in the '90s when we actually did free ourselves that we realized for all those years we were exactly like a Soviet country. The church and state were hand in hand just as the state and party were hand in hand there. And our lives were completely un-free.[64]

Such observations also find their way into the novels, with Quirke at one point warning Phoebe about the nature of the Catholic Church: "They're just the same as the Communists they're always warning us about—two sides of the same coin" (*ED*, 194).

And yet, nonetheless, Banville repeatedly rejects the suggestion that the Quirke novels are socially motivated and argues that the Church-linked corruption is "just material," denying, with respect to *Christine Falls*, that he had "a crusading social purpose" and explains instead that he "just wanted to write a novel, and the scandals that had just begun to be revealed at that time seemed ideal for my purpose, as they continued to be."[65] The logic that the function of the setting is primarily formal is also extended in his claim that he needed to give the character of Quirke a particular kind of troubled background: "I wanted to give him a past that was shadowed. First of all, to make him an orphan so he wouldn't know his background because that's the source of his curiosity, his urge to know, to find out secrets," but he also admits that a new awareness in Ireland of the horrors perpetrated by the Catholic Church "was preying on my mind."[66] Furthermore, while Banville has always asserted that subject matter is incidental, he has occasionally admitted to the indirect impact of political violence on his work. He admits, for instance, to the possibility of a certain ethical thread of significance in *The Book of Evidence*, when he eventually recognized that the novel may have been "about Ireland because it was about the failure of imagination and the failure to imagine other people into existence," which was a symptom, as he saw it, of the monstrosity of the Omagh bomb as well as all the horrors of the Northern Irish troubles. While he insists that he "didn't set out to do that in the book," he simultaneously accepts that "we're never free of our time. We like to think we are but we're not."[67] In all, Banville's positioning, particularly with respect to the sociohistorical significance of setting the Black novels in the 1950s and his choice of such a pronounced anti-Catholic Church narrative thread, requires some consideration. Despite his declared disinterest in social comment and an emphasis on the generic attributes of the form, the significance of his subject matter for a contemporary Irish audience familiar with myriad forms of church abuse ensures that his declared position may appear to be at odds with the novels themselves.

Banville's perspective on Picasso helps to clarify some of the apparent ambivalence in his statements. He cites Picasso's own claim that he preferred his painting "The Three Dancers" (1925) to the much more famous anti-war painting "Guernica" (1937): "It [the *Dancers*] was painted as a picture, without ulterior motive."[68] His reasoning is that "The Three Dancers" is "a fearsome, indeed a savage, work, but it is pure painting; "Guernica," for all its violence and power, was intended as a political statement as well as a work of art, and for that reason it is, essentially, kitsch." He warns that artists are sometimes "in danger of imagining that because they have achieved critical success and earned much money and fame, they must have profound things to say about the public life of their times."[69] The key here is not so much that the subject of "Guernica" is war, but that it was painted, unlike "The Three Dancers," with motive. Works of art frequently have discernible subject matter but the real question is whether they are motivated by rhetorical purpose *or* artistic

CHAPTER 6

intention. For Denis Donoghue these are fundamentally different processes: rhetoric "has an aim, to move people to do one thing rather than another," while eloquence (synonymous with art for Donoghue) "has no aim: it is a play of words or other expressive means. It is a gift to be enjoyed in appreciation and practice. The main attribute of eloquence is gratuitousness: its place in the world is to be without place or function."[70] Donoghue's suggestion that a "speech or an essay may be eloquent, but if it is, the eloquence is incidental to its aim"[71] importantly raises the term "incidental." The inverse of his statement also holds: an eloquent work of art may contain subject matter which remains peripheral to its primary function—eloquence. The subject matter of the Benjamin Black novels arguably remains incidental to Black's primary aim, which is to create works of art, primarily because they are not imbued with a clear rhetorical purpose. Some of Banville's essays and reviews make overt claims about his work—rhetorical statements, in fact—but no such rhetorical purpose is foregrounded in the novels and, despite their resonance for contemporary Irish readers' sense of injustice about the ethical contagion that the Catholic Church came to represent, the novels do not explicitly take up a persuasive ideological position. As with Joyce and Beckett, of course, this in no way means that the works don't offer suitable fare for sociopolitical critical analysis, which is an entirely different matter.

Several critics have argued that the Benjamin Black novels are really just "Banville-lite"[72] with one suggesting that Banville might be "an interesting bet for one of the Bond continuations recently commissioned by the Fleming estate."[73] But this kind of critique fails to see the point of the whole endeavor. It appears that the more clearly defined plots of the Black novels have encouraged readers to look no further than plot, and Banville has certainly contributed to this impression by his somewhat ambiguous representation of the novels as being straight crime novels.[74] Other critics, however, have observed similarities between Banville's and Black's work. John Kenny, for example, acknowledges that Black is "only a partially cloaked Banville," pointing to the characterization of Quirke and his relationship with Phoebe as bearing comparison with Banville's typical narrators.[75] Similarly, Joanna Kavenna argues that Banville's "obsession with scarcely knowable origins becomes, well, Black's obsession with scarcely knowable origins," and suggests that the "difference is in emphasis," that makes us think "that things are substantially different when really they are almost the same."[76] Kavenna and Kenny insightfully recognize some of the distinct echoes that ring across the apparent gulf between Banville and Black but the lines of connection are more expansive than character types and their relationships, or the parallel fascinations with solving mysteries.

Above and beyond their content—the material substance of his novels—Banville's primary desire has always been to fashion works of art, to infuse their earned harmony with a kind of strangeness. His position on the essential detachment of art is well established and he has repeatedly argued that the subject matter of a work of art is somehow "incidental."[77] Also significant, perhaps, is the texture of the art work, the aestheticized surface, and in this sense Black's world far more closely resembles Banville's than at first seems apparent. Black's heroes are certainly less self-conscious than Banville's, influenced, in part, by the absence of that haunting self-obsessive first-person voice that addresses readers in most of Banville's major novels. Banville's poetic intensity is also not quite as densely wrought in Black, though he too is capable of moments of arresting prose that exceeds the norms for the genre. There is little doubt, furthermore, that the Black novels are more resolved in general, but it is important to note the difference between plot resolution and the essentially and deeply unresolved selves that characters such as Quirke and Phoebe, in particular, carry forward with them at the close of each novel.[78]

Banville has admitted that there may be "permeability between the worlds of Banville and Black" but, more crucially, he has claimed that crime novels can "approach the condition of art,"[79] and that "High art can happen in any medium. I think that Simenon's *Dirty Snow*, for instance, is high art."[80] The subject matter of the Banville novels is incidental to their condition as art works, and so too with the Black novels. Pater argued that art strove to be independent of the "mere intelligence . . . to get rid of its responsibilities to its subject or material"[81] and that sense of self-containedness has always marked Banville's uniquely introspective universe, or what Susanne Langer has termed the virtual life, or the "world of its own" of poetry.[82] Whether we encounter Banville's intellectual adventurers or the erstwhile Quirke struggling through the 1950s grime of Dublin's crime worlds, the disinterested self-containment is the same. We experience the familiar harmonies built from fragments borrowed from the worlds of art and literature, and populated by the survivors from other worlds who bear the indelible mark of what Wallace Steven calls "the transposition of an objective reality to a subjective reality,"[83] or the mark of art. Benjamin Black's worlds are simply those of Banville reconstituted in modified form but the same sense of the "veiled and deceptive nature of things" (*EA*, 112) persists. This aesthetic imperative ultimately governs the

CHAPTER 6

shift from Banville to Black, a shift that is more apparent than real. The characters in Black's genre-fiction detective novels inhabit an intertextually framed universe just as their near relatives do in Banville's novels. The deployment of the overt detective form in Black too is an intellectual ruse of sorts because it echoes the quest motif that lies at the heart of Banville's work. In all, the Black novels amount to a formal reconstitution of Banville's overt philosophical and poetic framing. They are stripped of the high degree of self-consciousness that Banville has always exhibited, and are instead infused with the directness and sequential shape that the detective genre offers.

Notes

1. Immediately after winning the Booker Prize for his novel, *The Sea*, John Banville surprised the literary world by publishing his first "Quirke" crime novel, *Christine Falls* (2006), under the pseudonym Benjamin Black. He has since published a further eight crime novels, six of which retain the central figure, Quirke, the chief pathologist in the Holy Family Hospital in Dublin of the 1950s, a profession that inadvertently allows him access to the crime world. Perhaps the most peculiar aspect of Banville adopting a pseudonym lies primarily in his immediate announcement that it was he, John Banville, who was writing; John Banville's name even appears on the Benjamin Black novels ("John Banville writing as Benjamin Black"), a gesture which appears odd and begs the question, why bother using a pseudonym at all if both names appear on the cover anyway?
2. Seamus Deane observed that criminality spreads "like a stain" throughout Banville's work in a special John Banville episode of *Bookside*, RTÉ (March 1989).
3. Carol Dell'Amico, "John Banville and Benjamin Black: The *Mundo*, Crime, Women," *Éire-Ireland* 49, no. 1 & 2 (Spring-Summer 2014): 115.
4. Joseph McMinn, *John Banville: A Critical Study* (Dublin: Gill & Macmillan Ltd., 1991), 14–15.
5. Brian McHale, *Teaching Narrative Theory*, eds., David Herman, Brian McHale, and James Phelan (New York: Modern Language Association of America, 2010), 188.
6. Jon Wiener, "I Hate Genre: An Interview with John Banville/Benjamin Black," *LA Review of Books,* March 15, 2014, https://lareviewofbooks.org/article/hate-genre-interview-john-banvillebenjamin-black/ (accessed July 31, 2016).
7. P. D. James, *Talking about Detective Fiction* (Oxford: Bodleian Library, 2009), 15.
8. Banville has cited Chandler as follows: "It doesn't matter what a book is about. Style is the only thing that will endure in writing," interview with Christopher Cox, "*The Black-Eyed Blonde*: A Conversation with John Banville," *Harper's Magazine*, March 26, 2014, https://harpers.org/blog/2014/03/the-black-eyed-blonde-a-conversation-with-john-banville/ (accessed July 31, 2016).
9. John Scaggs, *Crime Fiction* (London: Routledge, 2005), 59.

10. Jon Thompson, *Fiction, Crime, and Empire: Clues to Modernity and Postmodernity* (Urbana and Chicago: University of Illinois Press, 1993), 27.

11. "Guest Profile: Benjamin Black Parts 1–4," interview with Jim Ruland, *The Elegant Variation: A Literary Weblog*, December 8, 2008, http://marksarvas.blogs.com/elegvar/2008/12/guest-profile-p.html (accessed July 31, 2016).

12. Ibid. In addition, see Mark Sarvas's interview with John Banville, http://marksarvas.blogs.com/elegvar/2005/09/the_longawaited.html (accessed June 18, 2014).

13. Simenon wrote seventy-five Maigret novels and a few dozen short stories between 1931 and 1972, many of which were adapted for television. Quirke is a modified version of Maigret with whom he shares a fondness for alcohol, although Quirke takes his alcohol dependence to further extremes, and gets far more intertwined with the crimes on a personal level than Maigret would allow. Simenon also has an Inspector Cadaver, a rival of Maigret's, who bears a striking resemblance to Inspector Hackett in the Quirke novels.

14. Weiner, "I Hate Genre."

15. Thompson, *Fiction, Crime, and Empire*, 4.

16. Ibid., 29.

17. David Platten, "Mediatized Realities: The Modern Crime Narrative," *Moving Worlds* 13, no. 1 (November 2013): 33.

18. Banville, *The Black-Eyed Blonde* (New York: Henry Holt, 2014).

19. Thompson, *Fiction, Crime, and Empire*, 2.

20. Andrew Kincaid, "'Down These Mean Streets': The City and Critique in Contemporary Irish Noir," *Éire-Ireland* 45, no. 1 & 2 (Spring-Summer 2010): 41.

21. Ibid., 47.

22. Elizabeth Mannion, "Introduction: A Path to Emerald Noir: The Rise of the Irish Detective Novel," in *The Contemporary Irish Detective Novel*, ed. Elizbeth Mannion (London: Palgrave, 2016), 4.

23. Audrey McNamara, "Quirke, the 1950s, and Leopold Bloom," *The Contemporary Irish Detective Novel*, ed. Elizabeth Mannion (London: Palgrave, 2016), 135–48.

24. Kincaid, "'Down These Mean Streets': The City and Critique in Contemporary Irish Noir," 47.

25. Scaggs, *Crime Fiction*, 70.

26. Ibid., 57.

27. Ibid., 58.

28. Thompson, *Fiction, Crime, and Empire*, 8.

29. Scaggs, *Crime Fiction*, 72.

30. Thompson, *Fiction, Crime, and Empire*, 2.

31. John T. Irwin, *The Mystery to a Solution: Poe, Borges, and the Analytic Detective Story* (London: Johns Hopkins University Press, 1996), 1.

32. Banville, *Even the Dead* (London: Penguin, 2016).

33. Stephen Knight, *Crime Fiction, 1800–2000: Detection, Death, Diversity* (Basingstoke: Palgrave Macmillan, 2004), 195.

34. Ibid., 195.

35. Cox, "The Black-Eyed Blonde."

CHAPTER 6

36. Knight, *Crime Fiction*, 196.
37. John T. Irwin, *The Mystery to a Solution*, 11.
38. Banville, *A Death in Summer* (London: Mantle, 2011).
39. This is only one of two crime novels by Black that do not feature Quirke. Benjamin Black, *The Lemur* (London: Picador, 2008). Subsequent page references are to this edition, abbreviated TL, and included in the text of the article.
40. I have written elsewhere about the significance of the repeated incarnations of characters in Banville's early fiction: "From *Long Lankin* to *Birchwood*: The Genesis of John Banville's Architectural Space," *Irish University Review* 36, no. 1 (Spring-Summer, 2006): 9–24.
41. Banville, *Holy Orders* (New York: Henry Holt, 2013).
42. John Banville, *Birchwood* (London: Panther Books, 1984).
43. See Mark Sarvas interview.
44. Cox, "*The Black-Eyed Blonde*."
45. John Banville's name appears on the covers of the Benjamin Black novels ("John Banville writing as Benjamin Black").
46. James Joyce, *A Portrait of the Artist as a Young Man* (Harmondsworth: Penguin, 1992), 230–31.
47. Cited in Hedda Friberg's "John Banville and Derek Hand in Conversation," *Irish University Review: A Journal of Irish Studies* 36, no. 1 (Spring-Summer 2006): 206.
48. Benjamin Black, *Elegy for April* (London: Picador, 2011).
49. Victor Shklovsky: "The purpose of art is to impart the sensation of things as they are perceived and not as they are known. The technique of art is to make objects 'unfamiliar,' to make forms difficult, to increase the difficulty and length of perception because the process of perception is an aesthetic end in itself and must be prolonged. Art is a way of experiencing the artfulness of an object; the object is not important." Victor Shklovsky, "Art as Technique," in *Modern Criticism and Theory: A Reader*, ed. David Lodge (London: Longmans, 1988), 20.
50. Friberg, "John Banville and Derek Hand in Conversation," 200.
51. In Banville's *Doctor Copernicus*, for example, the young Copernicus muses on "the thing itself, the vivid thing." John Banville, *Doctor Copernicus* (London: Secker & Warburg, 1976), 3.
52. Kevin Boyle, "Benjamin Black and John Banville: The Legitimacy of the Irish Literary Persona," *New Voices in Irish Criticism: Legitimate Ireland*. The Peter Froggatt Centre, Queen's University Belfast, 19 April 2012.
53. Fintan O'Toole, "From Chandler and the 'Playboy' to the contemporary crime wave," *Irish Times*, November 21, 2009, http://www.irishtimes.com/culture/tv-radio-web/from-chandler-and-the-playboy-to-the-contemporary-crime-wave-1.776393 (accessed July 31, 2016).
54. Elizabeth Mannion, "Introduction: A Path to Emerald Noir: The Rise of the Irish Detective Novel," in *The Contemporary Irish Detective Novel*, ed. Elizabeth Mannion (London: Palgrave, 2016), 3.
55. Platten, "Mediatized Realities," 35.
56. Kincaid, "'Down These Mean Streets': The City and Critique in Contemporary Irish Noir," 47.

57. Hugh Haughton and Bryan Radley, "An Interview with John Banville," *Modernism/Modernity* 18, no. 4 (November 2011): 857.

58. For example, Derek Hand, leveraging on Richard Kearney's work, insists on the essential Irishness of Banville's work in *John Banville: Exploring Fictions* (Dublin: The Liffey Press, 2002), 12–19. Similarly, John Kenny has considered the merits of historicizing Banville's work in *John Banville* (Dublin: Irish Academic Press, 2009), 55–57.

59. John Banville, "The Movies and Me," *Irish Times*, June 8, 2013, http://www.irishtimes.com/culture/john-banville-the-movies-and-me-1.1419028 (accessed August 24, 2016).

60. Banville, *Time Pieces: A Dublin Memoir*, 80.

61. Weiner, "I Hate Genre."

62. Ibid.

63. John Banville, "Quirke comes from the damaged recesses of my Irish soul," interview with Hannah Ellis-Petersen, *The Guardian*, 23 May 2014, https://www.theguardian.com/books/2014/may/23/john-banville-quirke-benjamin-black-bbc (accessed July 14, 2016).

64. Ruland, "Guest Profile: Benjamin Black."

65. "Q & A with Benjamin Black," *Crimespree Magazine*, January 27, 2016, http://crimespreemag.com/qa-with-benjamin-black/ (accessed July 31, 2016).

66. Ruland, "Guest Profile: Benjamin Black."

67. "Oblique Dreamer," interview with *The Observer*, *The Guardian*, September 17, 2000, https://www.theguardian.com/books/2000/sep/17/fiction.johnbanville/ (accessed July 31, 2016).

68. John Banville, "A True Picture of Picasso," *Irish Times*, January 4, 2014, http://www.irishtimes.com/culture/books/a-true-picture-of-picasso-1.1642473 (accessed July 31, 2016).

69. Ibid.

70. Denis Donoghue, *On Eloquence* (New Haven: Yale University Press, 2008), 135.

71. Ibid., 3.

72. John Connolly, "Joining the Criminal Fraternity," *Irish Times*, 30 September 2006. A review of *Christine Falls*, http://www.irishtimes.com/news/joining-the-criminal-fraternity-1.1009802 (accessed July 31, 2016).

73. Mark Lawson, "The Name's Quirke," *The Guardian*, 9 July 2011. R.10.

74. Banville has pointed to the importance of plot in his Black novels in the following terms: "For Black, character matters, plot matters, dialogue matters to a much greater degree than they do in my Banville books. One can, with skill and perseverance, give a sense of life's richness and complexity in noir fiction." Belinda McKeon, "John Banville: The Art of Fiction No. 200," *The Paris Review*, no. 188, http://www.theparisreview.org/interviews/5907/the-art-of-fiction-no-200–john-banville (accessed October 31, 2016).

75. John Kenny, *John Banville* (Dublin: Irish Academic Press, 2009), 9.

76. Joanna Kavenna, "Pseudonymously Yours: The Strange Case of Benjamin Black," *The New Yorker*, 11 & 18 July 2011, 93.

77. Haughton and Radley, 868.

78. See, for example, *The Silver Swan:* "She was his daughter. He must find a way to bring her back to life. That was how he thought of it, those were the words that formed

CHAPTER 6

themselves in his head: I must bring her back, bring her back, to life. . . . He tried to make himself move, to walk, to get away, but in vain: his body would not obey him. He stood there, paralysed. He did not know where to go. He did not know what to do" (344–45).
79. John Banville, "Personally Speaking I Blame Agatha for Turning Me to Crime," *Sunday Telegraph*, 11 February 2007.
80. McKeon, "John Banville: The Art of Fiction."
81. Walter Pater, *The Renaissance: Studies in Art and Poetry: The 1893 Text*, ed. Donald L. Hill (Berkeley: University of California Press, 1980), 106.
82. Susanne Langer, *Feeling and Form* (New York: Charles Scribner's Sons, 1953), 228.
83. Wallace Stevens, *Opus Posthumous* (New York: Knopf, 1989), 229.

CONCLUSION

As recently as 2009, John Banville suggested to Belinda McKeon that he had moved into "another area—pure fiction."[1] This would imply that *The Infinities*, *Ancient Light*, and *The Blue Guitar* (of the Banville novels) represent a shift in his work with respect to the diminished significance of subject matter. But Banville has always stressed the incidental nature of subject matter in his work; his novels have always flaunted their own fictionality and foregrounded the ineffectual nature of intellectual systems that seek to engage with "real" things. For example, in his essay "The Personae of Summer" (1996), he somewhat brashly declares, "Fictional characters are made of words, not flesh; they do not have free will, they do not exercise volition. They are easily born, and as easily killed off. They have their flickering lives, and die on cue, for us, giving up their little paragraph of pathos."[2] Similarly, a year later, he expressed his admiration for Beckett's "pure art," particularly with respect to the late "light works at the end of his life," which created a "house for being" that is "the ideal of what every artist should be."[3] More recently, in a review-essay he has argued, with respect to *Ulysses*, that Joyce's boast (that Dublin could be rebuilt, brick by brick, using his work) is "a hollow boast. . . . A book, even a book as minutely detailed as *Ulysses*, is built not of bricks but of words, and words, even James Joyce's words, are at best an approximate take on physical reality."[4] However, it is also clear that from *Eclipse* onward Banville's work turned inward on itself to a greater degree than previously, retreating from the practice of placing ostensibly coherent subjects like science, paintings, history, and morality at the center of his narrators' attention. Instead, they focused on the quality of their own perceptions and subjective imaginings, metaphorically resembling the late interiors of Bonnard in their narrowing of focus to the specificity of the imagining mind itself. What is it that the imagination does with the world that haunts it? How is the recalibrated world textured in these strange, illuminated spaces that emerge as compensatory gestures for a lost

CONCLUSION

world? Each of the fictions that were published since *Eclipse* circle around these questions in slightly modified ways but the primary focus remains similar. In keeping with Banville's continuous process of self-reference, this similarity is akin to Morrow's insistence in *Athena*, citing Adorno, that "works of art recall the theologumenon (sic) that in a state of redemption everything will be just as it is and yet wholly different" (*A*, 105), and Max's claim in *The Sea*, that "the uncanny is not some new thing but a thing known returning in a different form, becoming a revenant" (*TS*, 10). These statements echo a point that he has made in several of his essays and interviews. For example, when writing of Joyce he argues that art,

> Far from allowing us to know things with any immediacy, art, I believe, *makes things strange*. This it does by illuminating things, literally: the making of art is a process in which the artist concentrates on the object with such force, with such ferocity of attention, that the object takes on an unearthly—no, an earthly glow.[5]

Similarly, he argues that this kind of transformative act is the most appropriate way that art can respond to material reality: "This is the project that all artists are embarked upon: to subject mundane reality to such intense, passionate, and un-blinking scrutiny that it becomes transformed into some-thing rich and strange while yet re-maining solidly, stolidly, itself."[6] Banville has frequently acknowledged that there is a distinct continuity across his novels,[7] but the revisitation of the same core matters, the same landscapes and characters, and similar aesthetic positioning serves a more aesthetically ambitious end.

Banville's recent novel, *The Blue Guitar*, emphatically reconfirms the extraordinary interconnectedness of this most intricate of fictional universes. The novel features explicit references to other Banville novels like *The Sea*, *The Newton Letter*, *Athena*, and *The Infinities*,[8] while also revisiting many familiar tropes like the house, the circus, the scientific imagination, the lost daughter, and a pervasive sense of artistic crisis. Furthermore, familiar Banville allusive presences, both real and imaginary, return in the shape of Wallace Stevens, Rilke, Bonnard, Picasso, Watteau, Tiepolo, and Vaublin, while the sense of a haunted, defamiliarized world and a perpetual sense of bafflement are constituent features of Oliver Orme's narrative voice. One is thus again reminded of the essential sameness of Banville's extended fictional topos. Furthermore, Oliver acknowledges that he has always been a thief and the doubling with Banville, the author, is especially apparent here; he has not just constructed intertextual "tissues of quotations," but has formulated his aesthetic principles from a combination of concepts from Rilke, Wallace Stevens, Kleist, Nietzsche, the Russian formalist defamiliarization, the Freudian uncanny, Bonnard, Watteau, various still life painters, and Henry James, among countless others. *The Blue Guitar,* narrated—oddly enough—by Banville's first literal artist-narrator (all the others are impersonators), Oliver Orme (Or *me,* is surely self-reflexively intended) represents a kind of overview and itemization of all Banville's work. Oliver's unique contribution lies here, in the self-reflexive declaration that he, like Banville, has woven a long, extended sequence of interrelated, doubled fictional worlds that have long sought their own, borrowed, artistic significance. What they all share is an antirepresentational aesthetic, one in which the strangeness of existence is mirrored in an othered sense of reality that perpetually recurs, and which is given life *precisely* because of its strangeness. This position is also repeatedly articulated in Banville's reviews and essays. He argues, somewhat contentiously for Joyceans, one imagines, that the primary value in the old master's work is its mysteriousness and proceeds to identify the uncanny as an attendant feature:

> There is something uncanny about such art. It does not seem to have been produced by human hands but to have created itself out of nothing by some secret, unknowable means. And so the work stands before us, light and lightsome, glossy as an apple, full of chat—and utterly impenetrable.[9]

This echoes his subsequent observations about Picasso's *The Three Dancers* (1925), which he claims was painted without "ulterior motive," an example of "pure painting," unlike the more famous—and politically ambitious *Guernica* (1937), and is therefore a superior work of art.[10] For Banville, the subject matter ultimately does little more than to serve the entangled mesh of aesthetic principles that perpetually speak of the world's strangeness and the bafflement of a procession of narrators.

In *The Blue Guitar,* the correlation between painting and stealing is maintained throughout, facilitating a commentary on one aspect of Oliver's, and Banville's, aesthetic position. Oliver explicitly registers the connection via an elaboration of his aesthetic practice of assimilation of experiences and influences: "Painting, like stealing, was an endless effort at possession, and endlessly I failed. Stealing other people's goods, daubing scenes, loving Polly: all the one, in the end" (58). More specifically, he alerts us to the familiar Banvillean perspective that art is not intended to serve any particular purpose: "There are many kinds of theft, from the whimsical through to the malicious, but there's

CONCLUSION

only one kind that counts, for me, and that's the theft that is utterly inutile. The objects I take must be ones that can't be put to practical use, not by me, anyway" (22).[11] Echoing the Kantian-derived concept of "purposiveness without purpose,"[12] and Banville's insistence that his work is disengaged from utility,[13] Oliver echoes a particular aesthetic position which strongly resonates with the inward gaze of all of the author's narrators. Banville's "purposiveness" is instead primarily aimed at the craft of the work that he is engaged with at any given time: "Fiction is a kind of infinitesimal calculus, approaching nearer and ever nearer to life itself and yet never really having anything of real life in it at all, except the fictionist's obsessive and doomed determination to get it right (if that really is a human desideratum)."[14]

Oliver's Orme's role as an artist-in-crisis serves as a key enabler of a retrospective artistic commentary and offers an intriguing opportunity to articulate several of the key aesthetic positions that permeate Banville's body of work. For example, Oliver admits that he hadn't always painted the world "but the world as my mind rendered it" (38), echoing the subjectivist position that defines all of Banville's major narrator-artists. Similarly, he suggests, recalling a key fascination of the science tetralogy, that he had long ago realized "that there was no such thing as the thing itself, only effects of things, the generative swirl of relation" (57). He concludes that there is "the world without, the world within, and betwixt them the unbridgeable, the unleapable, chasm. And so I gave up" (59). This recalls Banville's observations about the aspirations of science in several commentaries:

> Science keeps uncovering more and more secrets, keeps getting closer and closer to . . . well, to something, in the same way that computations in the infinitesimal calculus keep approaching nearer and nearer to infinity without ever getting there. Progress must be progress toward something, surely, some final end to the quest for knowledge? But to my mind the world has no meaning.[15]

He has also argued that he ultimately found the language of science too systematized[16] but an aspiration toward progressive levels of meaning is also at odds with the kind of evolution that one finds in the novels.

Banville's perpetual fascination with the ontological layering of "reality" repeatedly finds expression in his doubled fictions, in the infusion of intertextual moments, in the play with twins and mirrors, and in the malleability of temporality. *The Blue Guitar*, as a kind of cumulative statement, addresses all of these focuses. With Oliver the overt discourse is slightly modified because

CONCLUSION

he *is* an artist, while all of Banville's previous narrators are simply imbued with creative impulses in the context of their primary frames (science, history, mathematics, art history, art forgery, and acting). Oliver *is* an artist and this lends specificity to his observations, and offers him a vocabulary that is directly artistic in focus. Explaining his crisis, for instance, he articulates the sequence that delivered him to his current impasse:

> for what else was there to paint but the thing, as it stood before me, stolid, impenetrable, un-get-roundable? Abstraction wouldn't solve the problem. I tried it, and saw it was mere sleight of hand, meremost sleight of mind. And so it kept asserting itself, the inexpressible thing, kept pressing forwards, until it filled my vision and became as good as real. Now I realised that in seeking to strike through surfaces to get at the core, the essence, I had overlooked the fact that it is in the surface that essence resides: and there I was, back to the start again. So it was the world, the world in its entirety, I had to tackle. But world is resistant, it lives turned away from us, in blithe communion with itself. World won't let us in. (*BG*, 57–58)

Oliver's detailing of his aesthetic challenges can be read as an approximate itemization of the various artistic crises that Banville's narrators experience in all of his books, alerting his readers to the fact that his work has always been a demonstration of the inevitability of artistic failure rather than a genuine artistic quest for a solution to the unavoidable distinction between world and word. The work has always sought to explore the nature of that failure and to illustrate the manner in which art may act as an illuminated gesture of compensation that conveys a semblance of the strangeness of the world. And it is here, in the "betwixt," in the peculiar space that Banville manages to fashion for himself where an observation of the strangeness of existence may be eked out, not as a means to get at the world, ultimately, but as an end in itself.

The Blue Guitar, as a comprehensive self-reflexive sequence of observations about all of Banville works, simultaneously manages to both express the oddness of the tension between the world and our unfulfilled desire to name it. For example, the manner in which he witnesses Polly—effectively slipping through ontological levels (of within, without, and betwixt)—and himself, gazing at each other through reflected mirror eyes generates an intensely unsettling moment:

> When Polly stepped out of the lavatory, the door, before she closed it, was behind her, hiding her from my view, but in the mirror, to which she had turned—which of us can resist a glance at ourselves

CONCLUSION

> in the glass?—she was facing me, and our eyes met, our reflected eyes, that is. Perhaps it was the intervention of the mirror, or the interpolation of it, I should say, for the faint hint of treachery the word insinuates, that made us seem, just for a second, not to recognise each other, indeed, not to know each other at all. We might have been, in that instant, strangers—no, more than strangers, worse than strangers: we might have been creatures from entirely different worlds. And perhaps, thanks to the transformative sly magic of mirrors, we were. Doesn't the new science say of mirror symmetry that certain particles seeming to find exact reflections of themselves are in fact the interaction of two separate realities, that indeed they are not particles at all but pinholes in the fabric of invisibly intersecting universes? No, I don't understand it either, but it sounds compelling, doesn't it? (*BG*, 81–82)

The ontological oddness of their subsequent, post-mirrored moment also extends to Oliver's wondering "if Polly and I came back fully from whatever other reality, whatever looking-glass world it was, that we had strayed into, however briefly, in that instant" (82). Throughout the novel, this sense of slippage between different levels occurs on many occasions, lending a most peculiar density to the surface texture of the world. While the novel initially appears to be reminiscent of a nominally realist landscape, even to the point of name-checking various Irish contexts, as Eoghan Smith has shrewdly observed,[17] it soon becomes apparent that the surface reality shimmers with a strangeness that intensifies as the work proceeds. Andrew Riemer contends, for example, that in Banville's intertextually charged world, "people are transformed, at least in the artist's eyes, and become, poetically and symbolically, incarnations of the ancient gods."[18] The sense of an imaginatively transformed world is perhaps most strikingly rendered when Oliver encounters a strange procession of colored caravans and odd music while walking in the countryside, recalling the familiar presence of circuses and gypsy folk in several other Banville fictions (*Long Lankin*, *Birchwood*, and *Eclipse*). The peculiarity of the event isn't lost on Oliver:

> Had I chanced upon some crossing point where universes intersect, had I broken through briefly into another world, far from this one in place and time? Or had I simply imagined it? Was it a vision, or a waking dream?
> Now I walked on, heedless of the encroaching dark, unnerved by that hallucinatory encounter and yet strangely elated, too. (*BG*, 168–69)

CONCLUSION

The precise ontological status of this moment is unclear, even to Oliver, but in Banville's layered fictional universe, characters and incidents like this frequently bleed into one another and rupture the primary diegetic level. Oliver's primary narrative level is already deeply compromised by his continual observations about the chasm between the world and his art. The one certainty is the strangeness of what it means to exist, a condition of being that has become the dominant mode of fictional consciousness in Banville. In moments like this, the text declares a sense of its own strangeness as primary constituent of the telling.

This sense is evident throughout the novel, most unnervingly perhaps in Oliver's sense of dislocation in Grange Hall, yet another house resonant with an essentially aesthetic function:

> Take that strange afternoon at Grange Hall, with Polly and her parents, and the even stranger hours that followed. I should have made my getaway at the end of that gruesome tea-party—at which I felt like Alice, the Mad Hatter and the March Hare all rolled into one—but the atmosphere of Grange Hall held me fast in an unshakeable lassitude. (*BG*, 140)

Here again the slippage between worlds, even intertextually, informs his sense of being. Like most of his predecessor-narrators, he exists in a perpetual "daze of bafflement" (184), which becomes the central aesthetic focus of their fictional world. As Banville puts it: "Good art recognizes, as I say, our peculiar predicament in the world, that we're suspended in this extraordinary place, we don't know what it's for or why we're here. We know vaguely, but there is no answer to it."[19] It has long been clear that Banville's aesthetic sense, his understanding of what the nonrepresentational fictional mode can achieve, is to speak of the strangeness of being, of the dizzying state that permeates the self-conscious space between an unreachable world and its fictional representations. In his self-reflexive worlds, it is precisely the unrepresentable that is given utterance, and his work over the past two decades has increasingly sought to find a vocabulary to speak of this.

Such a position has long been present in Banville's sense of how the novel form evolved: "There is a profound mystery about the best of Henry James' books, even though they are perfectly comprehensible. The object itself stands in its own mystery."[20] Similarly, Banville has often insisted that the reason he writes is precisely to express his own state of confusion: "I don't understand people. That's probably why I write novels. Not to try and understand

CONCLUSION

them, but to express my incomprehension."[21] The strangeness of being, the incomprehension, are constituent parts of the process of illuminating, rather than reflecting, reality. Or, as Oliver insists, "My only aim always, from the very start, was to get down in form that formless tension floating in the darkness inside my skull, like the unfading after-image of a lighting-flash" (103). The formless tension in Banville is always troubled, mysterious, and ultimately unreachable and, in the nonreferential tradition from which he emerged, the work seeks to express the very fact of the world's mysteriousness in the forms of art. As Banville insists, "All—all!—art attempts to do is to quicken the sense of life, to make vivid for the reader the mysterious predicament of being alive for a brief span in this exquisite and terrible world,"[22] and the novels perpetually circle around this predicament, never moving beyond it in any essential sense. Banville's world is thus of the half-seen and the inarticulate, his role is to populate the "incoherent space" of art with his "creatures, or inventions."[23]

That Oliver is a visual artist affords us both a glimpse of how he conceives of the world as a particular kind of artist, and it also permits Banville to revisit the manner in which his own narrative forms are sometimes formulated in conversation with the visual arts. While the ghost of Picasso's 1903–1904 painting, *The Old Guitarist* (Figure 5), clearly hovers in Banville's novel, in much the same way that it does in Stevens's poem, "The Man with the Blue Guitar,"[24] the painting that is most significantly present is Manet's *Déjeuner sur l'herbe* (1863) (Figure 6). In a manner similar to the infusion of Bonnard, Vermeer, and others in *The Sea*, on a number of occasions *The Blue Guitar* substitutes its sequential narrative for a spatial appropriation of Manet's painting. Early in the novel Oliver imaginatively reconstructs a picnic with his wife, Gloria, Polly, his future lover, and her husband, Marcus by fusing the event with Manet's painting:

> Inevitably, I see the occasion in the light of old man Manet's *Déjeuner sur l'herbe*—the earlier, smaller one—with blonde Gloria in the buff and Polly off in the background bathing her feet. Polly that day seemed hardly more than a girl, pink-cheeked and creamy, instead of the married woman that she was. Marcus was wearing a straw hat with holes in it, and Gloria was her usual glorious self, a big bright beauty shedding radiance all round her. And, my God, but my wife was magnificent that day, as indeed she always is. . . . In fact, she is a Tiepolo rather than a Manet type, one of the Venetian master's Cleopatras, say, or his Beatrice of Burgundy. (*BG*, 9)

His imaginative vision alternates between the remembered event itself and the painting, with neither fully asserting primary authority in the novel's narrative, a point that is emphasized even further when he later recalls both the picnic and the painting:

> Cast your mind back to my mentioning, oh, ages ago, that the first encounter I could recall between the four of us, that is, Polly, Marcus, Gloria and me, was a little outing to a park somewhere that we went on together one intermittently rainy summer afternoon. I spoke of it then as a version of *Le déjeuner sur l'herbe*, but time, I mean recent time, has mellowed it to something less boldly done. Instead, picture it, say, as a scene by Vaublin, *mon semblable*, nay, my twin, not in summer now but some other, more sombre, season, the crepuscular park with its auburn masses of trees under big heapings of evening cloud, dark-apricot, gold, gesso-white, and in a clearing, see, the luminous little group arranged upon the grass, one idly strumming a mandolin, another looking wistfully away with a finger pressed to a dimpled cheek. (*BG*, 223)

Not only does Manet now transform into another of Banville's familiar presences, the painter Vaublin, usually associated with Watteau as we have seen, the switch to the present tense more completely assimilates the ekphrastic mode into the novel's own temporal and spatial zones. George Steiner likens such a quality to what he terms the condition of "free time" as articulated through poetics:

> Even more than in philosophy, it is through poetics that human consciousness experiences free time. Syntax empowers a multitudinous range of "times." Remembrance, a frozen present, futurities (as in science fiction) are obvious examples of the free play with time without which the epic poem, the universe of narrative fiction or the film would be impossible.[25]

For Steiner, these possibilities are even more evidently present in the visual. For example, he claims, that "certain paintings 'temporize,' generate their own time within time, even beyond the powers of language. . . . Such paintings draw us into a time-grid integral wholly to themselves."[26] Much of Oliver's reconstitution of the events of his life, and especially his affair with Polly, is filtered through a series of moments that seem integral to themselves. Similarly, his character-depictions are loaded with aesthetic implications: Gloria has a "big bright beauty shedding radiance all around her" (9); Polly seemed to "radiate something" (6) and later, "the skin at the outer corners of her eyes became slightly stretched and shiny, which gave to her features a curiously lacquered, Oriental cast"—an observation that reminds one of an

CONCLUSION

almost identical description of the woman in the painting in *The Book of Evidence* (78). The presence of Manet's and Vaublin's paintings in the narrative world of *The Blue Guitar* further contributes to a sense of the poeticization of space that occurs throughout the novel, and indeed in all of Banville's mature works.

Collectively, Banville's work seeks to demonstrate the chasm between reality and the subjective imagination—"a chilly pane of glass between me and longed-for world," as Oliver Orme has it—and not a series of earnest, ineffectual journeys to discovery. He has known from the outset that the pane of glass will always stand between the mind and the world, so art is instead offered up as the great, illuminating, consoling fiction. Oliver repeatedly insists that everything is a question of "aesthetics" after all (21, 172, 237), in the face of an incalcitrant or indifferent world. In many respects these are essentially the problems that so defined postmodernism. Theorists of postmodern fiction have primarily conceived of the self-reflexive mode—a key formal marker of the form—as an act of resistance toward, or subversion of realist modes of writing, and gestures of "incredulity toward metanarratives," as Lyotard has it.[27] This was certainly so in Banville's work for many years with the earlier novels, *Nightspawn, Birchwood, Doctor Copernicus,* and *Kepler* all corresponding to Larry McCaffery's understanding of the postmodern novel as featuring a "shared heightening of artifice, a delight in verbal play and formal manipulation of fictive elements."[28] But novels like *The Newton Letter* and *Mefisto* initiated a transitionary period in which Banville sought to evolve beyond acts of playful resistance in an effort to articulate, via the self-conscious mode, a new formulation about the meaning and significance of art. The novels of the Frames Trilogy placed art firmly at the center of their formulations, as primary subject, but the Cleave novels, *The Sea,* and *The Blue Guitar* all utilize the mode in different ways—they seek instead to demonstrate the complex act of apprehension in the process of the act itself, almost to the exclusion of all else. To some degree this corresponds with McCaffery's suggestion that postmodern fiction, after the 1980s, "incorporated postmodern experimental strategies into their structures so smoothly that they have often been seen as being quite traditional in orientation."[29] While Banville's work is certainly not traditional in orientation, many of the painters he folds into his narratives may be seen as such, and painters like Watteau, Bonnard, and even Picasso have never been associated with postmodernism.

Here lies the key to Banville's particular engagement with the postmodernism from which he emerged. After the early overtly metafictional novels, his work clearly evolved in a manner that sought to assimilate a range of aesthetic ideals, visual artists, and writerly influences (Kleist, Rilke, Stevens, Nietzsche, Kafka, Bonnard), none of which can be considered postmodern. And yet, the ostensibly postmodern mode remains implicit to all of the recent work, including *The Blue Guitar*, a novel that repeatedly draws attention both to its own constructed nature and the inevitability of one's failure to ever fully grasp the essence of things. Oliver is no nearer to grasping the true significance of existence than Banville's narrators have ever been; this is a philosophically postmodern point, but Banville has long since infused his variation of postmodernism with a compensatory gesture framed by the illuminations of art. It is in this sense that Banville's largely positive attitude toward Beckett's aesthetic achievement is revealing.[30] In an obituary essay penned upon Beckett's death, he suggests that the reason for his magnificence as an artist was precisely his success in achieving a "state of luminous absence" in the work. "It is a bad mistake," Banville argues, "to treat art as a commentary upon the life and times of the artist. Relevance is always an accident." Beckett's work only *seems* to us "a testament to the life of our execrable century," because of its "bleak refusal to turn aside from horrors."[31] The luminous absence, the "failing light and encroaching silence, the tedium and laughter and sorrow, these are not things transposed from the life into the work, but, rather, they are the processes of the work itself."[32] While there are obvious differences between Banville's and Beckett's work, the emphasis on aesthetic process rather than commentary is clear, as is what Banville views to be the essential value of Beckett's work: "No one else in this century has, in my view, expressed so unflinchingly the world's anguish or portrayed so movingly its tragic, fleeting beauty."[33] Banville's aesthetic synthesis represents a possible resolution of sorts for the postmodern predicament—the problem of representation and knowing—by renegotiating the value of the work of art in a manner that admits to the essential strangeness and mutability of existence. By creating fiction that places these essential characteristics at the heart of its world-making, it seeks to generate a special kind of aesthetic validation. Postmodern denials of meaning are not the central problem, but rather the assumption that one can establish fixed meaning, or locate the essence of things. Banville instead retains, like Beckett, a perpetual desire to name the world, in terms of its essential beauty, even in the face of the gaunt epistemological afterlife of the world after postmodernism.

The final pages of *The Blue Guitar* may be read both as a pivotal note of resignation and a statement of future intent by Oliver Orme *and* Banville:

CONCLUSION

> As I squatted there in the attic, musing on her image, with the soft smell of must in my nostrils and thronged around by the wreckage of the past, it occurred to me that perhaps that should be my task now, to burrow back into that past and begin to learn over again all I had thought I knew but didn't. Yes, I might embark on a great instauration. Hardly an original endeavour, I grant you, but why should I allow that to hinder me? I never aspired to originality, and was always, even in my paltry heyday, content to plough the established and familiar furrows. Who knows, the dogged old painster might even learn to paint again, or just learn, for the first time, and at last. I could sketch out a group portrait of the four of us, linked hand in hand in a round-dance. Or maybe I'll bow out and let Freddie Hyland complete the quartet, while I stand off to one side, in my Pierrot costume, making melancholy strummings on a blue guitar. (*BG*, 249)

The self-conscious doubling of intention is as perfectly integrated here as it has ever been; Banville, Oliver Orme, and the Pierrot reflect and re-reflect each other in a retrospective reckoning of sorts, making the nominal distinctions between author, narrator, and art-rendering invisible. Fictional self-consciousness always bears traces of the author's hesitancy, his ongoing artistic crisis. In Banville it is so prevalent, so deeply engendered, that it becomes a constituent part of the whole enterprise—it becomes, in itself, his "one true subject" (*BG*, 103–4). In Banville's later works, in particular, ontological levels shimmer and mirror each other, occasionally overlap; they simultaneously fail to represent meaning while emphatically illuminating a sense of being in the world. Fiction itself is, finally, Banville's most invasively potent metaphor for being, with its inherent doubleness, its ontological impenetrability, and its perpetual refusal to present certitude. In its capacity to retain an illuminated after-glow of the world from which in some strange relational sense it emerges, it illustrates how Banville has advanced the form of the novel.

Notes

1. McKeon, "John Banville. The Art of Fiction," interview with John Banville, *The Paris Review*, no. 188 (Spring 2009): http://www.theparisreview.org/interviews/5907/the-art-of-fiction-no-200–john-banville (accessed October 31, 2016).
2. John Banville, "The Personae of Summer," in *Irish Writers and Their Creative Processes*, ed. Jacqueline Genet and Wynne Hellegouarc'h (Gerrards Cross: Colin Smythe Ltd., 1996), 118.

3. Hedwig Schwall, "An Interview with John Banville," *European English Messenger* 6, no. 1 (1997):16.

4. John Banville, "James Joyce's Dublin," *Irish Arts Review* 21, no. 2 (Summer 2004): 87.

5. John Banville, "Survivors of Joyce," in *James Joyce: The Artist and the Labyrinth*, ed. Augustine Martin (London: Ryan Publishing, 1990), 78.

6. John Banville, "Beauty, Charm, and Strangeness: Science as Metaphor," *Science* 281, no. 5373 (July 3, 1998): 41.

7. In an interview with Breathnach, for example, Banville confirms that all of his novels "are Banvillian novels. They have to be. I can't write them in anybody else's voice. They all seem of a piece, part of one large volume somebody will perhaps bind into an enormous doorstopper after I've gone. There is continuity between them all, even though some of them are very different." Kevin Breathnach, "John Banville Interviewed," in *Totally Dublin*, June 28, 2012, http://totallydublin.ie/arts-culture/arts-culture-features/john-banville-interviewed/ (accessed September 31, 2016).

8. Several of these echoes involve intertextual interweavings as, for example, the reference to "Morden's monograph" on Oliver Orme (*BG*, 179). Morden is Max's original name in *The Sea*, in which he is writing a book on Bonnard. It appears that he has also written a book on Oliver Orme (or-me), who is, in fact, really just another emanation of Morden anyway—so in Banville's playful scheme of things he has effectively written a book about himself.

9. John Banville, "Survivors of Joyce," 74.

10. John Banville, "A True Picture of Picasso," *Irish Times*, January 4, 2014.

11. Even in earlier essays like "A Talk" and "The Personae of Summer," there is a persistent emphasis on the role of the aestheticized object. In "A Talk," for example, Banville cites Rilke's *Duino Elegies* as follows:

> Praise this world to the Angel, not the untellable: you
> can't impress him with the splendour you've felt;

Banville, "A Talk," *Irish University Review* 11, no. 1 (Spring 1981): 15. In "The Personae of Summer," similarly, Banville praises the "wrought and polished object itself, an astonishment standing in the world—a jar in Tennessee! That is what interests me." Banville, "The Personae of Summer," 119.

12. Immanuel Kant, *Critique of Judgement* (New York: Cosimo Classics, 2007), 74.

13. Banville, for example, insists that "As a writer I have little or no interest in character, plot, motivation, manners, politics, morality, social issues." Banville, "Personae of Summer," 118.

14. Ibid., 121.

15. John Banville, "Beauty, Charm, and Strangeness," 40.

16. "Master of Paradox: Interview with John Banville," interview by Helen Meany, *The Irish Times*, March 24, 1993, 12.

17. Eoghan Smith itemizes some of the Irish contexts as follows: "Local names such as Colfer and a reference to the sacking of Wexford Town by Oliver Cromwell's New Model Army in 1649 means the southeast of Ireland is once more identifiable as the setting. Indeed, the novel is filled with references to Ireland's colonial past, an emblem of

CONCLUSION

dispossession. Oliver's surname, Orme, suggests a non-Irish ancestry (there were Ormes of English descent in Wexford and Mayo; it is also an Old Norse word for serpent) and so he is posited as a cultural outsider, if only very distantly." Eoghan Smith, "It's That Man Again," *Dublin Review of Books*, no. 83 (November 2016).

18. Andrew Riemer, "The Blue Guitar Review: John Banville Generates Deep Aesthetic Satisfaction," *Sydney Morning Herald*, August 29, 2015, http://www.smh.com.au/entertainment/books/the-blue-guitar-review-john-banville-generates-deep-aesthetic-satisfaction-20150822–gj3ooo.html (accessed June 20, 2016).

19. Anne K. Yoder, "The Millions Interview: John Banville," *The Millions*, February 24, 2010, http://www.themillions.com/2010/02/the-millions-interview-john-banville.html (accessed June 20, 2016).

20. Schwall, "An Interview with John Banville," 17.

21. "Interview with a Writer: John Banville," by J. P. O'Malley, *The Spectator*, March 29, 2013, http://blogs.spectator.co.uk/2013/03/interview-with-a-writer-john-banville/ (accessed June 20, 2016).

22. "Fully Booked: Q & A with John Banville," interview by Travis Elborough, *Picador*, June 29, 2012.

23. McKeon, "John Banville."

24. Wallace Stevens suggested that Picasso's painting was but loosely connected to his poem. In a letter to Professor Renato Poggioli, Stevens explained, "I had no particular painting of Picasso's in mind and even though it might help to sell the book to have one of his paintings on the cover, I don't think we ought to reproduce anything of Picasso's." *Letters of Wallace Stevens*, selected and edited by Holly Stevens, with a new forward by Richard Howard (Berkeley: University of California Press, 1966), 786.

25. George Steiner, *Grammars of Creation* (London: Faber and Faber, 2001), 59.

26. Ibid., 59.

27. Jean-François Lyotard, *The Postmodern Condition: A Report on Knowledge*, trans. G. Bennington/B. Massumi (Minneapolis: University of Minnesota Press, 1989), xxiv–xxv.

28. Larry McCaffery, *Postmodern Fiction: A Bio-Bibliographical Guide* (New York: Greenwood Press, 1986), xiii.

29. McCaffery, *Postmodern Fiction*, xxvii.

30. For a comprehensive and insightful comparison of Banville's relative interest in Joyce and Beckett, see Kersti Tarien Powell's "'Not a son but a survivor': Beckett . . . Joyce . . . Banville," extract from *The Yearbook of English Studies* 35 (2005): 199–211. Powell cites Banville's admission that he went in a "Beckettian direction, rather than a Joycean one" (199).

31. John Banville, "The Painful Comedy of Samuel Beckett," review of *Damned to Fame: The Life of Samuel Beckett*, by James Knowlson, and *Samuel Beckett: The Last Modernist*, by Anthony Cronin, *The New York Review of Books*, November 14, 1996, 29.

32. John Banville, "Samuel Beckett dies in Paris aged 83," *Irish Times*, December 25, 1989, 19.

33. John Banville, "The Painful Comedy of Samuel Beckett," review of *Damned to Fame: The Life of Samuel Beckett*, by James Knowlson, and *Samuel Beckett: The Last Modernist*, by Anthony Cronin, *The New York Review of Books*, November 14, 1996, 29.

BIBLIOGRAPHY

Primary Works

AS JOHN BANVILLE

Time Pieces: A Dublin Memoir. Dublin: Hachette Books, 2016.
The Blue Guitar. London: Viking Penguin, 2015.
Ancient Light. London: Viking Penguin, 2012.
The Infinities. London: Picador, 2009.
The Sea. London: Picador, 2005.
Prague Pictures. London: Bloomsbury, 2003.
Shroud. London: Picador, 2002.
Eclipse. London: Picador, 2000.
The Untouchable. London: Picador, 1997.
Athena. London: Secker & Warburg, 1995.
Ghosts. London: Secker & Warburg, 1993.
The Book of Evidence. London: Secker & Warburg, 1989.
Mefisto. New Hampshire: David R. Godine, 1989.
The Newton Letter: An Interlude. London: Panther Books, 1984.
Kepler. London: Panther Books, 1985.
Doctor Copernicus. London: Panther Books, 1984.
Birchwood. London: Panther Books, 1984.
Nightspawn. London: Secker & Warburg, 1971.
Long Lankin. London: Secker & Warburg, 1970.

AS BENJAMIN BLACK

Even the Dead. London: Penguin, 2016.
The Black-Eyed Blonde. New York: Henry Holt, 2014.
Holy Orders. New York: Henry Holt, 2013.
Vengeance. London: Mantle, 2012.
Elegy for April. London: Picador, 2011.
A Death in Summer. London: Mantle, 2011.

BIBLIOGRAPHY

The Lemur. London: Picador, 2008.
The Silver Swan. London: Picador, 2007.
Christine Falls. London: Picador, 2006.

DRAMA AND SCREENPLAYS

Love in the Wars: After Kleist's Penthesilea. Oldcastle: Gallery, 2005.
God's Gift: A Version of Amphitryon by Heinrich von Kleist. Oldcastle: Gallery, 2000.
The Last September. Screenplay adapted from the novel by Elizabeth Bowen. Dir. Deborah Warner. Trimark Pictures, 1999.
Seachange. Television screenplay. Dublin: RTE, 1994.
The Broken Jug: After Heinrich von Kleist. Oldcastle: Gallery Press, 1994.
Reflections. Screenplay adapted from The Newton Letter. Dir. Kevin Billington. Court House Films/Channel Four, UK 1983. 90 min.

INTERVIEWS, REVIEWS, AND SELECTED ESSAYS

John Banville. "Quirke comes from the damaged recesses of my Irish soul." By Hannah Ellis-Petersen. *The Guardian,* 23 May 2014. https://www.theguardian.com/books/2014/may/23/john-banville-quirke-benjamin-black-bbc (accessed July 14, 2016).
"*The Black-Eyed Blonde*: A Conversation with John Banville." By Christopher Cox. *Harper's Magazine,* March 26, 2014 (accessed July 14, 2017).
"I Hate Genre: An Interview with John Banville/Benjamin Black." By Jon Wiener. *LA Review of Books,* March 15, 2014. https://lareviewofbooks.org/article/hate-genre-interview-john-banvillebenjamin-black/ (accessed June 14, 2016).
"A True Picture of Picasso." *Irish Times,* January 4, 2014.
"The Movies and Me." *Irish Times,* June 8, 2013. http://www.irishtimes.com/culture/john-banville-the-movies-and-me-1.1419028/ (accessed June 16, 2016).
"Interview with a Writer: John Banville." By J. P. O'Malley. *The Spectator,* March 29, 2013.
John Banville. "'I'm at Last Beginning to Learn How to Write, and I Can Let the Writing Mind Dream.'" Interview with Arminta Wallace. *The Irish Times,* June 30, 2012.
"John Banville: A Life in Writing." With Stuart Jeffries. *The Guardian,* June 29, 2012.
"Fully Booked: Q & A with John Banville." Interview by Travis Elborough. *Picador,* June 29, 2012.
"John Banville Interviewed." Interview by Kevin Breathnach. *Totally Dublin.* http://totallydublin.ie/arts-culture/arts-culture-features/john-banville-interviewed/ (accessed July 21, 2016).
"An Interview with John Banville." Interview by Hugh Haughton and Bryan Radley. *Modernism/Modernity* 18, no. 4 (November 2011): 855–69.
"The Millions Interview: John Banville." Interview with Anne K. Yoder. *The Millions,* February 24, 2010.

"15 Questions with John Banville." Interview by Michelle B. Timmerman. *The Harvard Crimson*, February 26, 2010.

"John Banville, The Art of Fiction No. 200." Interview by Belinda McKeon. *The Paris Review* 188, no. 1 (Spring 2009).

"Guest Profile: Benjamin Black Parts 1–4." Interview with Jim Ruland. *The Elegant Variation: A Literary Weblog*, December 8, 2008.

"Personally Speaking I Blame Agatha for Turning Me to Crime." *Sunday Telegraph*, 11 February 2007.

"John Banville and Derek Hand in Conversation." Hedda Friberg. *Irish University Review* 36, no. 1 (2006): 200–215.

"The Long-Awaited, Long-Promised, Just Plain Long John Banville Interview—Part Two." Interview by Mark Sarvas. *The Elegant Variation Blog*, September 19, 2005.

John Banville, "James Joyce's Dublin." *Irish Arts Review* 21, no. 2 (Summer 2004): 84–89.

"Interviewing John Banville." Interview by Laura P. Z. Izarra. *Kaleidoscopic Views of Ireland*, edited by Murina H. Mutran and Laura P. Z. Izarra (Sao Paulo: Humanitas, 2003), 226–47.

"Oblique Dreamer: Interview with John Banville." Interview by the Observer. *Observer*, 17 September 2000: 15.

"Beauty, Charm, and Strangeness: Science as Metaphor." *Science*, New Series 281, no. 5373 (July 3, 1998): 40–41.

"An Interview with John Banville." Interview by Hedwig Schwall. *European English Messenger* 6, no. 1 (1997): 13–19.

"The Painful Comedy of Samuel Beckett." Review of *Damned to Fame: The Life of Samuel Beckett*, by James Knowlson, and *Samuel Beckett: The Last Modernist*, by Anthony Cronin. *The New York Review of Books* (November 14, 1996): 29.

"The Personae of Summer." In *Irish Writers and Their Creative Processes*. Edited by Jacqueline Genet and Wynne Hellegouarc'h (Gerrards Cross: Colin Smythe Ltd., 1996): 118–22.

"Master of Paradox: Interview with John Banville." Interview by Helen Meany. *The Irish Times*, March 24, 1993.

"Samuel Beckett Dies in Paris Aged 83." *Irish Times*, December 25, 1989, 19.

"Survivors of Joyce." In *James Joyce: The Artist and the Labyrinth*. Edited by Augustine Martin (London: Ryan Publishing, 1990), 73–81.

"The Helpless Laughter of a Tragedian." *Irish Times*, December 3, 1988: W.9.

"Physics and Fictions: Order from Chaos." *The New York Times Book Review*, 21 April, 1985: 41–42.

"My Readers, That Small Band, Deserve a Rest." Interview by Rüdiger Imhof. In *Irish University Review* 11, no. 1 (Spring 1981): 5–12.

John Banville. "A Talk." *Irish University Review* 11, no. 1 (Spring 1981): 13–17.

"Novelists on the Novel: Ronan Sheehan talks to John Banville and Francis Stuart." Interview with Ronan Sheehan. *The Crane Bag* 3, no. 1 (1979): 76–84.

BIBLIOGRAPHY

Other Works

Abbott, H. Porter. *The Cambridge Introduction to Narrative*. Cambridge, UK: Cambridge University Press, 2002.

Acocella, Joan. "Doubling Down: John Banville's Complicated Lives." *The New Yorker*, October 8, 2012. http://www.newyorker.com/magazine/2012/10/08/doubling-down.

Amory, Dita. "Pierre Bonnard (1867–1947): The Late Interiors." In *Heilbrunn Timeline of Art History*. New York: The Metropolitan Museum of Art, 2000. http://www.metmuseum.org/toah/hd/bonn/hd_bonn.htm (November 2010).

Beckett, Samuel. *The Beckett Trilogy: Molloy, Malone Dies, The Unnamable*. London: Picador, 1979.

Bell, Julian. *Bonnard*. London: Phaidon Press Ltd., 2003.

Blackford, Holly Virginia. "Apertures in the House of Fiction: Novel Methods and Child Study, 1870–1910." *Children's Literature Association Quarterly* 32, no. 4 (Winter 2007): 368–89.

Boyle, Kevin. "Benjamin Black and John Banville: The Legitimacy of the Irish Literary Persona." *New Voices in Irish Criticism: Legitimate Ireland*. The Peter Froggatt Centre, Queen's University Belfast, 19 April 2012.

Bryson, Norman. *Word and Image: French Painting of the Ancien Régime*. Cambridge: Cambridge University Press, 1981.

Calvino, Italo. "Levels of Reality in Literature." In *The Literature Machine*. London: Secker and Warburg, 1989.

———. "Lightness." In *Six Memos for the New Millennium*. New York: Vintage, 1993.

Canon-Roger, Françoise. "John Banville's *Imagines* in The Book of Evidence." *European Journal of English Studies* 4, no. 1 (2000): 25–38.

Capra, Fritjof. *The Tao of Physics: An Exploration of the Parallels Between Modern Physics and Eastern Mysticism*, 3rd ed. Boston: Shambhala, 1991.

Carroll, Noël. "Identifying Art." In *Aesthetics: A Comprehensive Anthology*, edited by Steven M. Cahn and Aaron Meskin. Oxford: Blackwell Publishing, 2008.

Cheeke, Stephen. *Writing for Art: The Aesthetics of Ekphrasis*. Manchester: Manchester University Press, 2008.

Connolly, John. "Joining the Criminal Fraternity." *Irish Times*, September 30, 2006.

Connor, Steven, ed. *The Cambridge Companion to Postmodernism*. Cambridge: Cambridge University Press, 2004.

Constantine, David. "Notes to *Amphitryon*," in *Heinrich von Kleist: Selected Writings*. Translated and edited by David Constantine. Cambridge: Hackett Publishing Company, 2004.

Coughlan, Patricia. "Banville, the Feminine, and the Scenes of Eros." *Irish University Review* 36, no. 1 (Spring-Summer 2006): 81–101.

Dell'Amico, Carol. "John Banville and Benjamin Black: The *Mundo*, Crime, Women." *Éire-Ireland* 49, no. 1 & 2 (Spring-Summer 2014): 106–20.

D'Hoker, Elke. "Portrait of the Other as a Woman with Gloves: Ethical Perspectives in John Banville's *The Book of Evidence*." *Critique* 44, no. 1 (Fall 2002): 23–37.

———. *Visions of Alterity: Representation in the Works of John Banville*. Amsterdam-New York: Rodopi, 2004.

Doctorow, E. L. "Foreword" to *Heinrich von Kleist: Plays*, edited by Walter Hinderer. New York: Continuum, 1995: vii–x.

Donnelly, Brian. "The Big House in the Recent Irish Novel." *Studies* 254 (Summer 1975): 134.

Donoghue, Denis. *On Eloquence*. New Haven: Yale University Press, 2008.

———. *Speaking of Beauty*. New Haven: Yale University Press, 2003.

Elam, Keir. *The Semiotics of Theatre and Drama*. London and New York: Routledge, 1980.

Eliot, T. S. "Tradition and the Individual Talent." In Vol. 2 of *The Norton Anthology of English Literature*, 6th ed., edited by M. H. Abrams, 2170–75. New York: W.W. Norton & Co., 1993.

Facchinello, Monica. "'The Old Illusion of Belonging': Distinctive Style, Bad Faith and John Banville's *The Sea*." *Estudios Irlandeses*, no. 5 (2010): 33–44.

Fattori, Anna. "'A Genuinely Funny German Farce' Turns into a Very Irish Play: *The Broken Jug* (1994): John Banville's Adaptation of Heinrich von Kleist's Der zerbrochne Krug (1807)." In Vol. 4 of *Angermion: Yearbook for Anglo-German Literary Criticism, Intellectual History and Cultural Transfers/Jahrbuch für Britisch-Deutsche Kulturbeziehunge*, edited by Rudiger Gorner, 75–94.

Flaubert, Gustave. *The Letters of Gustave Flaubert: 1830–1857*. Translated and edited by Francis Steegmuller. Cambridge, MA: Belknap Press of Harvard University Press, 1982.

Frehner, Ruth. "The Dark One and the Fair: John Banville's Historians of the Imagination and their Gender Stereotypes." In *ELJLS: Barcelona English Language and Literature Series*, 2000111, edited by Mireia Aragay and Jaquelme A. Hurtley. Barcelona: PPU, 2000: 51–64.

Friberg-Harnesk, Hedda. "In the Sign of the Counterfeit: John Banville's *God's Gift*." *Nordic Irish Studies* 9 (2010): 71–88.

Friberg, Hedda. "'In the Murky Sea of Memory': Memory Miscues in John Banville's *The Sea*." *An Sionnach: A Journal of Literature, and the Arts* 1, no. 2 (2005): 111–23.

———. "Waters and Memories Always Divide: Sites of Memory in John Banville's *The Sea*." In *Recovering Memory: Irish Representations of Past and Present*, edited by Hedda Friberg, Irene Gilsenan Nordin, and Lene Yding Pedersen, 244–62. Newcastle: Cambridge Scholars Publishing, 2007.

Gefter-Wondrich, Roberta. "Postmodern Love, Postmodern Death and God-Like Authors in Irish Fiction: The Case of John Banville." In *BELLS: Barcelona English Language and Literature Series*. Edited by Mireia Aragay and Jaqueline A. Hurtley (Barcelona: PPU, 2000–2011), 79–88.

Gide, André. *The Immoralist*. Harmondsworth: Penguin, 1983.

Gilson, Etienne. *The Arts of the Beautiful*. Illinois: Dalkey Archive Press, 2000.

———. *Form and Substance in the Arts*. Translated by Salvator Attanasio. Illinois: Dalkey Archive Press, 2001.

BIBLIOGRAPHY

Graham, Gordon. *Philosophy of the Arts: An Introduction to Aesthetics.* New York: Routledge, 2007.

Hand, Derek. *John Banville: Exploring Fictions.* Dublin: The Liffey Press, 2002.

Haughton, Hugh. "The Ruinous House of Identity: The fictions of John Banville." *The Dublin Review*, no. 1 (Winter 2000–2001): 107–15.

Heller, Erich. *The Poet's Self and the Poem: Essays on Goethe, Nietzsche, Rilke and Thomas Mann.* London: Athlone Press, 1976.

Herman, David, Manfred Jahn, and Marie-Laure Ryan. *Routledge Encyclopedia of Narrative Theory.* London: Routledge, 2008.

Hinderer, Walter. "Introduction" to *Heinrich von Kleist: Plays*, edited by Walter Hinderer, xi–xvii. New York: Continuum, 1995.

Huiting, Pan. *Aesthetic Configuration.* M.A. Thesis, Nanyang Technological University Singapore, 2013.

Hutcheon, Linda. *Narcissistic Narrative: The Metafictional Paradox.* Waterloo: Wilfred Laurier University Press, 1980.

Hutcheon, Linda. *A Poetics of Postmodernism: History, Theory, Fiction.* London: Routledge, 1988.

Imhof, Rüdiger. *John Banville: A Critical Introduction.* Dublin: Wolfhound Press, 1989.

———. *John Banville: A Critical Introduction.* Dublin: Wolfhound Press, 1997.

———. "John Banville's *Athena*: A Love Letter to Art." *Asylum Arts Review* 1, no. 1 (Autumn 1995): 27–34.

———. *The Modern Irish Novel: Irish Novelists after 1945.* Dublin: Wolfhound Press, 2002.

———. "'The Problematics of Authenticity': John Banville's *Shroud*." *ABEI Journal—The Brazilian Journal of Irish Studies*, no. 6 (June 2004): 105–28.

———. "The Sea: 'Was't Well Done?'" *Irish University Review* 36, no. 1 (2006): 165–81.

Irwin, John T. *The Mystery to a Solution: Poe, Borges, and the Analytic Detective Story.* London: Johns Hopkins University Press, 1996.

Jackson, Tony E. "Science, Art, and the Shipwreck of Knowledge: The Novels of John Banville." *Contemporary Literature* 38, no. 3 (Autumn 1997): 510–33.

James, Henry. *The Art of Criticism: Henry James on the Theory and the Practice of Fiction*, edited by William Veeder and Susan M. Griffin. Chicago: Chicago University Press, 1986.

James, P. D. *Talking about Detective Fiction.* Oxford: Bodleian Library, 2009.

Jernigan, Daniel K. "Tom Stoppard's Fiction: Finding his Form." *The Review of Contemporary Fiction* XXXIV, no. 1 (2014): 141–59.

Joyce, James. *A Portrait of the Artist as a Young Man.* Harmondsworth: Penguin, 1992.

Kant, Immanuel. *Critique of Judgement.* New York: Cosimo Classics, 2007.

Kavenna, Joanna. "Pseudonymously Yours: The Strange Case of Benjamin Black." *The New Yorker*, July 11 & 18, 2011.

Kenny, John. *John Banville.* Dublin: Irish Academic Press, 2009.

Kermode, Frank. *The Sense of an Ending: Studies in the Theory of Fiction.* New York: Oxford University Press, 2000.

Kincaid, Andrew. "'Down These Mean Streets': The City and Critique in Contemporary Irish Noir." *Éire-Ireland* 45, no. 1 & 2 (Spring-Summer 2010): 39–55.

Kleist, Heinrich von. *Amphitryon* in *Selected Writings*. Translated and edited by David Constantine. Indianapolis: Hackett Publishing Ltd., 2004.

———. "The Puppet Theatre," *Selected Writings*. Translated and edited by David Constantine. Cambridge: Hackett Publishing Company, 2004.

Knight, Stephen. *Crime Fiction, 1800–2000: Detection, Death, Diversity*. Basingstoke: Palgrave Macmillan, 2004.

Kowsar, Mohammed. "Fugitive Desire: The Figural Component in Heinrich von Kleist's 'Penthesilea.'" *Theatre Journal* 40, no. 1 (March 1988): 61–76.

Kreilkamp, Vera. *The Anglo-Irish Novel and the Big House*. Syracuse: Syracuse University Press, 1998.

Kundera, Milan. *The Art of the Novel*. Translated by Linda Asher. New York: Perennial Classics, 2003.

Lamarque, Peter. *The Philosophy of Literature*. Oxford: Blackwell, 2009.

Langer, Susanne K. *Feeling and Form: A Theory of Art*. New York: Charles Scribner's Sons, 1953.

Lawson, Mark. "A Death in Summer by Benjamin Black—review." *The Guardian*, July 7, 2011, https://www.theguardian.com/books/2011/jul/07/death-summer-benjamin-black-review (accessed July 18, 2017).

Lessing, G. E. *Selected Prose Works of G. E. Lessing*. Edited by Edward Bell. Translated by E. C. Beasley and Helen Zimmern. London: G. Bell, 1879.

Lodge, David. *The Art of Fiction*. Harmondsworth: Penguin, 1992.

Lutostański, Bartosz. "Theatrical Narrative—Samuel Beckett's *Molloy*." *The Review of Contemporary Fiction* XXXIV, no. 1 (2014): 214–32.

Lyotard, Jean-François. *The Postmodern Condition: A Report on Knowledge*. Translated by Geoff Bennington and Brian Massumi. Minneapolis: University of Minnesota Press, 1989.

Mahlendorf, Ursula R. "The Wounded Self: Kleist's Penthesilea." *The German Quarterly* 52, no. 2 (March 1979): 252–72.

Mannion, Elizabeth. "Introduction: A Path to Emerald Noir: The Rise of the Irish Detective Novel." In *The Contemporary Irish Detective Novel*, edited by Elizabeth Mannion, 1–15. London: Palgrave, 2016.

McCaffery, Larry. *Postmodern Fiction: A Bio-Bibliographical Guide*. New York: Greenwood Press, 1986.

McHale, Brian. *Postmodernist Fiction*. London: Routledge, 2003.

———. *Teaching Narrative Theory*. Edited by David Herman, Brian McHale, and James Phelan. New York: Modern Language Association of America, 2010.

McKenna, John. "Rage for Order." In *Dublin* (November 13, 1986): 17.

McMinn, Joseph. *John Banville: A Critical Study*. Dublin: Gill & Macmillan Ltd., 1991.

———. *The Supreme Fictions of John Banville*. Manchester: Manchester University Press, 1999.

———. "An Exalted Naming: The Poetical Fictions of John Banville." *The Canadian Journal of Irish Studies* 14, no. 1 (July 1988): 17–28.

McNamara, Audrey. "Quirke, the 1950s, and Leopold Bloom." In *The Contemporary Irish Detective Novel*, edited by Elizabeth Mannion, 135–48. London: Palgrave, 2016.

Momoo, Mika. "Only Echoes and Coincidences: Textual Authority in John Banville's *Birchwood*." *Journal of Irish Studies* 22 (2007): 41–47.

Müller, Anja. "'You Have Been Framed': The Function of Ekphrasis for the Representation of Women in John Banville's Trilogy (The Book of Evidence, Ghosts, Athena)." *Studies in the Novel* 36, no. 2 (Summer 2004): 185–205.

Murphy, Neil. "Crimes of Elegance: Benjamin Black's Impersonation of John Banville." *Moving Worlds* 13, no. 1 (Spring 2013): 19–32.

———. "Contemporary Irish Fiction and the Indirect Gaze." In *From Prosperity to Austerity: A Socio-Cultural Critique of the Celtic Tiger and its Aftermath*. Edited by Eugene O'Brien and Eamon Maher, 174–87. Manchester: Manchester University Press, 2014.

———. "From *Long Lankin* to *Birchwood*: The Genesis of John Banville's Architectural Space." *Irish University Review* 36, no. 1 (Spring-Summer 2006): 9–24.

———. "John Banville and Heinrich von Kleist: The Art of Confusion" *The Review of Contemporary Fiction* XXXIV, no. 1 (2014): 54–70.

Myers, James P. *Writing Irish: Selected Interviews with Writers from the Irish Literary Supplement*. New York: Syracuse University Press, 1999.

Nabokov, Vladimir. *Despair*. Harmondsworth: Penguin, 1987.

———. *Lolita*. Harmondsworth: Penguin, 1988.

———. *Strong Opinions*. New York: Vintage, 1990.

———. *The Defense*. New York: Vintage, 1990.

O'Connell, Mark. *John Banville's Narcissistic Fictions*. London: Palgrave Macmillan, 2013.

O'Toole, Fintan. "From Chandler and the 'Playboy' to the contemporary crime wave." *Irish Times*, November 21, 2009.

Ortega y Gasset, Jose. *The Dehumanization of Art, and Other Writings on Art and Culture*. New York: Doubleday Anchor Books, 1956.

Pater, Walter. *The Renaissance: Studies in Art and Poetry: The 1893 Text*. Edited by Donald L. Hill. Berkeley: University of California Press, 1980.

Pedersen, Lene Yding. "Revealing/Re-veiling the Past: John Banville's *Shroud*." *Nordic Irish Studies* 4 (2005): 137–55.

Peters, Susanne. "John Banville, *The Sea*." In *Teaching Contemporary Literature and Culture*, 6 vols. Edited by Susanne Peters, Klaus Stierstorfer, and Laurenz Volkmann. Trier: Wissenschaftlicher, 2006–2008.

Pilling, John. *An Introduction to Fifty Modern European Poets*. London: Pan Books, 1982.

Platten, David. "Mediatized Realities: The Modern Crime Narrative." *Moving Worlds* 13, no. 1 (November 2013): 33–48.

Powell, Kersti Tarien. "'Not a Son but a Survivor': Beckett . . . Joyce . . . Banville." *The Yearbook of English Studies: Irish Writing since 1950* 35 (2005): 199–211.

———. "Trying to Catch Long Lankin by His Arm: The Evolution of John Banville's *Long Lankin*." *Irish University Review* 31, no. 2 (Autumn-Winter 2001): 386–403.

Quilligan, Maureen. *The Language of Allegory: Defining the Genre.* Ithaca and London: Cornell University Press, 1979.

Rabinowitz, Peter. "Narrative Difficulties in Lord Malquist and Mr. Moon." *The Cambridge Companion to Tom Stoppard.* Edited by Katherine E. Kelly, 55–67. Cambridge: Cambridge University Press, 2001.

Richardson, Brian. "Voice and Narration in Postmodern Drama." *New Literary History* 32, no. 3 (Summer 2001): 681–94.

Riemer, Andrew. "The Blue Guitar Review: John Banville Generates Deep Aesthetic Satisfaction." *Sydney Morning Herald*, August 29, 2015.

Rilke, Rainer Maria. *Selected Poems.* Edited by A. Alvarez. Harmondsworth. Translated by J. B. Leishman. Harmondsworth: Penguin, 1978.

Robbe-Grillet, Alain. *Topology of Phantom City.* Translated by J. A. Underwood. London: John Calder, 1978.

Scaggs, John. *Crime Fiction.* London: Routledge, 2005.

Schopenhauer, Arthur. *The Essays of Arthur Schopenhauer: The Art of Literature.* Selected and translated by T. Bailey Saunders. United Kingdom: Dodo Press, 2013.

Schwall, Hedwig. "'Mirror on Mirror Mirrored Is All the Show': Aspects of the Uncanny in Banville's Work with a Focus on *Eclipse*." *Irish University Review* 36, no. 1 (Spring-Summer 2006): 116–33.

———. "An Iridescent Surplus of Style: Features of The Fantastic in Banville's 'The Infinities.'" *Nordic Irish Studies*, Vol. 9 (2010): 89–107.

Shakespeare, William. *The Tempest.* New York: Signet/Penguin, 1982.

Shklovsky, Victor. "Art as Technique." In *Modern Criticism and Theory: A Reader.* Translated by Lee. T. Leman and Marion J. Reis. Edited by David Lodge, 16–30. London: Longmans, 1988.

Smith, Eoghan. "It's That Man Again." *Dublin Review of Books*, no. 83 (November 2016), http://www.drb.ie/essays/it-s-that-man-again (accessed March 21, 2017).

———. *John Banville: Art and Authenticity.* Oxford: Peter Lang, 2014.

Sontag, Susan. *Against Interpretation and Other Essays.* New York: Picador, 1966.

Steiner, George. *Grammars of Creation.* London: Faber and Faber, 2001.

Stevens, Wallace. *Letters of Wallace Stevens.* Selected and edited by Holly Stevens, with a new forward by Richard Howard. Berkeley: University of California Press, 1966.

———. *Opus Posthumous.* New York: Knopf, 1989.

———. *The Collected Poems of Wallace Stevens.* London: Faber and Faber, 1984.

Stewart, Victoria. "'I May Have Misrecalled Everything.' John Banville's *The Untouchable*." *English: Journal of the English Association* 52, no. 204 (Autumn 2003): 237–51.

Thompson, Jon. *Fiction, Crime, and Empire: Clues to Modernity and Postmodernity.* Urbana and Chicago: University of Illinois Press, 1993.

von Kleist, Heinrich. "On the Puppet Theatre." *In Heinrich von Kleist: Selected Writings.* Translated and edited by David Constantine. Cambridge: Hackett Publishing Company, 2004.

Walsh, Eibhear. "'A Lout's Game': Espionage, Irishness, and Sexuality in *The Untouchable*." *Irish University Review* 36, no. 1 (Spring-Summer 2006): 102–15.

BIBLIOGRAPHY

Wang, W. Michelle. "Writing for the Ear: Alasdair Gray the Playwright." *The Review of Contemporary Fiction* XXXIV, no. 1 (2014): 90–107.

Watkins, Nicholas. *Bonnard*. London: Phaidon Press, 2004.

Weretka, John. "The Guitar, the Musette and Meaning in the *fêtes galantes* of Watteau." In *EMAJ : Electronic Melbourne Art Journal*, no. 3 (2008): accessed April 23, 2016, https://emajartjournal.files.wordpress.com/2012/08/weretka.pdf (accessed October 2, 2016).

Wilkin, Karen. "Pierre Bonnard's Late Interiors." *The New Criterion* 36, no. 4 (March 2009), https://www.newcriterion.com/issues/2009/3/pierre-bonnardas-late-interiors (accessed July 12, 2016).

Wrethed, Joakim. "'A Momentous Nothing': The Phenomenology of Life, Ekphrasis and Temporality in John Banville's *The Sea*." In *The Crossings of Art in Ireland*. Edited by Ruben Moi, Brynhildur Boyce, and Charles I. Armstrong, 183–211. Bern: Peter Lang Publishing Group, 2014.

INDEX

Abbott, H. Porter, 148–49
Acocella, Joan, 23n48, 123
aesthetics, 10, 77, 126, 171, 196
Amory, Dita, 103

Banville, John, works of: *Ancient Light*, 5, 11, 14, 19, 38, 119–23, 126, 128–29, 131–33, 136, 139, 142, 159, 187; *Athena*, 12–13, 17–19, 33, 63–66, 70, 84–88, 108, 141, 165, 170, 188; *Birchwood*, 2, 7, 11, 16–18, 22n41, 27–28, 32–44, 48–49, 51, 53, 56–57, 65, 69–70, 84, 95, 111, 123, 125, 134, 152, 166, 192, 196; *The Blue Guitar*, 1, 14, 17, 38, 77, 88, 136n8, 142, 175, 187–91, 194, 196–98; *The Book of Evidence*, 5, 11–12, 18, 23n41, 38, 41, 63, 65–69, 71–72, 76–77, 79, 83–84, 140, 145, 159–60, 165, 170, 179, 196; *The Broken Jug*, 5, 61n64, 122, 139, 142–45; *Doctor Copernicus*, 17–18, 27, 30, 33, 41–49, 52, 58, 59n12, 60nn41–42, 184n51, 196; *Eclipse*, 5, 12, 19, 38, 61n64, 119–25, 128, 131–35, 137n25, 139–42, 165–66, 174, 187–88, 192; *Ghosts*, 12–13, 17–19, 25n99, 33, 38, 58, 63–66, 68–71, 77–84, 99, 121, 146–47, 152, 157n44, 165, 170, 175; *God's Gift*, 61n64, 139, 141–42, 144–50, 152–54; *The Infinities*, 13, 17, 19–20, 25n99, 61n64, 67, 88, 114, 133, 139, 141, 142, 144–45, 148–55, 159, 187–88; *Kepler*, 17–18, 27, 31, 34, 41–50, 52, 58, 60n41, 60n44, 196; *Long Lankin*, 27–33, 36, 41, 58n3, 78, 159, 192; *Love in the Wars*, 61n64, 139, 142–43; *Mefisto*, 17–18, 22n41, 27, 33, 38, 52–58, 63, 65, 70, 78, 139–40, 196; *The Newton Letter*, 5, 27, 31, 38, 42, 45, 49–53, 57, 65, 111, 152, 188, 196; *Nightspawn*, 16–17, 27–28, 31–33, 35–37, 40–41, 57, 59n16, 134, 165–66, 196; *The Sea*, 1, 4–5, 9, 14–15, 17, 19, 23n48, 33, 38, 77, 88–89, 93–118, 119, 141, 148, 151, 159, 165–66, 169, 172, 175, 182n1, 188, 194, 196, 199n8; *Shroud*, 13–14, 19, 119–23, 125–28, 132, 134–35, 139, 142, 159, 165; *Time Pieces: A Dublin Memoir*, 5; *The Untouchable*, 18, 58, 77, 88–89, 123, 142, 159

beauty, 2–3, 6–7, 9–10, 35, 40, 113, 140, 147, 194–95, 197
Beckett, Samuel, 2, 7, 16, 29, 32, 39, 53, 70, 89–90n8, 110, 143, 146, 149–50, 180, 187, 197
Bell, Julian, 104, 107–8
Berensmeyer, Ingo, 18, 43
big house, 27, 33–34, 37–38, 40, 49–53, 57
Black, Benjamin, 14, 19, 127, 140–41, 159–86
The Black-Eyed Blonde, 25n95, 161, 166–67, 182n8; *Christine Falls*, 141, 166, 168, 170, 172, 175, 178, 182n1; *A Death in Summer*, 165, 169, 171–72; *Elegy for April*, 173–74; *Even the Dead*, 164, 168–69, 174–75; *Holy Orders*, 166, 169–70, 173–74; *The Lemur*, 25n95, 165–66; *The Silver Swan*, 141, 165, 170–71, 185n78; *Vengeance*, 140, 169, 173, 175

INDEX

Blackford, Holly Virginia, 69
Bonnard, Pierre, 19, 94, 99, 101–8, 112–14, 169, 187–89, 194, 196–97, 199n8
Boyle, Kevin, 176
Browning, Robert, 82
Bryson, Norman, 82

Calvino, Italo, 6, 8, 17, 67, 89n5
Canon-Roger, Françoise, 76
Capra, Fritjoj, 61–62n71
Carroll, Noël, 6
Chandler, Raymond, 25n95, 160–61, 163–68, 182n8
Cheeke, Stephen, 77, 80, 153
Connolly, John, 162
Connor, Steven, 110
Constantine, David, 144–45
Coughlan, Patricia, 12–13, 88, 120
crime fiction, 19, 159–86

Dell'Amico, Carol, 13–14, 159
D'Hoker, Elke, 12, 72, 75, 135
Doctorow, E. L., 145–46
Donnelly, Brian, 33
Donoghue, Denis, 15, 109, 134, 180
Dostoevsky, Fyodor, 31
dramatic form, 148–50

ekphrasis, 12–13, 77, 81–83, 87, 98–99, 105, 107, 112, 122
Elam, Keir, 149
Eliot, T. S., 75, 90n15, 116n30

Facchinello, Monica, 98, 101–2
Fattori, Anna, 142–43
fictional ontologies, 40, 166
Flaubert, Gustave, 135
form, 3–4, 6–10, 14, 20–21, 27–28, 33, 35–40, 47–48, 57–58, 77, 102, 113, 115, 148–50, 154–55, 193–96
Frehner, Ruth, 11, 13
Friberg, Hedda, 112, 120
Friberg-Harnesk, Hedda, 142, 146

Gefter-Wondrich, Roberta, 89
Gide, André, 30, 32
Gilson, Etienne, 6–7, 9–10, 14

Goethe, 145
Graham, Gordon, 3–4, 9–10, 40, 124

Hammett, Dashiel, 160, 161, 163, 165
Hand, Derek, 11, 13, 35, 49, 52, 65, 89n4, 185n58
Hassan, Ihab, 29
Haughton, Hugh, 144, 177
Heller, Erich, 54, 140
Higgins, Aidan, 167
Hutcheon, Linda, 16, 42, 110

Imhof, Rüdiger, 15, 18, 28, 36, 40, 43, 47, 52, 55, 65, 73, 88, 96, 106, 111–12, 125–27
impersonality, 15, 75, 77, 109, 116n30, 126, 174; impersonal, 5, 74–75, 86, 93, 170
intertextual, 14, 16, 28, 31, 33, 36, 49, 51–52, 68, 76, 84–86, 95, 97, 105, 114, 121–22, 126, 139, 142, 146–47, 152, 165, 168–71, 177, 182, 188, 190, 192–93, 199n8
Irwin, John T., 164–65
Izarra, Laura P. Z., 115

Jackson, Tony E., 75
James, Henry, 7, 38, 69, 73, 193
James, P. D., 160
Jernigan, Daniel K., 148
Joyce, James, 2, 28–29, 75, 90n15, 116n30, 117n47, 163, 180, 187–89

Kant, Immanuel, 30, 39, 43, 143, 174, 190
Kavenna, Joanna, 180
Kearney, Richard, 185n58
Kenny, John, 28, 30, 50, 52, 57, 65, 72, 82, 84–85, 93–94, 125, 140, 180, 185n58
Kermode, Frank, 9
Kincaid, Andrew, 163, 177
Kleist, Heinrich von, 19, 54, 61n64, 65, 67, 114, 117n49, 122, 127, 139–55, 189, 197
Knight, Stephen, 165
Kowsar, Mohammed, 143

212

INDEX

Kreilkamp, Vera, 33
Kundera, Milan, 6–8, 10

Lamarque, Peter, 9
Langer, Susanne K., 15, 181
Leighton, Frederic, 82
Lessing, G. E., 79
Lodge, David, 42
Lutostański, Bartosz, 149
Lyotard, Jean-François, 196

Mahlendorf, Ursula R., 144
Manet, Édouard, 194–96
Mann, Thomas, 125
Mannion, Elizabeth, 163, 176
McCaffery, Larry, 196
McHale, Brian, 28, 41, 160
McMinn, Joseph, 11, 18, 28, 35, 40, 43, 50
McNamara, Audrey, 163
metafiction, 16–18, 20, 27–29, 31–32, 35–37, 42, 44, 48, 57, 88, 123, 134, 196
Momoo, Mika, 38

Nabokov, Vladimir, 6, 8, 22n41, 31–33, 49, 89n2
narrative, 2, 3, 10, 12, 16, 19, 28–31, 34, 36–37, 48–49, 58, 65, 68, 71–74, 77–84, 88, 94–96, 98–102, 104–6, 108, 114, 129, 134, 146–51, 159–62, 165–68, 193–96
Nietzsche, Friedrich, 3, 23n41, 55, 84, 126, 189, 197

O'Brien, Flann, 17
O'Connell, Mark, 44, 48, 72, 84, 93, 114, 122, 130, 132, 136n8
O'Toole, Fintan, 176–77
Ortega y Gasset, Jose, 20

Pan, Huiting, 97–98
Pater, Walter, 109, 181
Peters, Susanne, 98, 111
physics, 42–43, 55–56
Picasso, Pablo, 100, 105, 130, 179, 188–89, 194, 196, 200n24
Pilling, John, 52

Platten, David, 161, 176
postmodernism, 40, 104, 134, 165, 196–97; postmodern, 27–29, 39, 110, 134–35, 164–65, 167, 196–97
Powell, Kersti Tarien, 28

Quilligan, Maureen, 41

Rabinowitz, Peter, 148
realism, 6–7, 16, 29–32, 37, 99, 151, 161–62, 177
Richardson, Brian, 150–51
Riemer, Andrew, 192
Rilke, Rainer Maria, 46, 51, 54, 127, 188–89, 197, 199n11
Robbe-Grillet, Alain, 29
Russian formalism, 134–35, 189

Scaggs, John, 160, 163–64
Schopenhauer, Arthur, 20
science, 7–8, 18, 27–30, 41–44, 47–49, 55, 57, 63–64, 84, 108, 133, 148, 187, 190–92, 195
self-conscious, 2, 8, 11, 13, 16, 18, 20, 25n99, 27–28, 32, 35, 36, 40, 44, 47, 49, 54, 57, 63, 71–72, 82, 87, 89, 96, 101, 104, 107–8, 112, 119, 122, 124, 132, 140, 149–50, 153, 159, 161, 164–68, 171, 174–77, 181–82, 193, 196, 198
self-reflexive, 3, 16–19, 27–28, 30–31, 33, 35, 37–38, 40–46, 48–49, 51–52, 58, 63–65, 69, 77, 79, 81, 88–89, 95, 102, 104, 117n47, 122–23, 125–26, 129, 132–35, 142, 147–48, 151, 153, 169, 175, 189, 191, 193, 196
Shakespeare, William, 28, 36, 170
Shklovsky, Victor, 110, 116n38, 123–24, 134, 174, 184n49,
Simenon, Georges, 160–61, 165, 181, 183n13
Smith, Eoghan, 121, 129, 192, 199n17
Sontag, Susan, 14, 20–21
Stark, Richard, 161, 165
strangeness, 11, 15–16, 20, 57, 66, 82, 89n4, 109–11, 124, 134–36, 142, 145, 150, 155, 173–74, 181, 189,

INDEX

191–94, 197; strange, 66–67, 78, 124, 129, 134–35, 166, 173–74, 187–88, 193
Steiner, George, 29, 125, 195
Sterne, Laurence, 6, 8, 28, 104
Stevens, Wallace, 45–46, 48, 56, 60n42, 188–89, 194, 197, 200n24
Stewart, Victoria, 18
still life, 77, 79, 98–100, 152, 189

Thompson, Jon, 160–64
Tiepolo, Giovanni Battista, 9, 97, 188, 194

the uncanny, 109, 135, 175, 188–89

vanishing point, 100–102
Vermeer, Johannes, 73, 77, 98–100, 112, 152, 194
visual arts, 2, 9, 18–19, 58, 63–64, 68, 94, 97, 113, 121–22, 129, 133, 167, 194

Walsh, Eibhear, 18
Wang, W. Michelle, 149
Watkins, Nicholas, 103
Watteau, Jean-Antoine, 65, 78, 80–83, 85, 98, 100, 125, 152, 170, 188, 189, 195–96
Wilkin, Karen, 105, 107, 116n20
women, representation of, 10–14, 73–74, 88, 163
Wrethed, Joakim, 98–99, 107, 112

ABOUT THE AUTHOR

Neil Murphy is Associate Professor of English at NTU–Singapore. He is the author of *Irish Fiction and Postmodern Doubt* (2004) and editor of *Aidan Higgins: The Fragility of Form* (2010). He co-edited (with Keith Hopper) a special Flann O'Brien centenary issue of the *Review of Contemporary Fiction* (2011) and *The Short Fiction of Flann O'Brien* (2013), and a four-book series related to the work of Dermot Healy, including a scholarly edition of *Fighting with Shadows* (2015), *Dermot Healy: The Collected Short Stories* (2015), *Dermot Healy: The Collected Plays* (2016), and *Writing the Sky: Observations and Essays on Dermot Healy* (2016)—all with Dalkey Archive Press, USA.